THE ULTIMATE
MICROWAVE COOKBOOK

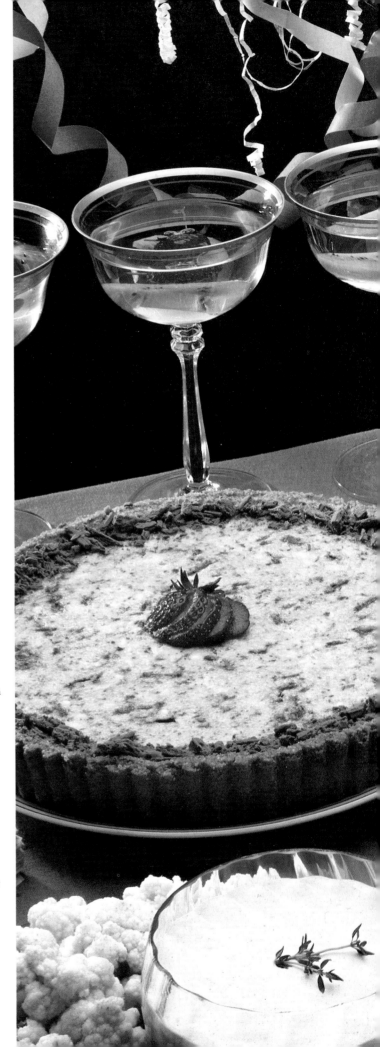

Photography by Ashley Barber
and Norman Nicholls

First published in 1985 by Bay Books
61-69 Anzac Parade,
Kensington 2033 NSW.

Publisher: George Barber

Copyright © Bay Books 1985
Copyright © Yvonne Webb (Microwave Cooking for One) 1984
National Library of Australia
Card number and ISBN 0 858 35 820 4

The publishers would like to thank the following for their assistance during photography of this book: David Jones Pty Ltd, Hale Imports, Mikasa Tableware, Peters of Kensington and The Bay Tree Kitchen Shop (for fine tableware, cutlery, glassware, dishes and kitchengoods); Breville and Kambrook Distributors Pty Ltd (for appliances); Fred Pazotti Tiles Pty Ltd (for tiles); Roden, Sanyo and Westinghouse (for microwave ovens). Crown Corningware and servingware is recommended for microwave cooking.

Food preparation and presentation: Douglas Marsland, Jan Wunderlich and Voula Kyprianou.

Photography assistant: Peita Littleton

Food testing: Gail Luck

THE ULTIMATE MICROWAVE COOKBOOK

Douglas Marsland — Yvonne Webb — Jan Wunderlich

Bay Books
Sydney & London

Contents

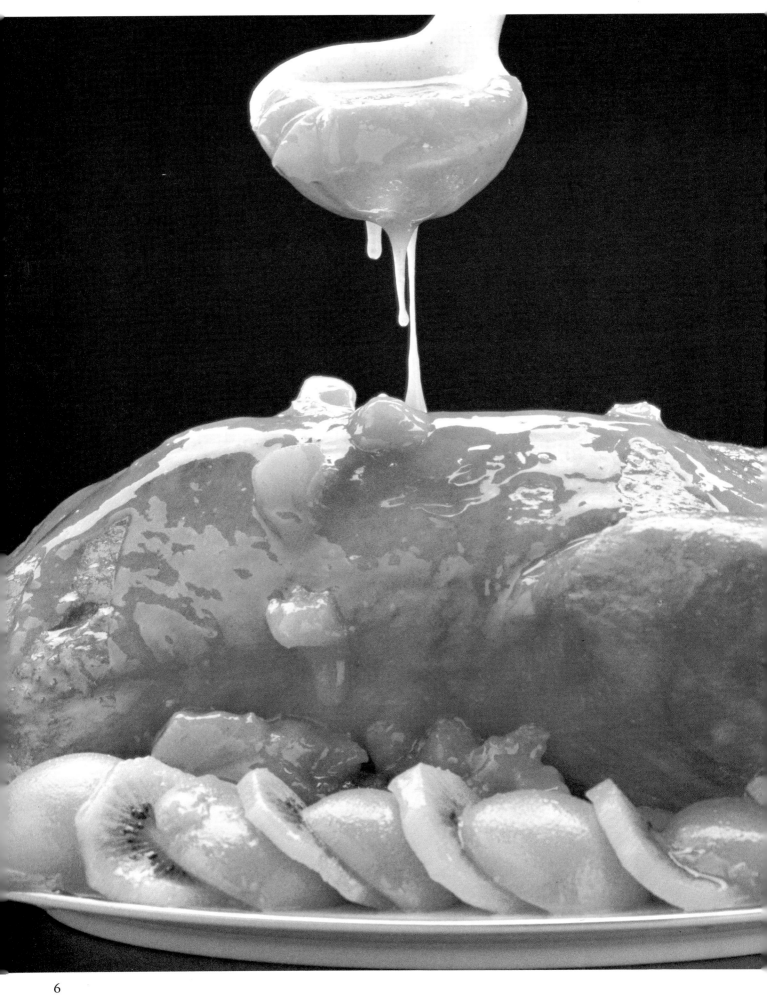

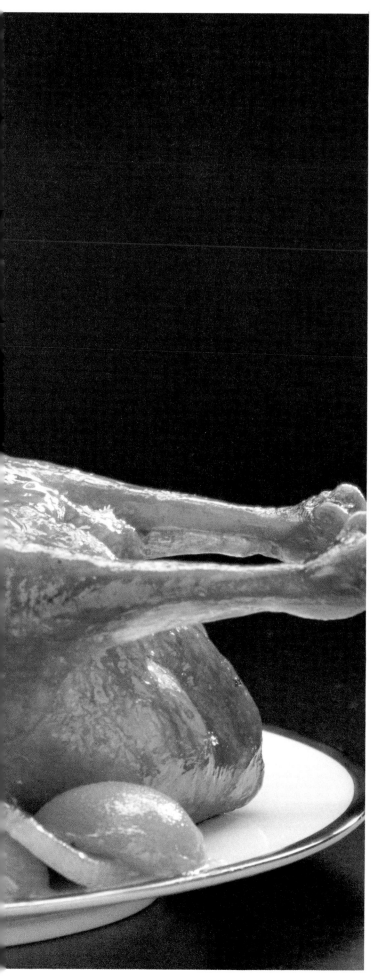

All about the Ultimate Microwave Cookbook

Over the last 25 years, microwave ovens have revolutionised kitchens in homes, restaurants and fast food outlets. The reasons for the boom are obvious: microwave ovens are quick, efficient, compact, clean and above all, allow the cook to work in a cool and comfortable environment.

Today's microwave ovens are even more flexible. There are models to suit every kitchen, every requirement. We can choose from 500 to 750 watt units which boast variable power, browners, computer memories and convection cookers. Microwave ovens are even available with combination gas/electric or electric models. The options are enormous.

This book is for those cooks who want to make the most of their culinary skills using their microwave oven. Divided into three sections with over 350 recipes for all occasions, the *Ultimate Microwave Cookbook* brings together the best from the Bay Books microwave cookery library including *Microwave Cooking Made Easy*, *Secrets of Microwave Cooking*, *Microwave Cooking for One* and *The Magic of Microwave Entertaining*. With over 150 colour photographs and step-by-step recipes the *Ultimate Microwave Cookbook* is simply that.

Roast Apricot Duck

The Microwave Story

The microwave oven is here to stay. This modern appliance is revolutionising kitchens and cooking as the sales figures show. It won't be too long before there's one in every home as we all discover how easy they are to use and just how naturally they fit into our busy lives. Microwave cooking is fast, efficient and economical. Microwave meals are delicious. In fact you can prepare any and every meal in your microwave — breakfast, lunch and dinner — as well as quick snacks, meals in moments and even elegant dinner parties.

This introductory section on microwave cooking has been prepared by the following home economists and microwave specialists: Jane Aspinwall, Mary-Lou Arnold, Douglas Marsland and Sheridan Rogers.

What are Microwaves?

A microwave is an electromagnetic wave within a particular frequency band. It is similar to electromagnetic waves found in radio, light and heatwaves. A microwave is generated by electricity passing through a special vacuum tube called a magnetron. Microwaves are short (hence the name 'micro'), high frequency waves which travel in virtually straight lines, and can be reflected, transmitted and absorbed. It is these special qualities which enable them to be used in ovens to cook food.

The Microwave Oven

Microwave ovens take advantage of microwave energy by trapping the waves which are then absorbed by the food. Once absorbed, the energy is converted into heat.

When you switch on the power, the electricity is converted to microwaves by a special tube called a **magnetron** — the heart of the microwave oven. (This only produces microwaves when the oven is switched on, the door properly shut and the timer set.) A **wave guide** directs the microwaves into the oven cavity. As the waves don't penetrate metal, they bounce off

How Microwaves Cook Food

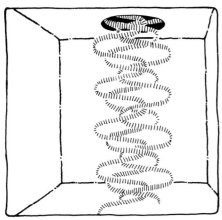

1. Microwaves are directed into the oven cavity by the wave guide

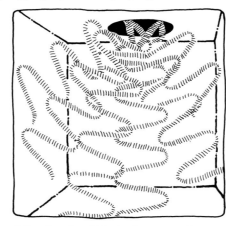

2. The stirrer fan distributes the waves. Some models also have a turntable to rotate food while cooking

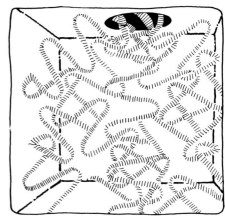

3. Microwaves cannot penetrate metal, so are randomly deflected off oven walls. This promotes even cooking.

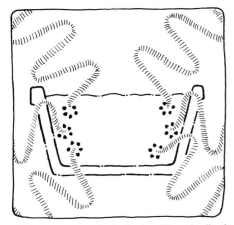

4. The waves penetrate the food to a depth of about 5 cm

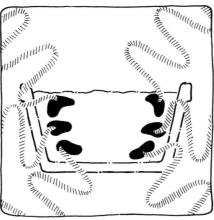

5. They produce friction which creates heat which cooks the food

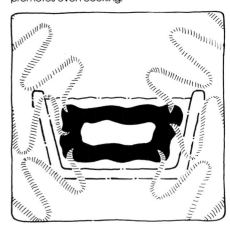

6. Heat spreads to the centre by conduction. Stirring food or turning it encourages even cooking.

the metal of the interior walls and the fine mesh door screen penetrating the food from all angles. With some models the waves are distributed by a fan-like **stirrer**; others have a **turntable** which rotates the food through either 180 or 360 degrees; some of the newer models have both.

Microwave cooking offers an exciting new approach to food preparation. You can cook and serve meals in the same dish, or cook and eat off the one plate. China, paper, plastic, heat-resistant glass can all be used for cooking or reheating in the microwave oven. Recipes are a little different, too. Times are shorter and less liquid is used.

In traditional conventional ovens the food slowly absorbs the heat from the oven or element. The food gets hot and so does the kitchen and the cook. In microwave cookery, because the heat is inside the food, the kitchen stays cool, likewise the cook.

The microwaves penetrate the food from all angles causing the water and fat molecules to vibrate. This produces friction which creates the heat which cooks the food. Because the heat is inside the food, it keeps cooking once you take it out of the oven. In fact standing time is an important part of the technique of microwave cooking: it completes the cooking.

Microwaves are odourless and tasteless. No residue remains in the food at all. In fact microwaved meals can be especially delicious and nutritious because the food is cooked quickly with all the flavour retained — not boiled or baked away.

Microwave breakfast with bacon, egg, sausages, tomato and a hot cup of coffee

Microwave Safety

Microwave ovens are among the safest of household appliances if used in accordance with the manufacturers' instructions. They are manufactured to meet stringent safety standards and in Australia for example must be approved for sale by the Electricity Supply Authorities in each state.

Manufacturers have gone to great lengths to make sure that microwaves stay inside the ovens. Safety devices, such as the door seal, are built-in to prevent any energy leakage. As soon as the door is opened the microwave energy stops. The following simple precautions are important.
• Do not try to operate the oven with the door open.
• Do not place any object between the front face of the oven and the door or allow any build up of dirt or cleanser residue to build up.
• Never try to operate the oven if it does not seem to be working properly.

The Advantages of Microwave Cooking

Time   Microwave cooking can save time. Superb meals for the family can be prepared in moments and that meat you forgot to take out of the freezer can be quickly defrosted.

Economy   Microwave cooking uses less energy. Because the energy output is less the oven consumes less power. And of course foods cook faster and unless you are using the browning dish, there's no preheating. Savings in energy and time mean savings with the power bill.

Convenience   Time, defrosting, reheating and shorter cooking times make the microwave oven ideal for today's busy lifestyle. Meals can be prepared, cooked, frozen and reheated all in the same dish then served piping hot.

Nutrition   Microwave ovens don't boil all the goodness away. The speed of cooking plus the small amount of liquid required means super-nutritious meals. Vegetables retain their vitamins and minerals. In addition, the colour of cooked vegetables is excellent and food presentation is thus enhanced. For many people the microwave is worthwhile just for cooking vegetables.

Diet   Because nutritious, low calorie foods can be ready in minutes, the temptation to reach for fattening snacks 'while waiting for dinner' is greatly reduced.

Cool cooking   The microwave is particularly useful during the hot summer months. No more slaving over that hot stove or in a steam-filled kitchen. Microwave ovens do not generate heat. All the energy produced is absorbed by the food. The kitchen remains cool and comfortable.

Quick cleanups   Food does not stick or bake on to casserole dishes in the microwave which makes cleaning up much easier. And because fewer dishes are used (one dish can go from freezer to oven to table) there's often less washing up. The ovens themselves just need a quick wipeover to clean.

Which Microwave?

Buying a microwave is much the same as purchasing another major household appliance. In making your selection, whether buying your first or updating an earlier model, consider your requirements and look carefully at all the options.

What wattage?
Power output is all important. The smaller 500 watt ovens are popular but less versatile. They are light, easy to move for cleaning and suitable for small kitchens, caravans or even to take outdoors for pool parties or barbecues where

food may need to be reheated. However, meals may take a little longer to cook and some of your larger casseroles or the useful microwave browning dish may not fit in the oven cavity.

In the higher powered ovens (now up to 750 watts), food cooks quickly and the larger ovens will readily accommodate a range of casseroles including all sizes of browning dishes.

Size

Oven capacity varies. Actual measurements can be deceptive as to the space available, especially if there is a turntable. Before investing, try out your favourite casserole dishes. Do they fit? Will they rotate on the turntable without touching the sides. An additional convenience with larger units is that you should be able to simply open the door and stir food without having to take the dish out.

Variable controls

Variable power controls (some of the latest models have up to ten!) allow you to prepare a wide range of foods very easily. Unfortunately, different manufacturers call the settings by different names, so you really need a basic guide as to the settings and their function. Check your instruction manual. In this book we use the following terms. We also include a basic guide to help you decide which setting on your microwave would be appropriate.

High	full power for quick cooking, vegetables, fish, meats, sauteeing and preheating browning dish
Medium high	for roasting and reheating
Medium	for baking cakes, bread, soups and stews
Medium low	for slow cooking or braising tougher cuts of meat
Defrost	for thawing frozen foods without cooking
Low	for small amounts of food that must be cooked slowly
Warm	for keeping food warm

Turntables

Turntables rotate the dish to ensure even cooking. Although this feature saves having to open the door and turn food frequently, the turntable itself takes up space and limits the size of dish that will fit in the oven. With some ovens you cannot use a temperature probe with the turntable. On other models you can immobilise the turntable. Some turntables can be removed for ease of cleaning.

Temperature controls

Temperature probes are inserted into the meat, measure its internal temperature and 'tell' the oven when to switch off. Some probes are designed to swivel so that they can be used with turntables.

Sensor controls let you cook automatically without having to check anxiously for doneness. The device 'senses' the temperature and automatically switches the oven off when the food is cooked.

Timer

All models have a timer — time is the essence of microwave cookery — and a buzzer or bell to let you know when cooking time has finished.

Browning element

The built-in browning element is just like the conventional griller. If you already have a good griller and/or you are planning to buy a browning casserole or dish then this feature may simply mean you are doubling up unnecessarily.

Combination cookers

The appliance for those who need both microwave oven and a new stove! Combination cookers provide the speed and efficiency of microwave plus the traditional benefits of conventional cooking with the turn of a switch.

A Microwave in your Kitchen

If you are like most people, you rush to open the box, put the oven on the table, plug in and switch on. Don't. It is essential to carry out a thorough post-delivery check and to read the instructions carefully.

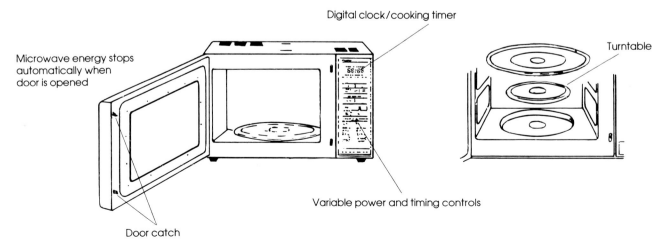

Digital clock/cooking timer

Microwave energy stops automatically when door is opened

Turntable

Variable power and timing controls

Door catch

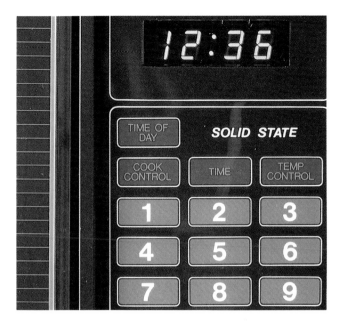

Installing your microwave

Microwave ovens need no special installation as they simply operate off normal household power supply. Place the oven on a strong, stable, level benchtop or table away from the sink and the gas or electric stove. For maximum operating efficiency, microwave ovens need breathing space. In general allow about 5 cm above the oven and 10 to 15 cm at the back and sides. Do not remove the feet or place books or bits and pieces over the air vents (they must be kept clear). Microwave ovens can be built in, but remember that doors open to the left and observe the manufacturer's ventilation requirements.

Using your microwave for the first time

First use is something that the manufacturer will discuss in detail. The two most important steps, however, are:
1. Read the instruction book carefully.
2. Do not operate the oven empty.

The standard first time test is boiling water. Having done this make a cup of tea or coffee (with your boiling water)

Grasshopper Torte *(see recipe)*
cooked in a heat-resistant glass pie dish

and sit down to fill in the warranty card while you recover your equilibrium. Keep your instruction booklet nearby so that you can refer to it just as often as you need to.

Which Dish?

Microwave-safe cookware

There's no need to rush out and buy special cookware for your microwave oven. The kitchen cupboard is probably full of bowls and casserole dishes which are ideal — Pyrex, Corning-ware, china bowls and plates and casseroles for example. Even ordinary items such as paper or plastic plates, wooden or wicker baskets can be used if you just want to warm food. For cooking, utensils need to be tough enough, however, to withstand extremely hot food or boiling water: with microwave, the food heats the dish. If food cooks or reheats in less than 5 minutes, however, the cookware may keep quite cool.

Microwave-safe materials include heatproof glass, glass ceramic, earthenware, stoneware, china (without a metal trim) and even porcelain (but don't use your finest). If you have a browning element, utensils must be non-flammable.

Plastic food storage containers or supermarket packages are fine just for defrosting but tend to melt or distort once cooking temperatures are reached. Do not use plastic containers, like ice cream buckets and take-away food and butter tubs, in the microwave.

Paper plates are useful for heating dry foods and paper napkins or kitchen paper for absorbing moisture.

Special microwave containers are available for freezer-to-table meals. You can mix, cook, freeze, defrost, reheat and serve all in the one dish.

Wooden or wicker baskets can be popped into the oven to heat up a bread roll, but crack if left in too long.

To find out whether or not a favourite dish is microwave safe, try this simple test. Place the dish in the oven on high with 150 mL of water for 2 minutes (china, pottery) or 20 seconds (glass, plastic). If the water heats but not the dish, then it is safe to use.

Shape is important in microwave cookery. Round dishes or ring dishes with straight (not bowl-shaped) sides give best results. If a recipe states a specific size or shape, use it. Cooking times can change when you use square or rectangular dishes and food can overcook at the corners with microwaves penetrating from both sides. Shallow dishes are best for foods like vegetables or portions of fish or meat. High-sided dishes are preferable for cooking rice, pasta, soups, stews and casseroles. Do not cook using a container with a restricted opening, such as a cordial or salad oil bottle.

What about metal?

Microwaves can't penetrate metal and metal can cause arcing if it comes in contact with the oven sides. Metal pots and pans and foil trays deeper than 5 cm form a barrier that microwaves can't pass through and reflect the energy back into the oven.

Decorative metallic trims can also cause arcing. This shouldn't harm the oven but it may pit the interior surface and the trim can peel off the plate leaving you without a pattern. Metal can be used to shield, reheat and even cook foods in a microwave oven. But certain rules must be followed. Check what the manufacturer recommends in your instruction book.

Basic Equipment for Successful Microwave Cooking

Item	Use
20 × 20 cm square dish	Cakes, slices, whole corn cobs, confectionery, vegetables, lasagna.
Roasting dish and rack	Pork, beef, lamb, chicken, duck, turkey and all roasts.
Browning casserole dish	Grilling chops and steaks, stews and curries, baking scones, frying seafood, crumbed foods, eggs and small quantities of chips.
3 litre casserole with lid	Soups, pasta, rice, casseroles, corned beef, vegetables, chowders.
Casserole lid	Pies, quiches, vegetables, omelettes, cheese cakes and for cooking small quantities of food.
Ring dish	Baked custards, breads, scone rings, cakes, whole potatoes.
Flan ring	Cheese cake, fruit flans, quiches, vegetables.
Loaf dish	Meat loaves, loaf cakes, breads.
Flat round platter	Fruit or savoury pizzas, vegetable platters, sweet and savoury biscuits fruit flambe.
Various sized basins 1 or 2 litre jugs	Melting, blanching, sauteeing. Savoury sauces, custards, reheating.
Souffle dish	Cakes, souffles, reheating soups, casseroles.

The browning dish

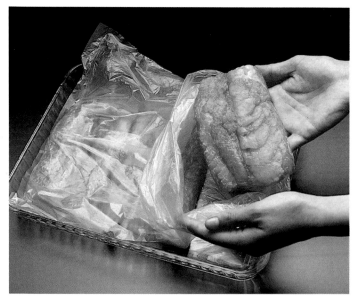

Cod fillets cooked in a plastic bag

12

Cover Story

Covering food with a lid or plastic wrap holds in steam keeping the food moist, tender and full of flavour. Loose coverings will also prevent splatters and small pieces of foil can be used to shield protruding angles or edges of roasts or poultry to prevent overcooking. You can also shield foods with a sauce to keep them moist.

Item	Use
Plastic wrap and plastic bags	Use recognised brand names for covering seafood, sauces and vegetables when no casserole lid is available. Lids are better if you need to turn or stir food during cooking. Plastic oven bags are microwave-safe so long as they are pierced. Tie bags with string — not metal ties. Plastic storage bags should be removed if you are heating food. Do not use plastic wrap and bags when cooking roasts and grills as the plastic can melt. Do not completely seal cake and bread dishes with plastic wrap as condensation can result.
White kitchen paper	Reheating dry foods such as cakes and breads. Lining dishes and covering food to prevent splatters. Absorbent paper allows steam to escape stops fat splattering and absorbs excess moisture. Greaseproof paper is less absorbent, provides a loose cover for preventing splatters and is useful as a lining.
Aluminium foil	When baking cakes. As long as the density of the food is greater than the amount of foil, foil can be used on the edges of roasts cakes and drumsticks. During standing time partially cover roasts so that heat is retained. Foil liners can also be used to prevent the sides of a fruit cake from drying out. Use foil to cover the cooked portion of a cake when the centre is still moist.

Practical Microwave

Standing Time

If you study microwave recipes or timecharts you will notice that 'standing time' is as important as 'cooking time'. With microwave cookery you can't stop cooking simply by taking the food out of the oven because the heat is inside the food. Standing time finishes the cooking. The heat cooks the centre of the food by conduction — a fuel saving bonus! Food can remain covered and left to stand in oven on warm or on bench.

With small items of food, standing time is a matter of minutes. Poultry or roasts of meat, however, require 15–20 minutes — or half the cooking time. These large items should be wrapped in foil for standing time to retain their heat. During this time the internal temperature will increase by 8–10°C, thus completing the cooking cycle. Standing time gives you time to cook vegetables and sauces.

Even Cooking

The following simple techniques for microwave cooking make sure that the food cooks evenly in the oven.

Arranging and spacing   Place individual portions such as potatoes or chops, an equal distance apart in the dish and in a single layer. Never stack foods for microwave cooking. With drumsticks, chops or similar portions, make sure that the thicker part faces the outside of the dish where it will receive most microwave energy.

Stirring   Stir food to spread and redistribute heat during cooking. As the outside will heat first, stir from the outside towards the centre. Rotate foods which can't be stirred — cakes and breads, for example — to prevent one side or corner overcooking.

Turning   Many recipes tell you to turn foods — usually about half way through the cooking time. This makes sure that top and bottom cook evenly.

Arrange food in layers

Piercing

Do not bake potatoes, tomatoes or apples unless the skins have been pierced. Be sure that all foods with an outer skin or membrane (this includes eggs) are pierced to allow steam to escape during cooking. Similarly, do not cook vegetables in a plastic bag or airtight container unless the bag or container has been pierced.

Pierce vegetables to let out steam

Is It Cooked?

For the novice, it can sometimes be a little tricky to determine if the food is cooked or not because some look different (usually paler) from conventionally cooked foods. A wise rule of thumb is to always undercook, to be patient and let food stand. If the dish is not cooked to your liking after standing time, you can always return it for further cooking. Undercooking at least gives you a choice. Once overcooked, there is little you can do for most foods. They taste spoilt and are usually tough.

Personal preference affects the degree of readiness to a certain extent. Some people prefer their foods underdone, so cooking times have to be adjusted to taste.

Many of the tests for 'doneness' or 'readiness' are the standard ones. However, some microwave ovens offer special features to take away the guesswork and help you determine whether or not food is cooked.

Probes are inserted in the meat or poultry which is cooked until a preset temperature is reached. They are specially constructed for use in microwave ovens. For an accurate reading, insert probe into centre of food away from fat or bone. (Do not use a regular meat thermometer in the oven while operating. Most meat thermometers contain metal. Special meat thermometers are available for use in microwave ovens.)

Electronic sensors inside the oven 'sense' the temperature. The oven switches off when the preset temperature is reached.

Recipe times and time charts When you start using your microwave, it is wise to follow cooking and standing times. As most cooking times given are only approximate, use your eyes and nose — if you can smell the food, then it is wise to check, as this usually indicates that it is done or ready to be stirred. Remember, the denser the food, the longer it will take to cook: for example, a 1 kg roast will take longer to cook than 1 kg of diced meat in a casserole. Foods that can be stirred will cook more quickly than foods which are whole.

After a while you will become an expert in timing foods in your microwave oven and learn how to adapt your favourite recipes to this new way of cooking.

Testing for 'Doneness'

When testing for 'doneness', always allow for the recommended standing time.

Cakes leave the sides of the dish when cooked and any moist spots on the surface will dry during standing time.

Egg mixtures Test quiche fillings and baked custard by inserting a knife one-third in from the edge. The knife should be clean when withdrawn. Stand cooked custard in cold water when cooking is complete to cool and to stop further cooking.

Seafood Green prawns, lobster and crabs turn pink when cooked. Cooked fish will flake easily when tested with a fork. Scallops, oysters and mussels become firmer when cooked.

Meats are fork tender when done. Always allow standing time. A final test for doneness can be carried out with a meat thermometer.

Drumsticks will move freely and juices will run clear when poultry is cooked.

Vegetables are brightly coloured when cooked. Overcooking discolours and dulls vegetables. Large vegetables like whole potatoes and beetroot and quartered pumpkin should be turned during cooking.

Jacket potatoes, which still feel firm when removed from the oven, will keep cooking during standing time, so don't overcook them. They will also keep hot if wrapped in foil for 30–40 minutes after cooking.

Browning

For those not familiar with modern microwave cooking, anxiety about how food will look when it is cooked is common. Many of us have visions of pale cakes, grey meat and wishy washy sauces.

The browning dish

Such anxiety was understandable back in the days when microwave ovens were first introduced, but microwave cooking has come a long way since then. One of the first major breakthroughs was the introduction of the browning dish (or skillet), making it possible to actually grill steaks and chops, make toasted sandwiches and cook bacon and sausages. These dishes, specially treated with a tin oxide coating, attract microwaves and become very hot. When food is put onto the hot surface, it sears or browns rapidly. Pizzas, sausage rolls, pies and other pastries can also be placed onto the dish to give a crisper base.

A great variety of shapes and sizes in browning dishes is now available including casserole-type browners, grill-type, sizzlers and minuettes (a small round casserole type browning dish with long handle and clear glass lid).

Use sauces to mask and enhance.
Beef Olives (see recipe)

Although such browning dishes are not essential, they certainly help to make foods which are normally grilled or fried look more attractive.

The browning element

Another breakthrough has been the introduction of the browner, a browning element or hot air blower in the top of the oven. This lets a limited amount of dry heat into the oven, enough to brown and crisp the outer surface of foods like cauliflower cheese, but not strong enough to cook a souffle.

The combination oven

Probably the most miraculous breakthrough has been the combination oven. This is a basic microwave oven combined with a convection oven. It includes all the cooking, baking and grilling features of a conventional oven, plus microwave cooking features which can be used separately or in combination with bake or grill heat. This results in a new kind of flexibility for microwave cooking and meal preparation. With roasts, for example, microwave energy and dry heat combine to give a perfect result. Pavlovas, sponges and pastries, never a great success in the microwave alone, can be cooked and browned to perfection using the convection oven.

Microwave Browning Tricks

If you don't have a browning dish, a browner or a combination oven, there are still a number of ways you can enhance microwaved food. If you use a little imagination, there are any number of things you can do to help brown food in microwave cooking. See what delicious and attractive ideas you can invent.

Meat and poultry

Meat and poultry due to longer cooking times will brown in their own fat, but not to the same extent as in a conventional or combination oven. However, if you brush with melted unsalted butter and sprinkle with paprika before cooking, this will help. Food can be coated with butter or Parisian essence, Worcestershire, barbecue or soy sauce, which not only add to the appearance but provide added flavour.

Chicken brushed with honey, brown sugar and soy sauce is delicious — and looks good too.

- To enhance the colour of chicken pieces dip the chicken in dried breadcrumbs or coating mixes.
- When roasting, use roasting bags (pierced) to increase colour.
- Cook sausages, chops and steaks in the microwave then complete browning under the conventional grill.
- Sear steak on the barbecue, freeze and defrost and finish cooking in the microwave when required.
- Ham and poultry can be brushed with jellies, preserves, glazes or marmalades after half the cooking time has elapsed.
- Soy, teriyaki and barbecue sauce are excellent brushed over hamburgers and other meats and poultry. Onion soup and gravy mix are also very good for colour.
- Small amounts of dried herbs or spices mixed in with melted unsalted butter or oil can also be used to give added colour.
- Dry poultry and meat with kitchen paper towels before cooking as this will aid browning.
- Casseroles can be made more interesting if sprinkled with breadcrumbs, Parmesan cheese, crushed corn chips or potato chips before serving.

Braised Lemon Chicken *(see recipe)*

Cakes, Bread and Pastry

- To colour cake tops sprinkle a mixture of cinnamon and sugar or cinnamon and coconut over the surface before serving.
- Cake recipes which contain colouring agents like chocolate, coffee, carrot, dates, or banana are always best in a microwave.
- Grease your cake or loaf container and sprinkle it with chopped nuts and brown sugar, toasted coconut or biscuit crumbs before pouring in the cake mixture.

- Before cooking savoury pastry brush it with a mixture of 1 egg yolk and 1 tablespoon soy sauce; for sweet pastry use molasses, maple syrup or a mixture of vanilla essence and beaten egg.
- Bread and bread rolls respond well to being brushed with beaten egg or milk and sprinkled with poppy seeds or toasted sesame seeds before cooking.

Carrot Cake *(see recipe)*

Micro/conversion

Converting conventional recipes is easy too, especially when you become familiar with your new appliance. Generally, microwave time will be one-quarter to one-third of conventional time. It is always best to undercook; overcooking cannot be corrected.

Only choose conventional recipes that will make, at most, 6–8 servings. Recipes yielding large quantities will not effectively use the convenience of flat microwave cooking. Select recipes which use ingredients with high natural moisture levels such as poultry, minced meats, vegetables, fruits and sauces. When you have found a recipe you wish to convert, find a similar microwave recipe and use it as a guide.

Basic Steps

Preparation   Always cut meat and vegetables into pieces the same size for casseroles and steaming in the microwave.

Liquids   Reduce liquid by one-third to one-half when converting recipes for microwave preparation as liquid attracts microwave energy and slows the cooking of other ingredients. If necessary add extra liquid towards the end of cooking. Reduce liquids in cakes by 2 tablespoons and replace with an extra egg. Thin liquids such as water, meat and fruit juices, stock and wine can be heated on high.

Fats and oils   Reduce those fats and oils which have been included in conventional cooking to prevent sticking. Add fats and oils only for their flavour qualities.

Delicate ingredients   Add delicate ingredients such as seafood, cheese, canned and fine cooked foods near the end of cooking to prevent toughening and overcooking.

Seasonings   Reduce salt by two-thirds for microwave cooking and adjust other seasonings before serving. Microwave cooking enhances the natural flavour of foods therefore conventional recipes can be over-seasoned.

Sauces   Sauces which contain cream, sour cream, yoghurt or moist cheese are cooked and then reheated on medium when other ingredients are added.

Major ingredients   Major ingredients like poultry, whole fish fillets and minced or cubed meats can be microwaved on high. Stir microwave-cooked foods that are stirred in conventional cookery. Soups, casseroles and roasts are best started on high for the first 5 minutes and finished on medium.

Cakes   Cakes are best cooked on medium and finished on high for the last 2–3 minutes. Foods that cannot be stirred should be cooked on medium and the dish rotated four times during cooking.

Oysters Kilpatrick *(see recipe)*

Menu Planning

- Prepare desserts, soups, rice, casseroles and sauces early in the day as these dishes can be reheated in just minutes.
- Wash and dry salad ingredients and place into plastic bags or wrap in foil and chill.
- One hour before serving assemble seafood dishes, meat and poultry. Cook jacket potatoes then wrap in foil to retain heat; then cook main course. During standing time

make sauces and toss salads. Allow 8–12 minutes to cook vegetable dishes. Reheat any pre-prepared foods just before serving.
- Take advantage of the space in your conventional oven to hold hot microwave food. Set oven at 100°C.
- Heat plates by placing a microwave casserole, soup or vegetable dish on top of them during standing time.
- Reheat desserts if necessary while clearing the table after the main meal.

Cooking Times

All cooking times given are approximate. However, the recipes in this book were prepared and tested in 600 and 650 watt microwave ovens and the times given are based on these. If you have a more powerful 750 watt oven, you will need to reduce times by a minute or two; if yours is a smaller 500 watt oven, add a minute or two. Remember, undercooking can be easily rectified, overcooking can't.

Beets with Orange Sauce *(see recipe)*

**Power Level Designations and Wattage Outputs
The following guide is based upon a General
Electric 650 watt microwave oven.**

Power Level	%	Wattage Output
Warm	10%	65
Low	20%	130
Defrost	30%	195
Braise	40%	260
Medium	50%	325
Bake	60%	390
Medium High	70%	455
Reheat	80%	520
Saute	90%	585
High	100%	650

Making the Most of Your Microwave

Making the Most of Your Microwave combines the recipes from *Microwave Cooking Made Easy* and *Secrets of Microwave Cooking* by microwave expert and teacher, Douglas Marsland. The delicious, mouthwatering recipes in this section have been selected so that microwave cooks — the novice and the experienced — can use their ovens and their skills to the fullest to make the most of their microwave. The delicious recipes and helpful hints reveal the secrets of perfect and exciting microwave cooking.

Coconut Prawn Cutlets

Breakfast

Breakfast is often a time when there is simply not much time. So, why not microwave that traditional cooked breakfast? The nourishing, economical egg is even more convenient when cooked in the microwave. Scrambled eggs are especially tasty. With a little butter, lots of whisking and careful timing they are extra light and fluffy. Some recipe books suggest that you cannot cook eggs in their shells in the microwave but this is not true. Just follow the directions for a perfect, no fuss, 3½ minute egg. Because egg whites and yolks cook at different speeds, pierce the yolk carefully with a toothpick if frying in the microwave.

Try some other delicious breakfast and brunch ideas by turning to the Eggs and Cheese and Snacks chapters.

Scrambled Eggs for 2

4 × 55 g eggs at room
 temperature
¼ cup milk or cream
½ teaspoon salt
1½ tablespoons butter

Time: 4 minutes. Serves 2

Combine eggs, milk, salt, in a bowl. Melt butter in a glass bowl for 30 seconds. Pour in egg mixture and cover with plastic food wrap. Cook 2 minutes, stir well and cook another 1½ minutes stirring 2 or 3 times. Remove eggs when softer than required and let stand 1 minute.

With Cheese
Add 1 tablespoon grated cheese to beaten eggs and milk. Add a few seconds to total cooking time.

With Bacon and Chives
Chop 1-2 rashers of bacon, cook 1-2 minutes. Cook eggs 1 minute, add bacon with 2 teaspoons chopped chives, stir well, continue cooking.

Fried Egg

1 × 55 g egg at room
 temperature
½ teaspoon butter

Time: 55 seconds. Serves 1

Melt butter on a plate for 25 seconds. Add egg, prick yolk 2-3 times with a toothpick. Cook 30 seconds.

> **HINT: FRIED EGGS**
> Allow the following times for frying eggs.
> 2 eggs—1 minute 5 seconds.
> 3 eggs—1 minute 35 seconds.
> 4 eggs—2 minutes.

Boiled Egg

1 × 55 g egg at room
 temperature
1 teaspoon salt
water to cover egg

Time: 3½ minutes

Boil water in small jug or bowl. Add 1 teaspoon salt, then the egg. Cook on defrost for 3½-4 minutes.

Grilled Grapefruit for 2

1 grapefruit
2 teaspoons brown sugar
2 teaspoons sherry

Time: 2 minutes

Cut grapefruit in half and segment. Place on plate and sprinkle with brown sugar and sherry. Cook on high 1½-2 minutes for 2 halves.

Oatmeal for 1

¼ cup quick cooking oats
½ cup water, at room
 temperature
⅛ teaspoon salt

Time: 1½ minutes

Place oatmeal, water and salt into a serving bowl. Cook 1 minute 30 seconds on high, stir, cover, and let stand for a few minutes before serving.

Note: May be cooked in advance and reheated.

Scrambled Eggs with Bacon and
Pineapple Sate and Savoury Scone
Ring

Grills

Sausages

Heat browning dish for 8 minutes on high. Lightly grease dish. Place up to 6 sausages in the dish and cook 3 minutes on each side on high.

Note: Prick sausages well before grilling and allow 2–3 minutes standing time.

Bacon

Place bacon on several layers of white kitchen paper on a flat dish with one layer of paper covering the bacon. Cook bacon for about 1 minute per slice on high.

Sliced Tomatoes

Heat browning dish for 6 minutes on high. Grease lightly with butter. Add 9 thick slices of tomato. Coat with buttered herbed crumbs. Cook 1 minute, turn slices and cook another 1–1½ minutes on high.

Note: Use 3 tomatoes cut into 3 thick slices each, cutting off top and bottom so that slices lie flat.

Pineapple and Bananas

Heat browning dish 5 minutes, lightly butter slices of fresh pineapple and cook 4 minutes on one side and 1–1½ minutes on the other. Reheat browning dish as above; using 3 bananas split lengthwise, cook 1–1¼ minutes on one side only.

Bacon and Pineapple Sate

Remove rind from thin strip of bacon. Cut into 3 or 4 pieces. Roll up and place onto bamboo sate stick. Place wedge of pineapple between bacon curls. Cook 3–4 minutes between white kitchen paper on high.

Note: Button mushrooms or cherry tomatoes could be used instead of pineapple wedges.

Microwave Grill Plate Vegetables

250 g button mushrooms
4–6 tomato halves

Time: 12 minutes. Serves 2–3

Preheat browning grill on high 5 minutes. Lightly butter grill. Microwave mushrooms on high 2–3 minutes.

Preheat browning grill on high 5 minutes. Top tomatoes with parsley.

Whole Mushrooms with French or Garlic Dressing

6 medium mushrooms
French dressing or garlic dressing

Time: 2 minutes

Arrange mushrooms in a circle on a plate and sprinkle each with ½ teaspoon of your favourite dressing and cook, covered, for 2 minutes on high.

Sliced Mushrooms

250 g mushrooms, thinly sliced
1 tablespoon lemon juice
1 tablespoon chopped parsley
60 g butter

Time: 2 minutes

Arrange mushrooms in a shallow dish. Sprinkle with lemon juice and parsley. Dot with butter and cook covered for 2 minutes on high.

Stuffed Mushrooms

6 medium mushrooms, whole
2 slices ham
125 g cream cheese
1 tablespoon chives

Time: 3 minutes

Remove stalks from mushrooms. Chop ham finely and combine with cheese and chives. Spread mixture into cavity of mushrooms and cook, covered, 3 minutes on high.

Stuffed Mushrooms

Scones

2 cups self-raising flour
1 tablespoon sugar
½ teaspoon salt
1½ tablespoons butter
¾ cup milk

Time: 10 minutes

Sift flour into basin, add sugar and salt. Cut butter into small cubes, rub into flour. Add milk, blend mixture with a tableknife. Turn onto floured board. Cut into rounds. Heat browning dish 8 minutes on high. Cook scones 1 minute on each side on high. 8 scones.

Chive and Ham Scones

Add 1 tablespoon cut chives and 1 tablespoon diced ham to mixture. Delete sugar.

Savoury Scone Ring

2 tablespoons butter
2 tablespoons sugar
1 cup pumpkin, mashed
1 small onion, finely cut
2 tablespoons chopped parsley
1 egg
½ cup milk
2½ cups self-raising flour
½ teaspoon salt

Time: 7 minutes

Cream butter and sugar. Add pumpkin, onion and parsley. Add well-beaten egg. Add milk slowly. Cut in sifted flour and salt. Place into a well-greased microwave baking ring. Cook 7–8 minutes, remove and let stand for 4 minutes.

Golden Corn Bread

2 tablespoons butter or
    vegetable oil
2 tablespoons sugar
1½ cups plain flour
4 teaspoons baking powder
1 cup cornmeal
¼ teaspoon salt
¼ teaspoon chilli powder
2 eggs, beaten
¾ cup milk
125 g cream style corn
¼ cup red capsicum, diced

Time: 7 minutes

Cream butter and sugar. Add sifted flour and baking powder. Add cornmeal, salt and chilli powder. Stir in eggs, milk and beat until smooth. Fold in corn and capsicum. Place into a well-greased microwave baking ring and cook 7–8 minutes on high. Remove and let stand 4 minutes.

Tea, Coffee or Cups of Soup

Fill cups or coffee mugs with cold water. Heat uncovered in the oven on high.
1 cup—approximately 2½ minutes, depending on size of cup.
2 cups—approximately 4½ minutes.
Then add your instant coffee, tea bag, or your single serving of instant soup mix.
    Note: Milk may be heated for coffee or tea, also for oatmeal.

HINT: HOT DRINKS
Hot drinks are quick and easy in a microwave. They can usually be drunk from the container in which they were heated. When making more than two cups always place them in a ring leaving the middle empty. Do not overfill or they will spill. Also ensure liquid has been stirred before heating.

Sausage Bacon and Eggs

Eggs and Cheese

Eggs cooked in a microwave will always be successful if you follow these rules. When poaching or frying cook the egg until the yolk is just how you like, then remove the egg from the microwave and allow standing time. During the standing time the white of the egg will continue to cook. To prevent the yolk from breaking during cooking, pierce it with a toothpick 2 or 3 times. Poached eggs are best cooked on the defrost setting in pre-boiled water. Allow 4 minutes cooking time for 2 eggs.

Boiled eggs should also be cooked on the defrost (4–6 minutes for 2 eggs) setting in pre-boiled salted water. Should the egg be uncooked when the shell is cut, prick the yolk then return it to the oven to cook for a few seconds more. To keep the eggs upright during continued cooking, put them into egg cups. Fried eggs can be cooked on a lightly buttered plate. Set the microwave on high and cook for only 65–70 seconds for 2 eggs.

For the complete egg and bacon breakfast use a preheated browning dish and cook the prepared rashers on high for 2 minutes. Remove the rashers and break 2 eggs into the browning dish. Prick the yolks before cooking and baste with bacon fat. Cook covered for 30 seconds and allow the eggs to stand for 2 minutes until set.

Cheese melts rapidly in a microwave oven, but because of its high protein content, cheese will toughen and become stringy if overheated. Always grate or crumble cheese before adding to sauces, soups and casseroles.

The true flavour of cheese is brought out if cheese is warmed before serving. To save effort cheese can be microwaved directly on a dry wooden board.

Asparagus Omelette

1½ cups roughly chopped,
    peeled, fresh asparagus
2 tablespoons water
⅓ cup grated Swiss cheese
4 eggs, separated
¼ cup chopped onion
¼ cup chopped green
    capsicum
⅓ cup milk
1 teaspoon flour
¼ teaspoon salt
⅛ teaspoon white pepper
1 tablespoon butter

Time: 14 minutes. Serves 4

Place asparagus and water in a 1 litre casserole dish. Cover and cook on high 6 minutes, or until tender. Stir after 3 minutes. Drain, stir in cheese, cover and let stand.

Combine egg yolks, onion, capsicum, milk, flour and seasonings. Set aside. In a bowl beat egg whites until stiff, then fold into yolk mixture.

Melt butter in a pie plate on high 1 minute or until melted. Tilt dish to coat. Pour egg mixture into buttered dish and cook on medium 7–10 minutes or until set, lifting edges every 2 minutes with a spatula so uncooked portion spreads evenly.

Top with asparagus and cut into wedges to serve.

Eggs Benedict

4 crumpets
4 slices leg ham
4 poached eggs
butter

Toast and butter crumpets. Top each with a thin slice of leg ham and cook on high 3 minutes. Place a poached egg on top of ham and spoon over hollandaise sauce.

Hollandaise Sauce

2 egg yolks
⅓ cup butter
2 tablespoons lemon juice,
    strained
¼ teaspoon salt

Time: 1 minute 45 seconds. Serves 2–4

Place butter in a small bowl and cook on high 45 seconds. Stir in lemon juice, egg yolks and whisk until well blended. Cook on high 1 minute, whisking every 15 seconds. Stir in salt half way through.

> **HINT: MELTING BUTTER**
> 1 tablespoon butter:
>   30–45 seconds on high
> ½ cup butter:
>   1 minute on high
> 1 cup butter:
>   1–2 minutes on high

Asparagus Omelette

Prawn Omelette

4 × 55 g eggs
140 g prawn meat
250 g fresh mushrooms, sliced
⅓ cup finely chopped shallots
1 cup bean sprouts
⅛ teaspoon white pepper
2 tablespoons oil
1½ teaspoons cornflour
2 teaspoons soy sauce
2 teaspoons oyster sauce
¼ cup chicken stock
1 teaspoon sugar

Time: 13 minutes. Serves 5

In a medium-sized bowl, beat eggs well. Fold in mushrooms, shallots, bean sprouts, pepper and prawn meat. Cook on high 4 minutes, stirring 3–4 times until soft set.

Preheat browning dish on high for 5 minutes then add oil. Using a half-cup measure, pour mixture into dish to make 5 omelettes. When sizzling stops turn omelette over and cook on high 1½ minutes until firm and set. Cover and set aside.

In a bowl combine cornflour, soy sauce, oyster sauce, chicken stock and sugar. Cook on high 2–3 minutes or until thickened, stirring during cooking.

Pour sauce over omelette to serve.

Poached Eggs

4 × 55 g eggs, room
    temperature

Time: 11 minutes. Serves 2–4

Pour 500 mL water into 1 litre casserole dish. Cover and cook on high 6 minutes or until boiling. Break in eggs and cover. Cook on defrost 5 minutes or until set.

Egg and Bacon Rounds

4 × 55 g eggs, room
    temperature
2 long rashers bacon
1 microwave muffin pan
¼ teaspoon paprika
½ teaspoon chopped parsley

Time: 2 minutes. Serves 2–4

Cut each rasher of bacon in half. Place each around the outer edge of 4 muffin rings. One shelled egg to each ring. Prick each yolk 3–4 times with cocktail stick or thin skewer. Sprinkle with paprika and parsley. Cook on high 2 minutes. Serve each on a round of buttered toast.

Step 1   Prawn Omelette. Add vegetables and prawns to beaten eggs

Step 2   Pour half cup measures of mixture into dish

Step 3   Cook omelettes on both sides until firm

28

Cheese Soufflé

6 eggs, separated
2 tablespoons butter
2 tablespoons flour
¾ teaspoon salt
⅛ teaspoon cayenne pepper
½ teaspoon dry mustard
1½ cups evaporated milk
1½ cups grated tasty cheese
¼ cup finely chopped chives or
     parsley
1 teaspoon cream of tartar

Time: 24 minutes. Serves 6

Place butter in a pyrex bowl and cook on high 1 minute. Stir in flour, salt, cayenne pepper and mustard. Cook 1 minute. Stir in evaporated milk and cook 4 minutes, stirring every minute. Stir in cheese.

Beat egg yolks and fold in 2 tablespoons of the cheese sauce. Stir yolks into remaining sauce and add chives.

Beat egg whites with cream of tartar until stiff peaks form. Fold whites into cheese mixture using a metal spoon.

Pour into an ungreased soufflé dish. Cook on low 18–20 minutes until top is firm.

HINT: WARMING, SOFTENING AND MELTING CHEESE

Warming cheese before serving brings out its full flavour. Here is a guide to warming some of our favourite cheeses:
Block Cheese (tasty or mild)
To warm: place 250 g block cheese on a plate. Cook on medium-low 45 seconds. Let stand for 5 minutes before serving. To melt: cut 250 g block cheese into 1 cm cubes. Place in bowl and cook on medium 2–3 minutes.
Camembert, Brie
To warm: place 250 g cheese on plate. Cook on medium-low 30–40 seconds. Let stand 5 minutes before serving.
Cream Cheese
To warm: Remove foil wrapper from 125 g cream cheese and cut into quarters. Place in bowl and cook on medium 45 seconds.
To melt: Remove foil wrapper from 250 g cream cheese and cut into eighths. Place in bowl and cook on medium 1–1½ minutes.

Cheese Fondue

250 g tasty cheese, cut into
     cubes
½ cup milk
1 teaspoon dry mustard
2 teaspoons Worcestershire
     sauce
1 teaspoon onion salt
2 tablespoons dry sherry or
     beer

Time: 8 minutes. Serves 4

In a large bowl combine all ingredients except dry sherry. Cook on medium low 8–10 minutes or until hot and smooth, stirring three times during cooking. Blend in sherry.

Serve with crusty bread cubes or blanched vegetables.

Welsh Rarebit

30 g butter
3 teaspoons flour
150 mL milk
125 g cheddar cheese, grated
1 egg yolk, beaten
4 tablespoons beer
½ teaspoon Worcestershire
     sauce
pinch salt
pinch cayenne pepper
pinch dry mustard

Time: 9 minutes. Serves 4

Place butter into bowl and cook on high 1 minute. Stir in flour and cook on high 1 minute. Blend in milk and cook on high 1½ minutes, stirring twice during cooking.

Add grated cheese and cook on medium 4–5 minutes to melt, stirring twice during cooking. Whisk egg yolk quickly into cheese sauce.

Place beer into small jug. Cook on high until reduced to 2 teaspoons. Add to cheese mixture with seasonings. Serve with triangles of buttered toast.

HINT: WARMING CHEESE

As cheese contains a high proportion of protein it will become tough and stringy if heated for too long or at too high a temperature.

Hors d'oeuvre

Most hors d'oeuvre ingredients can be prepared in advance and frozen until required. Melba toast and rounds, savoury butters and toppings, and meat and seafood balls can be stored carefully in the freezer and refrigerator and all that is needed to make you the perfect host is the microwave at the ready. And even those hors d'oeuvre which are at their best when freshly prepared will take only minutes to cook or heat in the microwave.

There are no set rules nowadays as to what should be served at cocktail parties or with pre-dinner drinks but the following selection of quick and exciting dips and finger foods have become firm party favourites.

Spicy Prawn Rolls

6 large green prawns
6 thin rashers bacon
6 pieces green capsicum,
  2 × 4 cm

Sauce

2 tablespoons light soy sauce
2 tablespoons dry sherry
1 tablespoon chilli sauce
2 tablespoons plum sauce

Time: 4 minutes. Serves 3–6

Arrange bacon rashers between double sheets of paper towel on a plate and cook on high 4 minutes.

Cut bacon rashers in half and remove rind. Wrap one prepared prawn and a piece of capsicum in each strip of bacon and fasten with a cocktail stick. Place in a bowl.

Combine sauce ingredients and spoon over prawn rolls. Allow to marinate 30 minutes. Cook on high 4 minutes or until prawns are cooked.

Bacon Puffs, Cheese Canapés,
Spicy Prawn Rolls, Crab Stuffed Zucchini

HINT: COOKING BACON
Cook bacon rashers between sheets of white paper towel as this will absorb the fat, prevent spattering and keep oven walls clean.

Caraway Crisps

½ cup flour
½ cup rye flour
½ teaspoon salt
1 teaspoon caraway seeds
3 tablespoons butter
1½–2 tablespoons cold water

Time: 3–6 minutes. Makes 24

Combine flours, salt and seeds in a mixing bowl and rub in butter to resemble breadcrumbs. Add water and blend together to form a dough.

Roll dough out thinly to form a rectangle on a floured board and cut into 2.5 cm squares. Arrange close together in circles on a large plate.

Cook on high 3–6 minutes or until dry and crisp. Remove carefully to a wire rack to cool.

Step 1   Caraway Crisps. Rub butter into dry ingredients

Hot Pizza Dip

200 g bacon
¼ cup chopped onion and
   capsicum
1 cup grated tasty cheese
¼ cup sliced stuffed olives
½ teaspoon chilli sauce

Time: 8 minutes. Serves 6

Cut bacon into 1 cm dice and place in a pyrex bowl. Cook on high 3 minutes. Drain off fat.

Stir in onion and capsicum and cook on high 2 minutes. Add cheese, olives and chilli sauce. Cook on medium 3 minutes or until cheese has melted. Serve hot with crackers or crisps.

Step 2   Use a knife to mix water into flour

Mushrooms with Pineapple Chicken Stuffing

6 large mushrooms, stalks
   removed
180 g canned crushed
   pineapple, drained
180 g cooked chicken, finely
   chopped
3 tablespoons mayonnaise
½ teaspoon lemon juice
pecan halves

Time: 7–8 minutes. Serves 6

Combine pineapple, chicken, mayonnaise and lemon juice. Spoon into mushroom caps and top each with a pecan nut.

Cook on high 2 minutes then on medium 5–6 minutes until hot. Rearrange mushrooms during cooking to ensure that all heat evenly.

Step 3   Cut pastry into 2.5 cm squares

Spinach Balls

1 × 300 g packet frozen
   spinach
¾ cup grated tasty cheese
¼ cup dry breadcrumbs
2 tablespoons Parmesan
   cheese
1 tablespoon finely chopped
   shallot
½ teaspoon salt
¼ teaspoon pepper
1 egg, beaten

Time: 12–13 minutes. Serves 6–8

Cook spinach in packet on high 5 minutes or until defrosted. Drain all excess liquid. Combine chopped spinach with remaining ingredients and shape into balls 2 cm in diameter.

Place onto baking tray lined with paper towel and cook on high 2 minutes then on medium 5–6 minutes, until hot. Rearrange balls during cooking to ensure that all heat evenly.

Crab Stuffed Zucchini

500 g even–sized zucchini, cut
   into 2 cm rings
360 g crabmeat
¾ cup finely chopped
   mushrooms
3 tablespoons butter
2 tablespoons flour
¾ cup milk, warm
½ cup finely chopped shallots
¼ teaspoon paprika
¼ teaspoon salt
⅛ teaspoon pepper
2 tablespoons white wine

Time: 13–14 minutes. Serves 8–10

Cook mushrooms and butter in a bowl on high 2 minutes. Stir in flour and cook on high 1 minute.

Blend in warm milk and add shallots, seasonings and wine. Cook on high 3–4 minutes or until thickened, stirring twice during cooking. Blend in crabmeat.

Hollow out half the centre of each piece of zucchini using a teaspoon.

Spoon crab mixture into zucchini cases and then place on a plate lined with paper towel. Cook on high 2 minutes, reduce to medium and cook 5 minutes or until hot. Rearrange during cooking.

HINT: WARMING MILK
Warm milk before blending into roux-based sauces. This avoids lumps and forms the sauce quickly. The sauce should always boil before serving.

Spinach Balls

Bacon Puffs

60 g bacon, finely chopped
20 small squares bread,
*   buttered on one side*
1 egg white
½ cup grated tasty cheese
¼ cup finely chopped
*   capsicum*
1 teaspoon chopped parsley
¼ teaspoon salt
pinch pepper

Time: 15 minutes. Serves 5

Beat egg white until stiff. Fold in cheese, capsicum, parsley, salt and pepper. Spoon mixture onto unbuttered side of bread. Sprinkle tops with bacon. Preheat browning grill for 5 minutes. Arrange canapés 10 at a time on preheated grill and cook on high for 10 minutes.

Cheese Canapés

16 prepared canapé bread
*   bases*
90 g cream cheese
1 shallot, finely chopped
1 teaspoon horseradish relish
16 small smoked oysters

Time: 7½ minutes. Serves 4

Cook cream cheese in bowl 30 seconds on high. Stir in shallot and horseradish relish and spread onto prepared canapé bases. Top each with a smoked oyster. Preheat browning grill on high for 5 minutes. Arrange canapés on preheated grill a few at a time and cook on high 2 minutes.

Devils on Horseback

4 long bacon rashers
12 prunes, pitted
12 toasted almonds
12 cocktail sticks

Time: 4 minutes. Serves 3–4

Derind bacon rashers and cut each rasher into 3 strips. Place an almond into each prune to replace the seed. Then wrap each prune in a strip of bacon. Secure with cocktail stick.

Place rolls onto a plate in a circle and cover with a paper towel. Cook on high 4 minutes.

HINT: CANAPÉ BASES
Most types of bread are suitable for microwave canapés. First remove crusts then cut the slices of bread into squares, rounds or rectangles. Butter bread thinly on one side only.

Step 1 Bacon Puffs. Add capsicum, cheese and parsley to beaten egg white

Step 2 Spoon mixture onto bread squares

Step 3 Sprinkle tops with chopped bacon

Snacks

A microwave oven is ideal for preparing snacks, either to welcome those surprise visitors or to delight at simple family meals. For quick lunches, appetising nibbles and snacks can be made in advance, frozen and simply reheated or defrosted when needed for a meal in a moment.

Anchovy Bread

1 loaf French bread
1 small can anchovy fillets
finely chopped parsley
90 g butter

Time: 1½ minutes

Mash anchovies with butter and parsley. Cut bread into slices ¾ through the loaf. Spread slices with butter. As the loaf will be too long for the microwave oven, cut loaf into four sections. Cook for 1½ minutes on high. Serve hot.

Creamy Smoked Ham Vol-au-vents

250 mL sour cream
1 tablespoon chopped parsley
freshly ground black pepper to
  taste
2 egg yolks, beaten
dash nutmeg
60 g smoked ham, diced
12 mini vol-au-vent cases

Time: 9 minutes. Serves 4–6

Combine sour cream, parsley, pepper, egg yolks and nutmeg in mixing bowl. Cook on medium high for 5–7 minutes, or until thickened, stir occasionally. Add ham. Cook 1–2 minutes on medium high.
Fill vol-au-vent cases and serve immediately.

Optional Fillings
As well as diced ham, the following ingredients make tasty fillings for vol-au-vent cases.

60 g smoked oysters
¼ cup chopped mushrooms
  and ¼ cup chopped
  asparagus
¼ cup crumbled blue vein
  cheese
½ cup chopped cooked chicken

Party Pizzas

Lebanese bread

Sauce

250 g can tomato paste
1 teaspoon sugar
½ teaspoon oregano
½ teaspoon freshly ground black
  pepper
½ teaspoon basil

Topping Suggestions

fresh mushrooms, sliced
onion rings
mozzarella cheese slices
capsicum rings
rolled or flat anchovies
ham, cut in strips
sliced continental salami
black or green stuffed olives
Parmesan cheese, cayenne,
  paprika
grated tasty cheese
parsley

Time: 6 minutes

Prepare sauce by combining ingredients. Arrange the toppings on a serving platter for guests to make their own selection.
Spread sauce over each bread round, add toppings and cook 6 minutes on high. Cut into wedges.

Tuna or Salmon Mornay

2 cups tuna or salmon
2 cups basic white sauce (see
  Sauces and Jams)
125 g tasty cheese, grated
lemon wedges, parsley and
  paprika for garnish

Time: 10 minutes. Serves 4

Layer half tuna, half sauce, and half cheese in a 20 cm × 20 cm baking dish. Repeat second layer. Cook 10 minutes on high. Garnish with parsley, paprika and lemon wedges.

Chinese Chicken Savouries

2 double chicken breasts
1 tablespoon oil
30 g butter
1 tablespoon finely chopped
   ginger
2–3 cloves garlic, crushed
2 tablespoons soy sauce

Time: 9 minutes. Serves 4

Remove chicken from bone. Cut into 2 cm pieces. Melt butter and oil in a pie dish. Add the ginger and garlic. Cook on high 1 minute. Add chicken pieces and soy sauce. Cover with plastic food wrap. Cook for 8 minutes. Stir halfway through cooking period. Do not overcook as chicken will toughen.

Macaroni and Cheese

1 cup macaroni, uncooked
1 litre hot water
½ teaspoon salt
2 cups cheese, grated
2 eggs
1 cup milk
½ teaspoon prepared mustard
dash of salt
dash of Worcestershire sauce
dash of paprika

Time: 18 minutes. Serves 4

Place macaroni into a 2 litre casserole with water and salt. Cook in oven 10 minutes on high or until macaroni is tender. Stir after 5 minutes. Drain, rinse in hot water.

Place a layer of macaroni in a baking dish and sprinkle with grated cheese. Repeat, alternating macaroni and cheese, ending with cheese. Beat eggs lightly in a bowl. Add milk, mustard, salt and Worcestershire sauce. Stir well. Drizzle mixture on macaroni. Sprinkle with paprika. Cook, covered, on high 8 minutes, stirring after 4 minutes.

Spicy Frankfurts

1 kg cocktail frankfurts
1 cup chilli sauce
¼ cup dry sherry
1 clove finely chopped garlic
grated rind ½ lemon

Time: 7 minutes. Serves 6–8

Combine chilli sauce, sherry, garlic and lemon rind. Place frankfurts in shallow baking dish and coat with chilli sauce mix. Cover and cook on high 5 minutes. Stir once.

Stand covered to marinate 1–2 hours. Reheat uncovered on high 2 minutes and serve immediately.

Tuna-stuffed Capsicums

4–6 large capsicums
500 g canned tuna
1 cup soft breadcrumbs
½ cup finely diced celery
⅓ cup mayonnaise
1 egg
2 tablespoons lemon juice
2 tablespoons prepared
   mustard
2 tablespoons soft butter
1 tablespoon finely chopped
   onion
¼ teaspoon salt
⅛ teaspoon tabasco sauce
2 slices cheese

Time: 18 minutes. Serves 4

Cut a slice from the upper third of each capsicum. Dice strips that have been cut off. Remove seeds and membrane from inside of capsicum. Parboil capsicum in oven for 5 minutes on high. Drain. Mix diced capsicum with remaining ingredients. Fill capsicums and stand them in a casserole dish. Cook covered on high 12 minutes.

Top with cheese strips in form of cross. Cook 1 minute on high.

Tuna Italian Style

1 × 500 g can drained tuna
2 tablespoons butter
2 tablespoons flour
½ cup cream
½ cup milk
1 cup fish stock
2 tablespoons dry vermouth
½ teaspoon onion salt
¾ cup grated tasty cheese
2 shallots, finely chopped
6 medium mushrooms, sliced
2 cups cook spaghetti or
   macaroni
2 tablespoons chopped Italian
   parsley

Time: 11 minutes. Serves 6

Place butter in a 2 litre casserole dish and cook on high 1 minute. Stir in flour and cook on high 1 minute. Blend in cream, milk, fish stock, vermouth and onion salt and cook on high 5 minutes, stirring twice during cooking.

Fold in cheese, shallots, mushrooms, tuna and cooked spaghetti. Cover and cook on high 4 minutes or until hot, stirring mixture during heating.

Serve garnished with chopped parsley.

Tuna Stuffed Capsicums

Cabbage Rolls

12 cabbage leaves, medium size
500 g topside, minced
250 g pork, minced
125 g chopped onion
¾ cup cooked rice
½ teaspoon cumin powder
1 egg
1 teaspoon thyme
1 tablespoon chopped parsley
1 clove garlic, chopped
1 tablespoon salt
¾ teaspoon pepper
2½ cups fresh tomato sauce
    (see recipe)
¼ cup butter

Time: 28 minutes. Serves 6

Place cabbage leaves in 2 tablespoons water in a casserole dish. Cook covered on high for 8 minutes or until soft. Combine mince, pork, onion, rice, cumin, egg, thyme, parsley, garlic, salt, pepper, and ½ cup of tomato sauce.

Place two tablespoons stuffing on each cabbage leaf and wrap leaves around mixture firmly. Place cabbage rolls in a casserole dish. Spread butter on top of rolls and remaining tomato sauce. Cook, covered, 20 minutes on high, or until meat is cooked and rolls are tender. Let stand, covered, 10 minutes.

Seafood Crepes

Crepes

60 g plain flour
150 mL milk
salt and pepper
parsley, finely chopped
1 egg
15 g butter, melted
30 g lard, to grease crepe pan

Filling

125 g cooked crabmeat, frozen
    or canned
125 g cooked prawns
125 g cooked scallops
2 cups cheese sauce (see recipe)
2 tablespoons finely cut chives
1–2 tablespoons finely chopped
    parsley
lemon wedges for garnish

Time: 5 minutes. Serves 6

Mix all crepe ingredients except lard to make a batter. Grease crepe pan with lard. Heat on range top. Add 1½–2 tablespoons of mixture. Cook until mixture bubbles, turn over and cook a further minute until lightly brown.

Combine all filling ingredients. Place 2 tablespoons mixture onto each crepe. Roll up and place side by side into a casserole dish and cook for 5 minutes on medium. Serve with lemon wedges.

Quiche Lorraine

Pastry

1¼ cups plain flour
¼ teaspoon baking powder
pinch of salt
⅓ cup margarine
2 tablespoons water
squeeze of lemon juice
1 egg yolk

Filling

3 eggs
1 cup cream
1 cup milk
pinch of nutmeg, sugar,
    cayenne pepper and white
    pepper
4 rashers bacon, chopped
1 cup grated tasty cheese
parsley for garnish

Time: 18 minutes. Serves 4–6

Sift dry ingredients for pastry into bowl. Rub in margarine using fingertips until mixture resembles fine breadcrumbs. Combine remaining pastry ingredients. Make a well in the centre of dry ingredients, gradually add liquid, mixing to form a dry dough. Turn onto a lightly floured surface, roll out to fit a deep 23 cm glass pie plate. Cook 6 minutes on high.

For filling, whisk eggs, cream, milk, and spices in mixing bowl. Lightly fry bacon. Sprinkle bacon and cheese over cooked pastry shell. Pour liquid mixture carefully into pastry shell. Cook, uncovered in microwave oven for 12 minutes on medium. Allow to stand 5 minutes before serving. Garnish with parsley and serve.

Lamb Pilaf

1½ cups cooked lamb cut in 2
    cm dice
1 medium onion, chopped
1 stalk celery, cut in 1 cm
    pieces
1 medium green capsicum, cut
    1 cm dice
1 tablespoon oil
1½ cups quick cooking rice
1 cup tomato puree
¾ cup beef consomme or stock
125 g mushrooms, cut in 1 cm
    pieces
2 teaspoons brown sugar
½ teaspoon basil
½ teaspoon salt
⅛ teaspoon pepper
1 bay leaf
⅛ teaspoon thyme
⅛ teaspoon cayenne pepper

Time: 13 minutes. Serves 4

In a 2 litre casserole combine onion, celery, green capsicum and oil. Cover and cook on high 3 minutes. Stir in remaining ingredients, cover and cook on high 5 minutes. Stir and re-cover.

Reduce power to medium. Cook 5–8 minutes until rice is tender and liquid absorbed.

Lasagne with Topside Mince

250 g lasagne noodles
8 cups boiling water
1 tablespoon salt
1 tablespoon oil
1 tablespoon butter, softened
1 cup sliced onion
¼ cup sliced mushrooms
500 g topside mince
1 clove chopped garlic
1 (250 g) can tomato puree
1 (180 g) can tomato paste
1½ cups beef stock
½ teaspoon sugar
½ teaspoon salt
dash of pepper
1 teaspoon basil
500 g cottage cheese
250 g mozzarella cheese slices
½ cup grated Parmesan cheese

Time: 48 minutes. Serves 6

Place lasagne noodles in a casserole. Pour over boiling water. Add salt. Cook 16 minutes on high until tender. Drain and mix with a little oil. Set aside.

Melt butter in casserole 30 seconds. Saute onion in butter 3 minutes. Add mushrooms. Cook 3 minutes. Remove from casserole. Cook topside mince and garlic in casserole 6 minutes, stirring every 2 minutes. Add onion and mushroom mixture, tomato puree, tomato sauce, stock, sugar, salt, pepper and basil. Stir well. Cook, covered, 10 minutes, stirring every 3 minutes to make meat sauce.

Layer meat sauce, noodles, cottage cheese and mozzarella cheese in a deep casserole dish. Repeat layers 3 times, ending with meat sauce. Sprinkle Parmesan cheese on top. Cook on high 10 minutes.

Moussaka

3 eggplants
4 tablespoons olive oil
500 g minced beef
1 small tin tomato paste
salt, cayenne and oregano
2 medium onions, sliced
1 egg
1 cup sour cream
1½ cups buttered breadcrumbs
tomato for garnish
parsley for garnish

Time: 30 minutes. Serves 6

Cut unpeeled eggplant into 1 cm slices. Sprinkle with salt and leave to stand for 30 minutes. Drain off liquid. Heat browning skillet 8 minutes, add oil and heat a further 3 minutes. Cook eggplant on each side 2 minutes on high. Combine meat, tomato paste and seasonings.

Place layers of eggplant, meat mixture and sliced onion in a greased casserole. Combine beaten egg with sour cream. Spread over mixture. Sprinkle thickly with buttered crumbs and cook 15 minutes on high. Serve hot garnished with tomato and parsley.

Spinach Pie

500 g precooked spinach leaves
  (see Vegetables)
1 onion, finely chopped
3 eggs
125 g feta cheese
1 cup cottage cheese
2 tablespoons Parmesan cheese
¼ cup chopped parsley
salt and pepper
¼ teaspoon nutmeg
1 packet filo pastry
½ cup butter, melted

Time: 15 minutes. Serves 6

Combine spinach, onion, eggs, cheese, parsley and seasonings into a bowl. Brush an oblong casserole dish with melted butter. Place 1 sheet filo pastry in dish so that it comes up to the top edges. Brush with melted butter and repeat until the base has 6–8 layers. Cook on high 2 minutes. Add filling to pastry, spreading evenly. Top with 6 more layers of buttered pastry. Trim edges. Cut into squares through the first four layers of pastry. Cook uncovered in oven 13 minutes. Cut into squares and serve warm.

Optional: Brown top of pie under heated grill for 2–3 minutes.

Crustless Ricotta Cheese Pie

1½ cups ricotta cheese
1 × 300 g packet frozen,
  chopped spinach
½ cup finely chopped onion
2 eggs
¼ teaspoon salt
¼ teaspoon pepper
¼ teaspoon nutmeg
2 teaspoons flour
1 finely chopped shallot
⅛ teaspoon paprika

Time: 15 minutes. Serves 8

Combine spinach and onion in a 1 litre casserole dish. Cover and cook on high 5 minutes, stirring after 2 minutes. Drain well.

Beat eggs with a fork in a medium-sized bowl. Stir in ricotta cheese, salt, pepper, nutmeg and flour. Blend in spinach and shallot.

Spread mixture on a 22.5 cm pie plate. Sprinkle with paprika and cook on high 4 minutes. Reduce to medium and cook 6 minutes or until centre is set. Let stand 5 minutes before serving.

Chilli con Carne

½ tablespoon butter
500 g topside, minced
1 small onion, diced
½ teaspoon garlic salt
1 tablespoon chilli powder
½ teaspoon dry mustard
salt and pepper
½ can tomatoes
250 g can kidney beans
250 g can baked beans
250 g can sliced mushrooms
2 stalks celery, diced
2 tablespoons tomato paste
1 teaspoon paprika
½ teaspoon oregano

Time: 13 minutes. Serves 6

Place butter, beef, diced onions and garlic salt into a 2 litre casserole dish. Cook on high 3 minutes until brown. Add chilli powder, mustard, salt, pepper and remaining ingredients. Cook for 10 minutes stirring after the first 5 minutes. Serve with rice or buttered toast.

Pork and Prawn Rolls

125 g pork mince
125 g prawns, shelled and
   finely chopped
3 sheets puff pastry
30 g butter
60 g mushrooms, finely
   chopped
1 tablespoon dry sherry
2 shallots, finely chopped
1 hard-boiled egg, chopped
½ cup grated carrot
egg to glaze

Time: 14 minutes. Serves 8

Place butter and pork in a bowl and cook on high 4 minutes. Drain. Add mushrooms and shallots and cook on high 2 minutes. Fold in remaining ingredients.

Cut each sheet of pastry into thirds and brush each sheet with beaten egg. Arrange filling along the strips and roll up carefully. Brush tops of rolls with egg and cut into 4 cm lengths.

Heat browning grill on high 5 minutes. Place rolls on grill and cook on high 1 minute on each side.

Ham Relish Finger Rolls

200 g ham, chopped
2 tablespoons gherkin relish
¼ cup mayonnaise
2 teaspoons finely chopped
   shallot
6 slices wholemeal bread
¼ cup butter
1 egg, beaten
1 cup poppy seeds

Time: 4 minutes. Serves 6

Combine ham, relish, mayonnaise and shallot in a small bowl.

Remove crusts from bread. Roll each slice out thinly with a rolling pin and spread thinly with ham mixture. Roll up and secure with two cocktail sticks.

Place butter in bowl and heat on high 1 minute. Blend in beaten egg.

Roll each sandwich in butter mixture, then coat generously with poppy seeds.

Chill for 15 minutes. Cut each roll into 4 pieces and arrange pieces 12 at a time on outer edge of a plate and cook on high 3 minutes.

Bread Cases

6 thin slices of brown or white
   bread
butter
1 micromuffin pan

Filling Suggestions

1 cup cheese sauce and add
   either:
1 cup of cream style corn
1 cup flaked salmon
1 cup assorted seafood
   (prawns, crabmeat, oysters)
1 cup chopped green asparagus

Time: 4 minutes

Remove crusts from bread. Place bread in oven and cook 1 minute to refresh. Butter bread. Place butter side down in muffin pan, so that the corners form four peaks. Place into oven and cook on high 2–3 minutes. Remove cases, which should be firm and crisp.

Rice and Pasta

Rice is available in many grades and varieties — local and imported, white and brown, short and long grain — but whatever variety, rice cooks far quicker in a microwave than it does on the conventional hot plate. It takes only 8 minutes to cook one cup of rice.

   Always use a large lidded casserole and it is a good idea to place a plain dinner plate under the casserole to catch any liquid that may boil over. Allow standing time for rice and before serving fork up grains.

   To add zest to rice dishes add whole or ground spices, curry powder, chopped fruit, nuts, vegetable juices, stock, wine or dressings to the rice before cooking.

   Dried pasta, unlike rice, does not cook quicker in a microwave. Always choose a large casserole or Pyrex basin that can hold at least 6–8 cups of salted water. If you are using fresh pasta reduce cooking time a little.

Cooking White Rice

1 cup long grain rice, washed
1¾ cups boiling water
1 tablespoon butter
½ teaspoon salt

Time: 8 minutes. Serves 6

Place all ingredients in a 1 litre casserole dish. Cover and cook on high 8 minutes. Let stand 4 minutes before serving.

Cooking Brown Rice

1 cup brown rice, washed
2 cups water
1 tablespoon butter
⅛ teaspoon salt

Time: 22 minutes. Serves 6

Place all ingredients in a 2 litre casserole dish. Cook on high 22 minutes. Let stand 5 minutes before serving.

HINT: KEEPING RICE HOT
Cooked rice will remain hot in a covered casserole dish for 30 minutes at room temperature. Take advantage of this time to cook or reheat accompanying food.

Fried Rice with Vegetables

Fried Rice with Vegetables

2 cups cooked rice
⅓ cup thinly sliced celery
⅓ cup chopped green
  capsicum
⅓ cup chopped shallots
1 small carrot finely chopped
1 × 250 g can sliced bamboo
  shoots, drained
1 tablespoon vegetable oil
1 teaspoon chopped parsley
⅛ teaspoon salt
⅛ teaspoon pepper
1½ tablespoons soy sauce
2 eggs, beaten

Time: 9 minutes. Serves 6

Combine vegetables, oil and seasonings in a bowl. Preheat browning dish on high for 3 minutes. Spoon in vegetable mixture and sauce, stir and cover. Cook on high for 3 minutes or until crisp but still tender. Set aside.

Place eggs into small bowl and cook on high for 1 minute, stirring every 20 seconds. Stir rice and eggs into vegetable mixture. Cook on high 2 minutes to reheat, stirring after 1 minute.

Wild Rice with Vegetables

1½ cups wild rice, washed
5 cups hot water
½ cup chopped onion
½ cup chopped celery
2 tablespoons butter
250 g fresh mushrooms, sliced
2 chicken stock cubes

Time: 40 minutes. Serves 6–8

Combine rice and hot water in a 3 litre casserole dish. Cover and cook on high 30 minutes or until rice is tender, stirring every 10 minutes. Let rice stand uncovered 15 minutes.

In a 2 litre casserole dish combine onion, celery and butter. Cover and cook on high 3 minutes. Add mushrooms and crumbled stock cubes and cook on high 3 minutes.

Drain and rinse rice with boiling water. Mix with vegetables, cover and cook on high 3–4 minutes until heated through.

> **HINT: REHEATING RICE**
> Cold cooked rice can be reheated on high. Add 1 tablespoon of warm water to rice, cover and heat for 2–3 minutes.

Step 1 Parsley Rice Ring. Add onion, parsley, rice and egg yolks to melted butter

Parsley Rice Ring

3 cups cooked rice
½ cup butter
2 tablespoons finely chopped
  onion
1 cup finely chopped parsley
3 × 55 g eggs, separated

Time: 6 minutes. Serves 6

Place butter into 2 litre bowl and cook on high 2 minutes. Add onion, parsley, rice and egg yolks and blend together.

Fold in stiffly beaten egg whites and pour mixture into a greased ring dish. Level top of mixture with a spoon and cook on high for 4 minutes. Unmould onto round platter to serve. Centre may be filled with various fillings.

Lemon Rice

1 cup white rice, washed
1 tablespoon butter
⅛ teaspoon cumin seeds
⅛ teaspoon coriander seeds
¼ teaspoon salt
½ teaspoon turmeric
1¾ cups boiling water
1 lemon, juiced
fresh coriander, chopped

Time: 10 minutes. Serves 6

Place butter in a 2 litre casserole dish and cook on high 1 minute. Add rice, cumin, coriander seeds, salt and turmeric and cook on high 1 minute. Stir in boiling water and cook on high 8 minutes. Let stand 4 minutes. Add strained lemon juice, forking in lightly. Sprinkle with coriander.

Step 2   Fold egg whites into rice mixture

Step 3   Spoon mixture into greased ring dish

Parsley Rice Ring

Fried Rice

3 rashers bacon
30 g fresh mushrooms
1 small onion
2 shallots
30 g shelled prawns
2 eggs
3 cups cold cooked rice, cooked
    with 1 chicken cube
1 tablespoon dark soy sauce

Time: 11 minutes. Serves 4

Dice bacon, mushrooms, onions, shallots and prawns. Place bacon on glass dish, cover with white kitchen paper and cook 3 minutes on high. Remove from dish, add onion, mushrooms and cook 2 minutes.

Fold lightly beaten eggs into rice, and add to dish. Cook on high 2 minutes, then stir, add bacon, soy sauce and stir mixture again. Cook 2 minutes. Stir in shallots and prawns Cook 2 minutes to reheat. Season.

Saffron Rice

15 g butter
1 small onion, chopped
¼ teaspoon powdered saffron
    or turmeric
1 cup washed rice
30 g currants or sultanas
2 cups boiling chicken stock
    (can use stock cube)
30 g almond slivers, toasted

Time: 11 minutes. Serves 4

Place butter into 1 litre casserole dish and cook 15 seconds. Add onion, saffron and cook on high 3 minutes. Add rice, currants and boiling stock. Cook covered 8 minutes. Allow to stand 10 minutes. Sprinkle with almonds before serving.

Ginger Saffron Rice

1 cup washed rice
pinch of salt
2 tablespoons diced red
    capsicum or crystallised
    ginger
½ teaspoon powdered saffron
nob of butter
2 cups boiling water

Time: 8 minutes. Serves 4

Place rice into a 1 litre casserole, add salt, capsicum or ginger, saffron, butter and boiling water. Cook on high 8 minutes. Allow to stand 10 minutes before serving. Can be moulded and turned out on serving plate.

Tomato Rice

1 cup washed rice
½ teaspoon sugar
pinch oregano
pinch onion salt
nob of butter
1 cup tomato juice
1 cup chicken stock
chopped parsley

Time: 8 minutes. Serves 4

Bring tomato juice and chicken stock to the boil on hotplate. Place rice into a 1 litre casserole dish, add sugar, spices, butter and tomato juice and stock. Cook covered on high 8 minutes. Allow to stand 10 minutes. Sprinkle with chopped parsley. Serve with chicken dishes or casseroles.

Basic Rice Pilaf

60 g butter
1 small onion, chopped finely
1 cup long grain rice, washed
2 cups boiling chicken stock
salt and pepper

Time: 14 minutes. Serves 4

Place 30 g butter and the onion into a casserole dish. Cook 3 minutes on high, stir in rice. Cook a further 3 minutes on high. Add stock, seasonings, cover with a lid and cook 8 minutes. Mix in remaining butter, allow to stand 5 minutes before serving.

Mushroom Pilaf

125 g sliced fresh mushrooms can be added to the rice and cooked as above.

Vegetable Pilaf

30 g cooked peas
30 g diced capsicum
30 g diced tomato
60 g grated cheese

Prepare Rice Pilaf as above. After cooking, fold all Vegetable Pilaf ingredients into rice with remaining butter and allow to stand 5 minutes before serving to heat through.

Ginger Saffron Rice

Vegetarian Rice

Vegetarian Rice

2 tablespoons butter
1 carrot, diced
2 large mushrooms, finely
   minced
1 onion
½ red capsicum
½ green capsicum
1 cup corn kernels
1 cup peas
3 cups cooked rice
salt and pepper
1 clove garlic, finely minced
1 slice ginger, finely minced
2 tablespoons chopped parsley
hard-boiled eggs

Time: 9 minutes. Serves 4–6

Dice all vegetables to the size of the corn. Wash and drain. Place butter into a 2 litre casserole. Cook 15 seconds. Add all the vegetables and cook on high covered 4 minutes. Fold in rice and add salt, pepper, garlic, ginger and parsley. Cook 5 minutes, covered. Garnish with diced, hard-boiled eggs.

Paella

3 tablespoons oil
1 cup sliced onion
1 clove garlic, minced
1 cup uncooked rice, washed
2 cups boiling chicken stock
1½ teaspoons salt
¼ teaspoon saffron
⅛ teaspoon pepper
1 can (125 g) prawns, drained
1½ cups cooked chicken, 2 cm
   cubes
6 mussels, in the shell
1 cup peas
½ cup sliced stuffed olives

Time 13 minutes. Serves 4–6

Heat oil in a 2 litre casserole for 3 minutes. Add onion, garlic and heat a further 2 minutes. Add rice, chicken stock, salt, saffron, pepper and cook for 3 minutes. Stir. Fold in prawns, chicken, mussels and peas and cook a further 5 minutes, stirring after 2½ minutes. Add olives. Remove from oven and allow to stand 10 minutes before serving.
   Note: Keep casserole covered while cooking.

Paella

Cooking Pasta

Pasta should be cooked in a large casserole dish with a lid. Place casserole onto a large plate during cooking to catch any spillover.

6–8 cups water
250 g pasta
2 teaspoons salt
cooking oil

Serves 4–6

Place water and salt in casserole. Allow 2½ minutes cooking time on high for each cup of water. When water is boiling add pasta and cover. Cook on high for 16 minutes or until tender.

Drain, rinse well in hot water, drain again and stir in 1–2 teaspoons cooking oil. This keeps the pasta separate.

Macaroni with Tomato Sauce

250 g large macaroni shells
60 g grated cheese
60 g butter
1½ cups tomato sauce (see recipe Tomato Sauce)

Time: 26 minutes. Serves 4–6

Cook macaroni in boiling salted water until tender. Drain well and return to casserole dish. Mix in butter and tomato sauce. Correct seasoning. Add tomato concassée and cook on high 4 minutes to reheat. Serve grated cheese separately.

Tomato Concassée

30 g chopped onion
30 g butter
250 g tomatoes, peeled and chopped
salt
freshly ground black pepper

Time: 6 minutes

Place onion and butter in a bowl and cook on high 2 minutes. Add chopped tomatoes and cook on high 4 minutes. Season with salt and pepper.

Tomato Sauce

15 g butter
½ clove garlic, chopped
15 g flour
375 mL stock
30 g tomato paste
salt and pepper
15 g bacon pieces
60 g onion, chopped
60 g carrot, chopped
30 g celery, chopped
½ teaspoon dried basil

Time: 21 minutes

Place butter in casserole. Cook on high 45 seconds then add bacon pieces, onion, carrot, celery and basil. Cover and cook on high 5 minutes, stirring after 2 minutes. Blend in flour and cook on high 1 minute. Add tomato paste, stock, garlic and seasonings and cook on high 4–5 minutes until boiling.

Reduce power to medium and cook 10 minutes. Purée sauce. Serve with pasta, eggs, fish or meat.

Fettuccine Carbonara

250 g fettuccine, cooked (still hot)
4 rashers bacon
150 mL cream
2 eggs
½ cup fresh Parmesan, grated
parsley

Time: 4 minutes. Serves 4

Cook bacon between sheets of paper towelling on high 4 minutes. Place pasta in bowl, add beaten eggs, cream, cheese and chopped bacon. Toss through pasta. Garnish with finely cut parsley and serve immediately.

HINT: WARMING SLICED BREAD AND DINNER ROLLS
Arrange 6 dinner rolls or 6 slices of bread in a napkin-lined bread basket and microwave on high 15 seconds. Warm uncut French and garlic bread on high for 30 seconds. Avoid overheating.

HINT: CONVENTIONAL TIME-SAVER
If you are preparing a large meal it can be more efficient to cook the pasta conventionally, while you use the microwave for sauces and other dishes.

56

Soups

Perfect soups can be cooked in the microwave oven in minutes and the variety is endless. Everything from clear consommés to chowders and rich cream soups can be prepared in a flash by using a food processor alongside your microwave.

Because vegetables retain their colour, flavour and goodness when cooked in a microwave, vegetable soups always look great and taste delicious. Soups can be made in advance and frozen and by taking advantage of the defrost cycle, a hot snack will only be minutes away.

Prawn Bisque

500 g prawn meat, chopped
2 tablespoons butter
1 onion, chopped
1 stalk celery, diced
2 tablespoons flour
3 cups milk
½ teaspoon salt
pinch white pepper
½ cup fish stock (see recipe
Quick Fish Stock)

Time: 16½ minutes. Serves 6–8

Place butter, onion and celery in a 2 litre casserole dish. Cover and cook on high 4 minutes. Stir in flour and cook on high 2 minutes.

Stir in milk, salt and pepper. Cook on high 7½ minutes, stirring every 2 minutes to make a white sauce.

Blend in fish stock and prawns. Cook on medium 3–4 minutes. Garnish with sliced pimiento and parsley to serve.

Minestrone

1 medium–sized onion,
chopped
1 clove garlic, finely chopped
½ cup chopped celery
¼ cup diced green capsicum
1 tablespoon cooking oil
1 × 440 g can kidney beans
1 × 440 g can tomato pieces
1 medium–sized zucchini,
diced
¼ cup white rice
3 cups beef stock or
consommé
¼ cup red wine
1 tablespoon chopped parsley
pinch dried oregano
½ teaspoon sugar
¼ teaspoon white pepper
¼ cup grated Parmesan
cheese

Time: 26 minutes. Serves 8

Place onion, garlic, celery, capsicum and oil in a 3 litre casserole dish. Cover and cook on high 6 minutes.

Add remaining ingredients except Parmesan cheese. Re-cover and cook on high 20 minutes, stirring 3 times during cooking.

Sprinkle with extra parsley and serve with Parmesan cheese.

HINT: TO CHANGE YIELD

To increase or decrease the yield of a microwave recipe follow these hints:

Decreasing yield by half — use only ½ the specified quantity of ingredients and reduce cooking time by ⅓.

Doubling yield — double quantity of solid ingredients, increase liquids by 1⅔ to 1¾ and increase cooking time by about ½ to ⅔.

HINT: INDIVIDUAL INSTANT SOUPS

Pour cold water or stock into cup until ¾ full. Microwave on high 1½–2 minutes, until boiling. Add contents of individual soup packet. Microwave on medium for 1–2 minutes to infuse.

Minestrone

Borscht

250 g beetroot, grated
2 medium-sized carrots,
* thinly sliced*
1 large onion, shredded
1 medium-sized potato, cut in
* 1 cm cubes*
1½ cups shredded green
* cabbage*
1 clove garlic, finely chopped
½ teaspoon salt
¼ teaspoon marjoram
⅛ teaspoon white pepper
1 large bay leaf
2½ cups water
1 × 440 g can beef consommé
sour cream
freshly cut dill

Time: 27 minutes. Serves 6–8

Step 1   Borscht. Prepare vegetables

Place beetroot, carrots, onion, potato, cabbage, garlic, seasoning and ½ cup water into a 3 litre casserole dish. Cover and cook on high 17 minutes or until vegetables are tender.

Add remaining water and beef consommé, cover and cook on high 20 minutes. Stir twice during cooking.

Remove bay leaf. Top individual servings with sour cream and dill to serve.

Quick Fish Stock

100 g white fish fillets
1 tablespoon chopped onion
1 bay leaf
1 teaspoon lemon juice
4 parsley stalks
3 peppercorns
2 cups water

Time: 11 minutes. Makes 3 cups

Step 2   Place vegetables in casserole

Place all ingredients in a 2 litre casserole dish. Cover and cook on high 6 minutes. Stir. Cook on medium 5 minutes, then strain. Correct seasonings before using.

HINT: DON'T OVERCOOK THESE FOODS

When using ingredients like asparagus, mushrooms, cheese, strawberries or shellfish it is always best to add them to the mixture toward the end of the microwaving process so that these fairly sensitive foods are not overcooked.

Step 3   When vegetables are tender, add beef consommé

Borscht

Cheese and Almond Soup

60 g butter
⅓ cup finely chopped onion
¼ cup grated carrot
*2 tablespoons chopped
    blanched almonds*
¼ cup flour
¼ teaspoon white pepper
⅛ teaspoon salt
1½ cups milk
*350 mL canned Cream of
    Chicken soup*
2 cups grated tasty cheese

Time: 17 minutes. Serves 4–6.

Place butter, onion, carrot and almonds in a 2 litre casserole dish. Cook on high 4 minutes, stirring every minute. Stir in flour, pepper and salt and then stir in milk and chicken soup.

Cook on high 8 minutes, stirring every 2 minutes. Add cheese, stir until melted. Cook on medium 5 minutes.

Mulligatawny Soup

60 g butter
125 g onions, chopped
1 clove garlic, finely chopped
60 g flour
2 teaspoons curry powder
1 tablespoon tomato paste
*1 litre brown stock or
    consommé*
30 g peeled, chopped apple
2 teaspoons fruit chutney
salt to taste
30 g cooked rice
1 tablespoon chopped parsley

Time: 36 minutes. Serves 6–8.

Place butter, onion and garlic in a 2 litre casserole dish. Cook on high 6 minutes. Blend in flour and curry powder. Cook a further minute.

Add tomato paste and stock and cook on high 15 minutes or until boiling. Stir in apple, chutney and salt. Cook on medium 10 minutes.

Purée ingredients in a food processor. Correct seasonings. Cook on reheat 5 minutes. Fold in rice and parsley.

Chilled Strawberry Soup

3 cups sliced strawberries
1 cup sugar
½ cup water
2 teaspoons arrowroot
2 tablespoons cold water
1 cup red wine
1 cup orange juice
1½ cups sour cream
strawberries for garnish

Time: 14 minutes. Serves 8

Place strawberries, sugar and water in a 2 litre casserole dish. Cover and cook on high 3 minutes or until boiling. Cook 5 minutes on medium.

Blend arrowroot with water, then blend with wine and orange juice into strawberry mixture. Cook on high 6 minutes or until boiling. Chill mixture.

Purée in food processor. Stir in cream and serve chilled, garnished with sliced strawberries.

Cream of Asparagus Soup

250 g asparagus, fresh or
　canned
60 g butter
60 g onion, chopped
60 g celery, cut in 1 cm pieces
60 g flour
1 litre white stock
1 bouquet garni
½ teaspoon salt
¼ teaspoon white pepper
150 mL cream or milk

Time: 35 minutes. Serves 6–8

Place butter, onion and celery into a 2 litre casserole dish. Cook on high 6 minutes.

Stir in flour, cook a further minute on high. Stir in stock, cook on high 15 minutes or until boiling.

Add roughly chopped asparagus, bouquet garni and seasoning. Cook on medium 10 minutes. Remove bouquet garni. Purée ingredients in food processor. Add cream or milk. Cook on reheat 5 minutes. Serve with croûtons.

Bouquet Garni

10 × 5 cm parsley stalks
3 large bay leaves
2 × 5 cm pieces celery

Place parsley stems and bay leaves into the hollow of one piece of celery. Place second piece of celery on top. Secure with elastic band or string. Use to flavour soups, stocks and casseroles.

Step 1　Strawberry Soup. Place strawberries, sugar and water in casserole

Step 2　Pour arrowroot, wine and orange juice over strawberries

Step 3　Purée soup in food processor

Crab and Sweet Corn Soup

6 cups chicken stock
1 cup crabmeat
1 cup cream style corn
1 tablespoon cornflour, water
1 tablespoon sherry (dry)
½ teaspoon salt
½ teaspoon oil
½ teaspoon sesame oil
2 eggs, beaten
½ cup shallots, finely chopped

Time: 20 minutes. Serves 6

Place stock into a large casserole dish and cook 15 minutes or until boiling on high. Add crabmeat and corn and cook a further 2 minutes. Add blended cornflour, sherry, salt and oils and bring to the boil, approximately 3 minutes. Remove from oven and add egg slowly to form egg flower. Add shallots. Serve hot.

Cream of Mushroom Soup

125 g mushrooms
4 tablespoons butter
4 tablespoons plain flour
1½ cups milk
1½ cups chicken stock
1 cup cream
salt and pepper
chopped chives

Time: 17 minutes. Serves 4

Slice and dice mushrooms. Place butter into a 2 litre casserole dish and cook 1 minute to melt. Add mushrooms, and cook on high covered 3 minutes. Stir in flour, cook a further 2 minutes. Blend in milk and stock. Cook 9 minutes on high. Add cream and cook 2 minutes to reheat. Season with salt and pepper. Add a few chopped chives before serving.

Clam Chowder

3 rashers rindless bacon,
    diced 1 cm
¼ cup finely chopped onion
¼ cup finely chopped celery
¼ cup finely chopped carrot
¼ cup diced 1 cm potato
3 tablespoons flour
1 cup clam juice
2¾ cups milk
1 × 250 g can clams
½ teaspoon thyme
1 bay leaf
1 teaspoon salt
½ teaspoon pepper
¼ cup cream
1 tablespoon finely chopped
    parsley

Time: 20 minutes. Serves 6

Sprinkle bacon into 2 litre casserole dish, cook 2 minutes. Add vegetables and cook 1 minute. Blend in flour, add clam juice and milk, stir to blend. Add clams and cook on high 5 minutes. Add thyme, bay leaf, salt and pepper. Cook 12 minutes, stirring after every 3 minutes. Let stand covered 5 minutes. Remove bay leaf, stir in cream, correct seasoning, sprinkle with parsley and serve.

Vegetables

When cooking vegetables in the microwave always use the freshest vegetables available so that your cooked vegetables remain moist and succulent. Microwave vegetables on high and use as little water (or whatever liquid you are using in which to cook the vegetables) and salt as possible.

If you are using pre-cooked canned vegetables simply reheat the vegetables in 2 tablespoons of their own liquid on a medium setting. Stir vegetables twice during reheating. For frozen packaged vegetables, snip off the corner of the plastic bag (this will prevent the bag from splitting) before placing in the microwave oven.

Pumpkin Cheese Ring

½ cup chopped shallots
2 tablespoons butter
4 cups cooked, mashed
  pumpkin
½ teaspoon salt
¼ teaspoon cayenne pepper
¼ teaspoon nutmeg
1 cup freshly grated Parmesan
  cheese
4 × 55 g eggs

Time: 19 minutes. Serves 6–8

Place shallots and butter in a medium–sized bowl. Cook on high 1 minute. Stir in remaining ingredients.

Pour into a greased 22.5 cm ring mould. Cook on high 18 minutes or until set. Let stand 8 minutes before turning out.

Jerusalem Artichokes

500 g artichokes
1 teaspoon lemon juice

Time: 8–9 minutes. Serves 4

Scrub artichokes thoroughly with a brush under running water. Peel if desired and cut into 1 cm slices. Cover with cold water and a squeeze of lemon juice to prevent discolouring. Drain.

Place into a 2 litre casserole on dish with ¼ cup water and lemon juice. Cover. Cook on high 8–9 minutes, until fork tender. Let stand 4 minutes.

Serve with hollandaise sauce *(see recipe Eggs Benedict)*, melted butter, salt and pepper or Parmesan cheese.

Mushroom and Artichoke Casserole

2 cups sliced fresh mushrooms
½ cup chopped onion
½ cup chopped celery
2 tablespoons butter
1½ cups seasoned
  breadcrumbs
¼ cup hot water
4 slices bacon, cooked and
  crumbled
⅛ teaspoon salt
2 cans artichoke hearts,
  drained and quartered
3 tablespoons Parmesan
  cheese

Time: 10 minutes. Serves 6–8

Combine mushrooms, onions, celery and butter in a bowl. Cover and cook on high 3 minutes, stirring after 2 minutes.

Stir in seasoned breadcrumbs, hot water, half the bacon and salt. In a casserole dish, layer half the mushroom mixture, artichokes and cheese. Repeat layers.

Cover and cook on high 6 minutes. Sprinkle with remaining bacon and cook, uncovered, on high 1 minute.

HINT: CUTTING VEGETABLES
When preparing vegetables for casseroles bear in mind that smaller, evenly cut pieces microwave faster than large, irregularly cut vegetables.

Pumpkin Cheese Ring

Vegetable Lasagna

250 g ricotta cheese
125 g mozzarella cheese,
  grated
2 teaspoons chopped parsley
3 long zucchini
2 large ripe tomatoes, sliced
250 mL tomato sauce (see
  recipe Macaroni with
  Tomato Sauce)
3 tablespoons grated
  Parmesan cheese

Time: 24 minutes. Serves 6

Combine ricotta, mozzarella cheese and parsley. Cut ends from zucchini and slice lengthwise into 5 mm strips. Arrange strips in a 20 cm square dish. Cover with plastic wrap and cook on high 6 minutes. Rearrange strips during cooking. Drain well and cool slightly.

Place a layer of sliced zucchini on the bottom of the dish and spread ricotta mixture over. Cover with tomato slices and spread half tomato sauce over sliced tomatoes. Top with remaining zucchini strips. Pour over remaining sauce and sprinkle with Parmesan cheese.

Cook uncovered on medium for 20 minutes. Let stand 5 minutes before serving.

Step 1 Vegetable Lasagna. Combine ricotta, mozzarella and parsley

Vegetable Lasagna

Step 2 Place a layer of sliced zucchini in dish

Step 3 Cover cheese mixture with sliced tomato

Cauliflower Snow

2–3 cups cauliflower florets
60 g butter
1 onion, chopped
2 medium–sized tomatoes,
  chopped
30 g flour
300 mL milk
⅛ teaspoon salt
⅛ teaspoon white pepper
⅛ teaspoon cayenne pepper
⅛ teaspoon dry mustard
125 g cheese, grated
4 eggs, separated
60 g extra cheese
chopped parsley

Time: 20 minutes. Serves 6–8

Place cauliflower in casserole with water and cook on high for 6 minutes. Drain off liquid.

Combine 30 g butter and onion in bowl and cover with plastic wrap. Cook on high 3 minutes then add tomatoes. Cook 2 minutes and set aside. Melt remaining butter in jug on high for 1 minute. Stir in flour and cook 1 minute. Blend in milk, salt, pepper, cayenne and mustard. Cook on high 2½–3 minutes until thick and boiling. Fold in cheese.

Arrange cauliflower in casserole dish. Spoon over onion mixture and coat with cheese sauce. Beat egg whites until stiff and spread over sauce. Make 4 indents into egg whites with a soup spoon and carefully place 1 yolk into each hollow. Prick yolks 3–4 times and sprinkle with extra cheese. Cook on medium 4 minutes. Garnish with parsley.

Parsnips with Pineapple

500 g parsnips, peeled and cut
  into Julienne strips
2 tablespoons butter
½ cup water
2 tablespoons brown sugar
2 teaspoons cornflour
250 g canned crushed
  pineapple
1 teaspoon orange zest
⅛ teaspoon salt

Time: 10 minutes. Serves 4–6

In a 1.5 litre casserole dish combine parsnips, butter and ¼ cup water. Cover and cook on high 7 minutes.

In a medium–sized bowl combine brown sugar and cornflour. Stir in remaining water, pineapple, orange zest and salt and cook on high 3–4 minutes, stirring after 2 minutes. Drain parsnips and add to pineapple mixture.

HINT: ARRANGING VEGETABLES FOR COOKING

Arrangement is the secret of microwave-cooking many foods with different cooking times. Place larger items around the edge of the plate. Make a second ring of vegetables with medium cooking time inside these and place quicker cooking vegetables in the centre. Arranged thus the vegetables will cook evenly and look attractive.

69

Brussels Sprouts with Lemon Butter

500 g fresh, even–sized
   Brussels sprouts
¼ cup water
1 tablespoon butter
1 tablespoon honey
1–2 tablespoons lemon juice

Time: 9 minutes. Serves 4–6

Wash sprouts, remove loose leaves and trim stems. Cut a cross into stem end for even cooking. Place into casserole dish, add water, cover and cook on high 8 minutes. Let stand 3 minutes and drain.

Heat butter and honey in small bowl on high 1 minute. Add strained lemon juice. Pour mixture over sprouts and toss to coat.

Baked Potato with Chicken Topping

4 medium–sized baking
   potatoes
¼ cup chopped capsicum
¼ cup chopped celery
¼ cup chopped shallot
¼ cup grated carrot
250 g mushrooms, sliced
½ chicken stock cube
2 tablespoons flour
¼ cup hot water
¾ cup milk
1 tablespoon white wine
1 teaspoon curry powder
¼ teaspoon salt
¼ teaspoon pepper
2 cups cooked, diced chicken
chopped parsley

Time: 22 minutes. Serves 4

Cook potatoes on high for 12 minutes, turning halfway through cooking. In a 1 litre casserole dish combine capsicum, celery, shallot, carrot and mushrooms and pour over hot water. Cover and cook on high 4 minutes. Drain off liquid.

In a medium–sized bowl, combine chicken cube, flour and water. Blend in milk and cook on high 2 minutes until thickened, stirring during cooking. Stir in wine and seasonings. Add sauce to chicken and vegetables and cook on high 4 minutes.

Halve each potato lengthwise and using a fork coarsely break up the centre. Spoon topping over. Serve garnished with parsley.

Beetroot with Dill Sauce

500 g fresh beetroot
½ cup water
½ teaspoon salt

Time: 26 minutes. Serves 4–6

Wash beetroot and cut off stalks 4 cm above the bulb. Place evenly apart in a 2 litre casserole. Stir salt into water and pour over beetroot. Cover and cook on high 15–20 minutes, turning beetroot over half way through cooking. Let stand, covered, 5 minutes.

Remove tips, skin and root ends and cut each bulb into quarters. Arrange in casserole dish and serve with dill sauce. (See recipe following.) Cook on medium 2–3 minutes to reheat.

Dill Sauce

1 tablespoon butter
1 tablespoon flour
½ teaspoon onion salt
dash pepper
¼ teaspoon sugar
¾ cup milk
2 teaspoons chopped fresh dill

Heat butter in a small bowl on high 1 minute. Stir in flour, seasonings and sugar. Blend in milk. Cook on high 2 minutes or until thickened. Stir in chopped dill.

Sweet Potato and Pineapple Bake

1 kg orange sweet potato
½ cup brown sugar
4 rashers bacon, diced into
   2 cm pieces
6 pineapple rings, diced into
   2 cm cubes
¼ cup pineapple juice
2 tablespoons butter
chopped parsley
¼ cup brown sugar

Time: 20 minutes. Serves 6–8

Peel potatoes and cut into even-sized dice. Place in a buttered casserole dish.

Arrange alternate layers of bacon, pineapple and brown sugar in the dish. Dot with butter and extra brown sugar. Pour over pineapple juice, cover and cook on high 20 minutes or until potato is fork tender.

Sprinkle with chopped parsley to serve.

Beetroot with Dill Sauce

Vegetable Platter

200 g cauliflower
200 g broccoli
2 medium-sized carrots
200 g small new potatoes
1 cup peas, beans or zucchini
    rings

Time: 12-14 minutes. Serves 6

Wash vegetables and cut into serving size. Prick potatoes with a skewer. Arrange cauliflower, broccoli, carrots and potatoes around edge of plate. Place peas in centre. Add 2 tablespoons cold water and season lightly.

Cover with lid or a double thickness of plastic wrap. Cook on high 12-14 minutes. Serve with butter or hollandaise sauce *(see recipe Eggs Benedict)*.

Kohlrabi

1 kg kohlrabi bulbs

Time: 15-20 minutes. Serves 6-8

Trim roots and stems from even-sized bulbs. (The leaves may be cooked like spinach leaves.) Peel and scrub bulbs and cut into slices. Place in casserole with ¼ cup water to cover.

Cook on high 12-15 minutes, or until tender, stirring every 4 minutes. Drain and serve with dill sauce *(see recipe Beetroot with Dill Sauce)*, cheese and caraway sauce *(see recipe following)* or sour cream and chives.

Cheese and Caraway Sauce

2 tablespoons butter
2 tablespoons plain flour
pinch salt
¼ teaspoon dried mustard
⅛ teaspoon cayenne pepper
2 cups milk
½ teaspoon caraway seeds
½ cup grated tasty cheese

Time: 6 minutes. Serves 6-8

Melt butter in a jug and cook on high 1 minute. Stir in flour, salt, mustard powder, cayenne pepper and cook for 1 minute on medium heat. Blend in milk and cook on high 4 minutes, stirring every minute or until sauce thickens. Stir in cheese and caraway seeds.

Peas French Style

1 cup shelled peas
⅓ cup thinly sliced celery
2 tablespoons water
3 cups shredded lettuce
1 tablespoon butter
1 tablespoon flour
½ teaspoon sugar
¼ teaspoon salt
dash lemon pepper
¼ cup sour cream

Time: 9 minutes. Serves 6

In a 1.5 litre casserole dish combine peas, celery and water. Cover and cook on high 6-7½ minutes, or until tender. Stir in lettuce, recover and cook on high 2 minutes, stirring after 1 minute. Set aside.

In a small bowl, combine butter, flour, sugar, salt and pepper. Blend in cream and cook on high 1 minute or until thick. Drain vegetables and fold in sauce to coat.

Baked Stuffed Potato

4 large potatoes
4 tablespoons butter
6 tablespoons sour cream
salt
pepper
4 tablespoons grated tasty
    cheese
2 rashers bacon, cooked and
    diced
chopped chives

Time: 16 minutes. Serves 4

Pierce potatoes several times with a metal skewer. Arrange potatoes 2.5 cm apart in a pie plate to enable microwaves to penetrate from all sides. Cook on high 12 minutes, turning potatoes over half way through cooking.

Slice the top off each potato and scoop out centre. Set shells aside. Mash potato centres with butter and sour cream. Season, add cheese and bacon pieces and spoon into shells.

Reheat on high 4 minutes. Serve with chopped chives.

HINT: BLANCHING CAPSICUMS
It is always best to blanch capsicums before cooking to prevent indigestion.

HINT: WRAP COOKED POTATOES IN FOIL
Wrap cooked jacket potatoes in foil after cooking. They will retain their heat for 30 minutes and leave the microwave oven free for other cooking.

Baby Squash Provençal

500 g baby squash,
  even–sized
60 g chopped onion
1 clove garlic, chopped
⅛ teaspoon salt
⅛ teaspoon pepper
60 g butter
½ teaspoon basil
500 g tomatoes, chopped
chopped parsley

Time: 10 minutes. Serves 6–8

Pierce each squash 5 times with a skewer. If large, cut into quarters. Heat butter, onion and garlic on high 4 minutes in medium–sized bowl. Add chopped tomatoes, basil, salt, pepper and squash.

Cover and cook on high 5–6 minutes until squash is fork tender. Sprinkle with chopped parsley to serve.

Step 1   Baby Squash Provençal. Pierce each squash 5 times with a skewer

Carrot Curls with Honey Sauce

4 large carrots, peeled
2 tablespoons water
1 tablespoon butter
2 tablespoons golden syrup
2 tablespoons vinegar
2 tablespoons orange or
  pineapple juice
2 teaspoons arrowroot
toasted sesame seeds

Time: 12 minutes. Serves 6–8

Using a vegetable peeler, cut carrots lengthwise into long thin strips. Place into cold water to form curls. Transfer carrots to casserole dish with 2 tablespoons water. Cover and cook on high 6–8 minutes. Drain.

Blend butter, syrup, vinegar, juice and arrowroot together in medium–sized bowl. Cook on high 1 minute, stirring after 30 seconds. Pour over carrot curls.

Cook on medium 2–3 minutes to reheat. Sprinkle with toasted sesame seeds to serve.

Step 2   Heat butter, onion and garlic

HINT: PRICKING VEGETABLES

Certain vegetables such as tomatoes, zucchini, baby squash and potatoes should be pierced with a skewer before cooking. This enables steam to escape during cooking and prevents the vegetables from splitting.

Step 3   Add squash, tomatoes, basil and seasoning

Cabbage

500 g shredded cabbage,
   washed and drained
2 cloves garlic, chopped finely
1 tablespoon butter
2 large peeled tomatoes,
   roughly chopped
salt to taste

Time: 7 minutes. Serves 4–6

Place all ingredients in a small casserole dish or an oven bag lightly tied with string or an elastic band. Prick bag once or twice near opening. Cook 7 minutes on high, turning once during cooking.

Leaf Spinach

500 g spinach leaves, no stalks,
   washed and drained
1 tablespoon butter
1 small onion, finely chopped
¼ teaspoon nutmeg
60 g peanuts, roughly chopped

Time: 7 minutes. Serves 4

Place spinach, butter, onion, and nutmeg into an oven bag. Fasten with an elastic band. Prick twice near opening. Cook 7 minutes on high, turning once during cooking. Top with roughly chopped peanuts.

Vegetable Medley

250 g cauliflower florets
125 g carrots, sliced crosswise
250 g Chinese cabbage, sliced
125 g sliced mushrooms
1 small can asparagus spears
2 slices ham, diced
chopped parsley

Sauce

2 tablespoons butter
2 tablespoons flour
1 cup chicken stock
2 cups milk

Time: 20 minutes. Serves 4–6

Place cauliflower and carrots into a casserole dish. Add 2 tablespoons water and cook covered 6 minutes on high. Place carrots and cauliflower into a larger casserole, cover with cabbage, mushrooms and asparagus spears. Spoon sauce over, top with ham and parsley. Cook covered 6 minutes.

Cook butter for sauce to melt 20 seconds. Stir in flour and cook 2 minutes on high. Stir in stock and milk. Cook 6 minutes until thick and boiling. Stir during cooking.

76

Beets with Orange Sauce

4 precooked beetroots (see
   Cooking Chart)
2 tablespoons brown sugar
1 cup orange juice
2 tablespoons tarragon vinegar
1 tablespoon butter
1 tablespoon cornflour

Time: 17 minutes. Serves 4

Use a melon baller and scoop out balls of beetroot from cooked beets. Combine sugar, juice, vinegar, butter and cornflour in a bowl. Cook 3 minutes on high, stir and cook until boiling. Add beets, cook further 2 minutes and serve.

Parsley Potato Balls

750 g potatoes
water
2 tablespoons butter
2 tablespoons finely chopped
   parsley
salt to taste

Time: 12 minutes. Serves 4–6

Cut potatoes into balls using a melon baller. Place into casserole with water. Cook covered on high for 12 minutes, stirring twice during cooking. Cook butter 20 seconds to melt. Add parsley and salt. Pour over drained potatoes. Stir to coat.

Note: Chopped mint may be used in place of parsley.

Cauliflower au Gratin

2 tablespoons butter
500 g cauliflower florets
¼ teaspoon garlic salt
pepper
2 large peeled tomatoes, sliced
1 cup cheese sauce (see Sauces
   and Jams)
chopped parsley
paprika

Time: 9 minutes. Serves 4–6

Cook butter in casserole 20 seconds to melt. Add cauliflower, garlic salt, pepper and cook covered for 6 minutes. Top with sliced tomatoes, cheese sauce and parsley. Cook 3 minutes on high. Dust lightly with paprika before serving.

Parsley Potato Balls and Glazed Carrots

Glazed Carrots

500 g carrots, cut into strips

Honey Sauce

1 tablespoon butter
2 tablespoons honey
2 tablespoons vinegar
2 tablespoons orange juice
salt
2 teaspoons cornflour

Time: 10½ minutes. Serves 4

Place carrots in casserole dish with 1 tablespoon water. Cook covered 7–8 minutes on high, stir twice during cooking, drain.

Combine all sauce ingredients, place into glass dish and cook 1 minute on high. Stir after 30 seconds. Pour over carrots, cook 2 minutes to reheat.

Carrots with Marsala

500 g carrots, sliced crosswise
1 onion, finely chopped
1 tablespoon brown sugar
75 mL Marsala
1 tablespoon butter

Time: 8 minutes. Serves 4–6

Combine all ingredients and place in casserole dish just large enough to hold all ingredients. Cook 7–8 minutes on high, stirring twice during cooking.

Scalloped Sweet Potatoes

750 g orange sweet potatoes,
*   sliced thinly*
2 rashers of bacon, diced and
*   precooked*
2 tablespoons flour
1 teaspoon salt
½ cup finely cut shallots
2 cups milk
1 cup tasty cheese, grated
*   nutmeg and paprika*
chopped parsley

Time: 15 minutes. Serves 6

Combine all ingredients in a greased casserole dish. Cover and cook 15 minutes on high, stirring every 4 minutes. Sprinkle with extra nutmeg, paprika and chopped parsley.

Sweet Potato Parmesan

1 medium sweet potato
1 medium parsnip
1 bacon rasher, chopped
½ cup grated Parmesan cheese
2 tablespoons water
1 small onion, chopped

Time: 8 minutes

Wash, peel and cut sweet potato and parsnip into rounds. Place in large glass bowl or casserole and add bacon, onion and water on high. Cover with lid or paper towel and cook 6 minutes.

Top with Parmesan cheese. Cook for 2 minutes or until cheese begins to melt. Garnish with snipped chives.

Served with extra Parmesan cheese and a glass of white wine this dish is a meal in itself.

Variation: For extra colour and flavour add some diced capsicum to the mixture before cooking.

Sweet Potato Parmesan

Step 1 Wash and peel sweet potato and parsnip and cut into rounds

Step 2 Place vegetables in bowl and add chopped bacon and onion

Step 3 Top with Parmesan cheese and cook for 2 minutes

Scalloped Sweet Potatoes

Braised Red Cabbage

½ head sliced red cabbage
2 tablespoons butter
2 green apples, peeled and
    sliced
1 small onion, chopped
½ teaspoon salt
¼ teaspoon pepper
2 cloves
1 bay leaf
2 tablespoons tarragon vinegar
1 cup dry red wine
1–2 tablespoons brown sugar

Time: 12 minutes. Serves 6

Combine all ingredients in casserole. Cook covered 12 minutes on high, stirring every 4 minutes.

Vegetable Kebabs

Time: 6 minutes. Serves 4

Spear a variety of vegetables onto bamboo sate sticks: cherry tomatoes, mushroom caps, chunks of red and green capsicums, canned mini corn, small onions, and zucchini. Layer in dish and cook 6 minutes on high, turning every minute and basting with a mixture of melted butter and lemon juice.

Herbed Jacket Potatoes

4 even-sized potatoes, unpeeled
peanut oil
herbed butter
4 tablespoons sour cream
2 rashers bacon, diced,
    precooked
chopped chives

Time: 11 minutes. Serves 4

Prick potatoes, brush with oil and wrap in plastic food wrap. Place in a circle on oven tray and cook 5 minutes on high. Turn over and cook a further 6 minutes. Remove wrap and cut a cross on top of each potato. Squeeze firmly so that the centre will pop up. Top with herb butter, sour cream, bacon and chives.

Zucchini Special

500 g unpeeled zucchini, sliced
1 tablespoon butter
onion or garlic salt
1 teaspoon fresh chopped dill
1 large peeled tomato, seeds
    removed, roughly chopped

Time: 8 minutes. Serves 4

Place all ingredients into a small casserole. Cover and cook 8 minutes on high

Fresh Broccoli Hollandaise

500 g fresh broccoli
1 tablespoon water
2 tablespoons butter
onion salt

Time: 8 minutes. Serves 4

Cut broccoli into even lengths, remove skin from stalk and split ends with a knife. Place into a covered casserole dish or oven bag, with water, butter and onion salt. Cook 8 minutes on high. Arrange onto serving dish and mask with hollandaise sauce (see recipe).

Cooking Chart for Fresh Vegetables

ITEM	QUANTITY	DIRECTIONS	SUGGESTED COOKING TIME IN MINUTES
Asparagus	500 g	¼ cup water, ⅓ teaspoon salt in covered casserole	5–6
Beans	750 g	⅓ cup water, ¼ teaspoon salt in covered casserole	12–14
Beetroot	4 whole medium	Wrap each bulb in plastic wrap	12–16
Broccoli	1 small bunch	Cut away stalk, ½ cup water, 1 teaspoon salt in covered casserole	8–11
Brussels sprouts	500 g		
Cabbage	750 g chopped	3 tablespoons water, ⅓ teaspoon salt in covered casserole	8–10
Carrots	4 medium sliced	¼ cup water, ⅓ teaspoon salt in covered casserole	8–10
Cauliflower	750 g	⅓ cup water, ⅕ teaspoon salt in covered casserole	10–12
Celery	6 cups	¼ cup water, ⅓ teaspoon salt in covered casserole	10–12
Corn	3 ears	Remove silk, leave husk on and tie with elastic band	12
Corn kernels	3 cups	⅓ cup water, ⅓ teaspoon salt in covered casserole	8
Eggplant	1 medium	¼ cup water, ⅓ teaspoon salt in covered casserole	8–10
Onion	2 large (cut in quarters)	½ cup water, ⅓ teaspoon salt in covered casserole	8–10
Parsnips	4 medium (cut in quarters)	½ cup water, ⅓ teaspoon salt in covered casserole	8–10
Peas	500 g	⅓ cup water, ⅓ teaspoon salt in covered casserole	6–8
Potatoes	1 medium 2 medium 3 medium 4 medium 5 medium 6 medium 7 medium 8 medium	Scrub potatoes, and place on paper towel leaving a 2.5 cm space between potatoes. Note: Prick potatoes before placing in oven	5 7 9 12 14 16 20 22
Potatoes	4 medium (thinly sliced)	2 tablespoons butter in casserole, sprinkle with salt and dot with butter. Cover	11
Sweet Potatoes	2 medium	Place on paper towel, leaving 2.5 cm space between potatoes	7–8
Spinach	500 g	Put in casserole with water to cling to leaves, ⅓ teaspoon salt and cover	6–7

Meat

Lamb is one of the all-time family favourites for roasts, casseroles and grills. Legs and shoulders (boned and rolled) can be cooked uncovered on a roasting rack, and a sheet of white kitchen paper can be placed on top to absorb any fat splatters.

To avoid meat drying, cover the thin shank end of the leg with a 5 cm wide strip of foil. The foil should be removed after half the cooking has elapsed and before the roast is turned. On completion of cooking, place a sheet of foil over the roast, leaving the ends uncovered, and allow 10–15 minutes standing time before carving.

Lamb chops, stews and curries cook well in a preheated browning casserole dish. To cook 4 lamb chops (chops can be marinated in lemon juice, oil and garlic), cook on one side on high for 1 minute, then turn and cook the other side, also on high, for 3–4 minutes.

Seal lamb for casseroles and curries in a browning dish with a small amount of oil or ghee. Add remaining ingredients and cook on high for the first 3–5 minutes and finish cooking on medium. Cook covered and stir.

Tender cuts of beef are dry roasted on a roasting rack and foil can be used to prevent meat from drying. As salt draws out liquids and can cause drying it is best to season with garlic and fresh or dried herbs.

To defrost large pieces of beef, place on a roasting rack and cook on medium for 5–8 minutes for each 500 g. Defrosting steaks and chops takes only 3–4 minutes for each 500 g but should the meat start to brown while the centre is still frozen, cover the cooked sections with foil.

Steaks and chops and burgers are cooked in a preheated browning dish but less tender cuts are best pot roasted, braised or stewed and the cooking technique is the same as for conventional range-top cooking.

Roast pork will dry if overcooked and all care should be taken to monitor the internal temperature. When the temperature reaches 165°C remove the pork from the microwave and allow it to stand for 5–10 minutes before carving. During the standing time the temperature will increase to 170°C. To cook, place fat side down on roasting rack in roasting dish and cook on high for the first 5 minutes. Complete cooking on medium and turn the roast half way through cooking. Allow 12–16 minutes cooking time for each 500 g.

It is up to you whether you remove the rind but should you want crackling, score the rind with a sharp knife and rub in oil and salt before cooking.

Hams are available canned, boned, rolled, on the bone, cooked and uncooked and your microwave oven can successfully enhance the flavour of any ham. The flavour of canned or boneless rolled cooked ham is increased when heated. Allow 5–8 minutes for each 500 g and cook on medium. Shoulders and pieces of leg ham can be heated if you allow 15 minutes for each 500 g. In this instance, cook for the first 5 minutes on high, then set the microwave to medium.

For raw picnic hams and leg hams allow 16–18 minutes cooking time for each 500 g. Cook on high for the first 5 minutes and complete cooking on medium.

Veal is the most tender of all meats and extra care should be taken to make sure that this very lean meat does not dry due to overcooking. When cooking thin steaks of coated veal for schnitzels preheat the browning dish for 6–8 minutes before adding a cup of oil. Heat on high for a further 3 minutes and add a slice of green ginger. When the ginger is brown the oil is the correct temperature for frying. Cook steaks 3–4 minutes on each side on high.

Grilled cutlets should be cooked on high in a preheated browning dish for 1 minute each side. Cook each side for further 5 minutes on medium.

When roasting veal allow 13–17 minutes for each 500 g. Commence cooking on high for the first 5 minutes and complete on medium. Turn the roast half way through cooking and remove roast from the oven when the internal temperature reaches 160°C. During standing time the internal temperature of the veal will increase by 5–10°C. For cubes or slivers of veal, cook on medium for 10–15 minutes for each 500 g.

Cooking Times for Beef Fillet Roasts

7½–9½ minutes per 500 g : rare
8–10 minutes per 500 g : medium rare
9½–11½ minutes per 500 g : medium

If beef is under 1 kg, cook on high for first 3 minutes; finish on medium. If beef is over 1 kg, cook on high for first 5 minutes; finish on medium. Test for doneness with meat thermometer: on standing the internal temperature will rise 20° for rare or medium rare, 15° for medium, 10° for well done.

Savoury Beef Roll, Lemon Lamb Sate

Step 1 Fillet of Beef Wellington. Turn beef 4 times while cooking

Step 2 Pour warmed brandy over beef

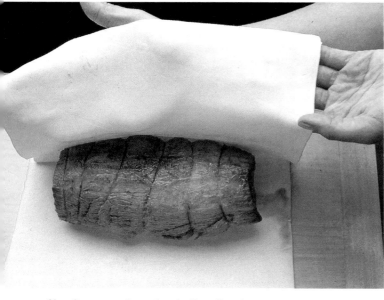

Step 3 Cover beef with puff pastry

Fillet of Beef Wellington

Fillet of Beef Wellington

1.5 kg middle cut fillet in one
  piece
2 cloves garlic, peeled
¼ cup brandy
2 tablespoons oil
2 tablespoons French mustard
2 sheets puff pastry
1 egg, beaten

Time: 45–47 minutes. Serves 6–8

84

Cut each clove of garlic in four. Make 4 small cuts in each side of beef and insert garlic. Tie roast at 5 cm intervals with kitchen string. This holds the beef in shape while browning. Cook in browning casserole on high 6 minutes.

Remove beef, add oil and cook on high 2 minutes. Return beef to casserole and cook on high 4 minutes, turning fillet four times during cooking for even browning. Cook on medium 20 minutes. Remove string.

Place brandy in jug and cook on high 15–20 seconds to warm. Ignite with flaming taper. Pour over fillet and let stand 5 minutes, turning beef twice.

Place beef onto sheet of puff pastry. Spread top and sides with French mustard. Brush edges of pastry with beaten egg and shape second sheet of pastry over beef. Seal edges and cut off excess pastry. Brush pastry with beaten egg and decorate with excess pastry.

Bake in convection microwave 200°C until pastry is well risen and golden. Serve with demi-glacé sauce.

Savoury Beef Roll

750 g lean minced beef
2 eggs
¼ cup dry breadcrumbs
1 tablespoon barbecue sauce
1 teaspoon beef seasoning
¾ cup chopped green
    capsicum
¾ cup chopped red capsicum
1 onion, chopped
1 cup grated cheese

Time: 32 minutes. Serves 4–6

Combine mince, eggs, breadcrumbs, sauce and seasoning. On a sheet of plastic wrap pat out to a rectangle 2 cm thick.

Cook capsicum and onion on high 2 minutes. Cool. Place onto meat leaving 2.5 cm border on all sides. Roll up and press edges together to seal. Place in baking dish seam side down.

Cook on high 5 minutes, then on medium 25–30 minutes. During the last 10 minutes of cooking time sprinkle with grated cheese.

Beef Bourguignonne

1 kg sirloin steak, cut into
    thin strips
4 slices bacon, cut into 2 cm
    pieces
⅓ cup flour
250 g mushrooms, sliced
4 medium–sized onions, cut
    into sixths
1 medium carrot, sliced
1 clove garlic, finely chopped
1 cup dry red wine
½ cup beef consommé or stock
1 tablespoon chopped parsley
1 teaspoon salt
½ teaspoon thyme
¼ teaspoon pepper
2 bay leaves

Time: 48 minutes. Serves 6–8

Place bacon in 3 litre casserole. Cover and cook on high 3 minutes. Drain, leaving 1 tablespoon of dripping. Stir in beef strips, sprinkle with flour and toss to coat evenly.

Mix in remaining ingredients. Cover and cook on high 5 minutes. Stir. Cook on medium 40 minutes or until fork tender, stirring during cooking to thicken sauce evenly. Let stand 10 minutes before serving. Serve with buttered noodles or rice.

Note: For long slow cooking, microwave on low 60–75 minutes.

Filet Mignon

4 × 180 g filet mignon
1 tablespoon butter

Time: 15 minutes. Serves 2

Preheat browning grill on high 9 minutes. Butter one side of each mignon and place buttered side down on preheated grill. Cook on high 3 minutes. Brush tops with butter and turn mignons over. Cook on high 3 minutes for rare. Serve with mushroom sauce.

Mushroom Sauce

125 g mushrooms
1 tablespoon butter
1 tablespoon flour
300 mL canned beef
    consommé
1 egg yolk
2 tablespoons cream
⅛ teaspoon salt
⅛ teaspoon pepper

Time: 6–8 minutes. Yield 300 mL

Place butter in jug and heat on high 1 minute. Add mushrooms and cook 1 minute. Blend in flour. Cook a further minute on high. Stir in consommé and cook on high 3–4 minutes, stirring after 2 minutes.

Combine egg and cream in bowl. Add 2 tablespoons of sauce and blend well. Fold into remaining sauce. Season. Pour over mignons or other grilled meat.

Stroganoff

1 quantity basic beef mix,
    thawed (see recipe Basic
    Beef Mix)
125 g mushrooms, chopped
½ cup beef consommé
1½ tablespoons seasoned flour
1 teaspoon Worcestershire
    sauce
⅔ cup sour cream

Time: 8 minutes. Serves 4–6

In a 2 litre casserole combine beef mixture, mushrooms, consommé, flour and sauce. Blend well and cook on high 6 minutes, stirring twice during cooking.

Blend in sour cream and reheat on high 1–2 minutes. Serve with rice or pasta.

> **HINT:**
> Cut meat into slices parallel to the grain for tenderness and even cooking. Meat is easier to slice when partially frozen. Fully defrost before cooking.

Basic Beef Mix

1.25 kg lean minced beef
2 onions, sliced
2 cloves garlic, chopped
2 tablespoons peanut oil
1 tablespoon chilli sauce
1½ tablespoons onion soup
    mix
1½ tablespoons Gravox
    powder

Time: 16 minutes. Serves 8–12

Combine onion, garlic and oil in 2 litre casserole. Cook on high 3 minutes. Crumble in mince and cook on high 7–8 minutes. Stir in remaining ingredients and cook on high 6 minutes, stirring twice during cooking. Cool.

The mixture can now be placed in a plastic container and frozen until ready to use for savoury mince dishes such as lasagna or Bolognese sauce, or for stuffing vegetables.

Beef Roulades with Brazil Nut Stuffing

500 g rump steak, thinly
    sliced
1 small onion, finely chopped
½ cup celery, thinly sliced
2 tablespoons butter
⅓ cup beef consommé or stock
½ cup chopped Brazil nuts
1 cup prepared stuffing mix
1½ tablespoons seasoned flour
1 tablespoon peanut oil
125 mL beef consommé or
    stock
125 mL dry red wine
3 teaspoons arrowroot
1–2 tablespoons cold water
30 g sliced Brazil nuts

Time: 1 hour 47 minutes. Serves 4–6

Cut steak into 10 cm squares. Pound lightly with meat mallet. Combine onions, celery and butter in a medium-sized bowl. Cook on high 3–4 minutes. Add ⅓ cup of stock and cook on high 1 minute. Stir in ½ cup Brazil nuts and stuffing. Allow to cool.

Spread filling over meat slices, roll up and tie with string. Coat rolls evenly with seasoned flour. Heat browning dish on high 6 minutes. Add oil and heat 1 minute. Cook roulades 6 minutes, turning during cooking. Add 125 mL stock and wine and cook on medium 12 minutes.

Remove string from rolls and transfer to serving plate. Blend arrowroot with water, stir into pan liquids and cook on high 3 minutes or until boiling. Strain sauce and pour over roulades. Garnish with sliced Brazil nuts to serve.

HINT: MEAT BALLS
Roll meat balls with wet hands to prevent sticking.

Ginger Meatballs

500 g lean minced beef
3 shallots, finely chopped
1 egg, beaten
1 teaspoon green ginger, finely
    chopped
⅛ teaspoon garlic salt
½ cup beef consommé
2 teaspoons arrowroot
1 tablespoon soy sauce
1 teaspoon vinegar
1 tablespoon parsley

Time: 12 minutes. Serves 4–6

Combine mince, shallots, egg, ginger and salt. Form into 24 small balls. Arrange the meat balls around outer edge of a 25 cm pie plate. Cook on high 7 minutes, turning once during cooking. Remove to serving dish.

Blend consommé and arrowroot with meat juices in pie plate. Add soy sauce, vinegar and parsley. Cook on high 2–3 minutes until sauce has thickened, stirring twice during cooking. Coat meat balls with sauce and cook 2–3 minutes on high to reheat.

Calf's Liver and Bacon

375 g calf's liver
4 large bacon rashers
1 small onion, finely chopped
½ teaspoon freshly ground
    pepper
¼ teaspoon salt
50 mL sweet vermouth
1 tablespoon tomato paste
1 teaspoon Gravox powder
50 mL beef consommé or
    stock

Mustard Cream

1 cup sour cream
3 tablespoons French mustard

Time: 16 minutes. Serves 4

Soak liver in cold, salted water for 10 minutes. Remove skin and cut liver into thin slices. Derind bacon rashers and cut each rasher into 2.5 cm lengths.

Place bacon and onion in casserole and cook on high 4 minutes, stirring after 2 minutes. Add liver and cook on high 2 minutes. Add freshly ground pepper and salt, vermouth and tomato paste.

Blend in Gravox and consommé. Cover and cook on medium 10 minutes, stirring and rearranging liver every 3 minutes.

Serve with mustard cream — made by blending sour cream and French mustard.

Calf's Liver and Bacon

Roasted Ribs with Sweet Sour Sauce

1–1.5 kg beef ribs, cut in 5 cm
   lengths
1 medium–sized onion, thinly
   sliced
1 teaspoon basil
1 cup sweet sour sauce or
   barbecue sauce
1 tablespoon lemon juice,
   strained

Sweet Sour Sauce

¼ cup brown sugar
1 tablespoon cornflour
½ cup pineapple juice
¼ cup vinegar
2 tablespoons soy sauce

Time: 40–46 minutes. Serves 4–6

Arrange ribs in roasting dish in a single layer for even cooking. Top with onion rings and basil and cook on high 5 minutes. Reduce power to medium and cook for 15 minutes.

Rearrange and turn ribs over. Cook on medium 15–20 minutes. Drain off liquid.

To make the sauce combine sugar and cornflour in a jug. Blend in remaining sauce ingredients and cook on high 3 minutes or until thickened, stirring every minute.

Pour sauce over ribs and cook for a further 6 minutes.

Roasted Ribs with Sweet Sour Sauce

Stuffed Capsicums

1 quantity basic beef mixture,
   thawed (see recipe Basic
   Beef Mix)
1¼ cups cooked rice
250 g tomato paste
½ teaspoon chopped basil
   leaves
1 teaspoon sugar
¼ teaspoon salt
¼ teaspoon pepper
4–6 large capsicums
½ cup grated tasty cheese

Time: 12 minutes. Serves 4–6

In a 2 litre casserole combine beef mixture, rice, tomato paste, basil, sugar, salt and pepper.

Cut tops from capsicums, remove seeds and fill each capsicum with mixture. Place into casserole, cover and cook on high 12 minutes. Top each with cheese during the last minutes of cooking.

T-bone Steak

2 T-bone steaks, 2 cm thick

Time: 15 minutes. Serves 2

Preheat browning grill on high 9 minutes. Butter grill and cook steaks on high 3 minutes on first side, 2 minutes on second side for rare. Serve with herb butter.

90

Tongue

1.5–1.75 kg beef tongue
1½ cups water
½ teaspoon salt
¼ teaspoon pepper
2 bay leaves
1 onion, quartered   Time: 73–83 minutes. Serves 4–6

Wash tongue and trim off fat. Place into a 2 litre casserole with water, salt, pepper, bay leaves and onion.

Cover and cook on high 3 minutes. Reduce power to medium and cook 70-80 minutes, or until tender, turning tongue half way through cooking. Let stand 5 minutes before removing skin.

Cooking Times For Lamb

8-11 minutes per 500 g : rare
9-13 minutes per 500 g : medium
10-14 minutes per 500 g : well done

Cook 5 minutes on high to begin. Finish on medium.

Shoulder Cooking Time

9-13 minutes per 500 g : rare : first 4 minutes on high —
finish cooking on medium.
10½-14½ minutes per 500 g : medium : first 4 minutes on
high — finish cooking on medium.
12-15½ minutes per 500 g : well done : first 4 minutes on
high — finish cooking on medium.

Colonial Goose

1 × 2 kg leg lamb, boned

Stuffing

*30 g butter
1 tablespoon honey
125 g dried apricots, chopped
1 onion, finely chopped
125 g white breadcrumbs
¼ teaspoon lemon pepper
¼ teaspoon salt
¼ teaspoon dried thyme
1 egg, beaten*

Marinade

*1 onion, sliced
1 carrot, sliced
1 bay leaf
3 crushed parsley stalks
1 cup red wine
1 cup consommé
2 teaspoons arrowroot
1 tablespoon water*

Time: 56 minutes. Serves 6-8

Combine butter and honey in a bowl and cook on high 1
minute. Blend in remaining stuffing ingredients and force
prepared stuffing into boned cavity of lamb leg. Tie firmly
with string and place meat in roasting dish. Combine marinade ingredients, pour over meat and leave in cool place
to marinate for 6 hours, turning leg occasionally. Remove
from marinade. Reserve marinade. Weigh leg to calculate
cooking time.

Place lamb on roasting rack in baking dish, fat side
down. Divide cooking time in half. Cook on high 5 minutes
then reduce power to medium for remaining first half of
cooking time. Turn roast over and cook on medium for
remaining time. Let stand 10 minutes, lightly covered with
foil, before carving. Arrange lamb on serving plate.

Remove fat from roasting dish and deglaze dish with 3
tablespoons of strained marinade and 1 extra cup consommé. Thicken lightly with extra blended arrowroot and
cook on high 3-4 minutes. Strain and serve with lamb.

Shoulder of Lamb Duxelle

*2 kg boneless rolled shoulder
   of lamb
1 clove garlic, quartered
1 tablespoon melted butter
1 teaspoon ground ginger
60 g tasty cheese
60 g Parmesan cheese*

Stuffing

*300 g mushrooms, chopped
1 tablespoon butter
¼ cup finely chopped shallots
½ teaspoon dried thyme
1 tablespoon chopped parsley
½ cup soft white breadcrumbs*

Time: 36-73 minutes. Serves 8-10

To make stuffing, melt butter in bowl on high 1 minute.
Add mushrooms and herbs and cook on high for 1 minute.
Add shallots and breadcrumbs.

Weigh lamb. Make 4 small cuts on each side of the rolled
shoulder and insert a piece of garlic in each one. Heat butter on high 1 minute and brush over lamb. Sprinkle with
ginger.

Place lamb, fat side down, on roasting rack in baking
dish and cook on high for 3 minutes. Reduce to medium
and continue cooking for remaining first half of cooking
time.

Turn shoulder over and continue cooking on medium for
remaining cooking time. Remove string from shoulder. Cut
three-quarters of the way through the shoulder into slices,
insert stuffing between each slice and reshape. Combine
tasty and Parmesan cheese. Sprinkle over top of shoulder
and cook on medium for 6 minutes until cheese melts and
lamb reheats. Serve with gravy.

Lamb Burgers

*500 g minced lamb
4 slices bacon
½ cup finely chopped shallots
1½ teaspoons Worcestershire
   sauce
½ teaspoon lamb seasoning
   salt
4 slices cheese*

Time: 12 minutes. Serves 4

Arrange bacon between two layers of white paper towel
and cook on high 3 minutes.

Preheat browning grill on high 5 minutes. Combine
lamb, shallots, sauce and seasoning and shape into 4
burgers. Place on preheated grill and cook on high 2
minutes.

Cut bacon slices in half and place 2 pieces on each patty.
Top each with cheese and cook on high 2 minutes for well
done. Serve on hot toasted buns.

Lamb Casserole

500 g lean lamb shoulder, cut
    into 2 cm cubes
2 tablespoons flour
½ teaspoon salt
¼ teaspoon lemon pepper
1 × 500 g can tomato pieces
¾ cup consommé or stock
250 g sliced mushrooms
1 medium–sized onion,
    quartered
½ teaspoon oregano
1 sprig fresh rosemary
1 × 300 g packet frozen
    chunk–style beans, thawed

Time: 65 minutes. Serves 6

In a 2 litre casserole place lamb, flour, salt and pepper and stir to coat lamb. Add tomatoes, consommé, mushrooms, onion, oregano and rosemary.

Cover and cook on high 5 minutes. Reduce to medium and cook 20 minutes. Stir, re-cover and cook on medium 30 minutes. Add beans and cook on medium 10 minutes until beans are cooked.

Lemon Lamb Sate

500 g lean lamb, cut into
    2.5 cm cubes
½ green capsicum, diced
1 medium–sized onion, cut
    into eighths
1 lemon, cut into 8 wedges
4 bamboo sate sticks

Lemon Marinade

½ cup lemon juice
½ cup olive oil
2 cloves garlic, crushed
2 bay leaves
1 teaspoon oregano
½ teaspoon salt
¼ teaspoon freshly ground
    black pepper

Time: 14 minutes. Serves 4

Combine all marinade ingredients in a 2 litre bowl. Add lamb cubes and marinate four hours. Discard marinade.

Thread marinated lamb cubes and vegetables onto sate sticks. Place on roasting rack and cook on medium 6 minutes. Turn over and rearrange. Cook 8-9 minutes. Serve with lemon wedges.

Lamb Kebabs

500 g lean boneless lamb, cut
    into 24 cubes
1 small can pineapple pieces
    in juice
2 teaspoons lemon juice
2 teaspoons soy sauce
¼ teaspoon ground ginger
¼ teaspoon dried oregano
8 cherry tomatoes
½ green capsicum, cut into
    eighths
4 wooden sate sticks

Time: 10 minutes. Serves 4

In a bowl combine ⅓ cup pineapple juice, lemon juice, soy sauce, ginger and oregano. Stir in lamb and cover. Marinate overnight in refrigerator. Remove meat and discard marinade.

Thread lamb, tomatoes, capsicum and pineapple pieces on sate sticks and arrange on roasting rack. Cook on medium 10 minutes.

Veal Mozzarella

500 g veal escalopes
¾ cup grated mozzarella
    cheese
1 tablespoon finely chopped
    parsley

Sauce

250 g tomato paste
¼ teaspoon oregano
½ teaspoon basil
¼ teaspoon garlic salt
½ teaspoon sugar
⅛ teaspoon white pepper

Time: 22 minutes. Serves 4

Combine all sauce ingredients in a medium–sized bowl and cook on high 2 minutes. Reduce power to medium and cook 6 minutes. Set aside.

Place veal escalopes in a single layer in baking dish and cook on medium 8-9 minutes. Drain.

Spoon sauce over veal. Sprinkle with cheese and parsley and cook on medium 6-7 minutes until cheese melts.

HINT: TESTING THE VEAL IS COOKED
Veal is cooked when the internal temperature reaches 160°–180°C. Let stand covered until temperature rises to 185°C.

Standing time tenderises veal.

Veal and Ham Terrine

750 g veal, minced
6 bacon rashers, rinds
    removed
1 clove garlic, finely chopped
2 eggs, beaten
¼ teaspoon dried tarragon
1 tablespoon chopped parsley
2 tablespoons brandy or
    sherry
¼ teaspoon salt
¼ teaspoon pepper
¾ cup soft white breadcrumbs
250 g ham, finely chopped
½ cup toasted almond slivers
½ cup drained crushed
    pineapple

Time: 20–25 minutes. Serves 8–10

Line a loaf dish with bacon. In bowl combine veal, garlic, eggs, tarragon, parsley, brandy, salt, pepper and breadcrumbs. Place ham, almonds and pineapple into a small bowl.

Place one-third of veal mixture onto bacon and cover with half ham mixture. Repeat with veal and ham mixtures and cover with remaining veal. Fold exposed ends of bacon over veal and cover with lid or plastic food wrap.

Stand terrine on plate to collect spillover and cook on medium–high 20–25 minutes. Let stand 10 minutes, then cool.

Remove lid. Place weight on top and refrigerate overnight to prevent crumbling when cut. Serve sliced with salad and toast.

Veal Niçoise

500 g veal steaks
1 medium–sized onion, sliced
    thinly in rings
4 tablespoons tomato paste
1 tablespoon flour
¼ teaspoon dried basil
1 teaspoon sugar
2 teaspoons chopped parsley
1 small clove garlic, chopped
¼ teaspoon salt
¼ teaspoon freshly ground
    black pepper
2 large tomatoes, peeled and
    chopped
½ medium–sized green
    capsicum, thinly sliced
½ medium–sized red
    capsicum, thinly sliced
¼ cup sliced stuffed olives
8 whole black olives
2 teaspoons finely chopped
    parsley

Time: 16–18 minutes. Serves 4

Pound veal with meat mallet to tenderise and flatten to 1 cm thickness. Place slices into baking dish and top with onion rings.

In a medium–sized bowl blend tomato paste, flour, basil, sugar, parsley, garlic, salt and pepper. Stir in tomato and capsicum. Spread veal with vegetable mixture and sprinkle with sliced and whole olives.

Cook on high 16–18 minutes until veal is fork tender. Sprinkle lightly with finely chopped parsley to serve.

Osso Bucco

4 × 300 g osso bucco (shin of
    veal slices)
seasoned flour
3 tablespoons olive oil
1 small onion, chopped
1 small carrot, cut into 1 cm
    pieces
1 stalk celery, cut into 1 cm
    pieces
1 bay leaf
⅔ cup dry vermouth or white
    wine
1 can peeled tomato pieces
1 tablespoon tomato paste
½ teaspoon salt
1 teaspoon freshly ground
    black pepper
1 clove garlic, finely chopped
zest ½ lemon
2 tablespoons finely chopped
    Italian parsley

Time: 75–85 minutes. Serves 4

Heat browning casserole dish on high 8 minutes. Add oil and cook on high 1 minute. Roll each piece of shin of veal in seasoned flour and place in oil. Cook on high 8 minutes, turning every 2 minutes. Transfer meat to a plate.

Add onion, carrot, celery and bay leaf to casserole dish. Cover and cook on high 5 minutes. Add wine, stir in and cook on high for 4 minutes. Stir in tomatoes and their juice, tomato paste, salt and pepper. Cover and cook on high 6 minutes.

Place meat in sauce mixture and baste. Cover and cook on high for 5 minutes. Reduce to medium and cook 44 minutes, turning and basting every 10 minutes.

Arrange meat on serving platter, purée vegetables and sauce in food processor. Correct seasoning and pour over meat.

Combine garlic, lemon zest and parsley. Sprinkle over meat just before serving. Serve with Lemon Rice (see recipe Lemon Rice).

Pork Fillets with Prune and Almond Stuffing

4 × 400 g pork fillets
16 prunes
4 anchovy fillets
16 toasted almonds
1 tablespoon butter
1 tablespoon flour
1 cup beef consommé
⅛ teaspoon salt
⅛ teaspoon pepper
6 tablespoons red wine
8 pickling onions, peeled

Time: 38 minutes. Serves 4

Cut each fillet lengthwise two-thirds through and open out. Remove seed from each prune. Cut each anchovy into quarters. Stuff one almond and a piece of anchovy into each prune and reshape.

Place 4 stuffed prunes into each cut fillet and tie each fillet with white string to enclose prunes. Preheat browning casserole on high for 8 minutes. Add butter and fillets and cook on high 4 minutes, turning every minute. Remove from casserole.

Blend flour into pan drippings and cook on high 1 minute. Blend in consommé, salt, pepper and red wine. Cook on high 4 minutes. Add fillets and pickling onions and mask with sauce. Cover and cook on high 3 minutes, then reduce to medium. Cook 18 minutes, turning 4 times during cooking.

Pickled Pork with Caper Sauce

2.5 kg lean pickled pork
1 tablespoon brown sugar
1 cinnamon stick
1 teaspoon peppercorns
6 whole cloves
3 bay leaves
1 onion, chopped
1 stalk celery, cut in 2 cm
    lengths
1 cup water
½ cup pineapple or orange
    juice

Time: 2–2½ hours. Serves 8–10

Place pork in a 2–3 litre casserole dish. Add remaining ingredients, cover and cook on high 10 minutes. Reduce power to medium and cook for 45 minutes.

Turn pork over and cover. Cook on medium 60–90 minutes or until pork is tender. Let stand 10–20 minutes, covered, before carving. Serve with caper sauce.

Caper Sauce

1 tablespoon capers
2 teaspoons chopped parsley
1 tablespoon butter
1 tablespoon flour
⅛ teaspoon salt
⅛ teaspoon pepper
250 mL milk

Time: 3 minutes 45 seconds. Makes 2–3 cups

Place butter into medium-sized bowl. Cook on high 45 seconds until melted. Stir in flour, salt, pepper and add milk. Cook on high 3 minutes or until boiling, stirring after each minute. Fold in capers and parsley.

Sweet and Sour Pork Casserole

750 g pork, cut into 2 cm
    pieces
2 tablespoons seasoned
    cornflour
3 tablespoons soy sauce
¼ cup brown sugar
¼ cup vinegar
¼ teaspoon ground ginger
1 × 440 can pineapple pieces
    in juice
1 onion, chopped
½ red capsicum, chopped
1 stalk celery, chopped
1 clove garlic, finely chopped

Time: 35 minutes. Serves 6

Toss pork in seasoned cornflour into a 2 litre casserole dish. Add remaining ingredients except capsicum. Cover and cook on high 5 minutes. Reduce power to medium and cook for 20 minutes, stirring twice during cooking.

Add capsicum, adjust seasonings and thickening if necessary and continue cooking on medium 10 minutes. Serve with rice or fried noodles.

> **HINT: ADDING THICKENING AGENTS TO CASSEROLES**
> Pour blended cornflour into casserole around outer edge. Cook on high 2 minutes. Stir through the other ingredients. Continue cooking 2–3 minutes.

Seasoned Shoulder of Lamb

1 boned shoulder of lamb
 — 2 kg

Seasoning

1 cup fresh breadcrumbs
1 tablespoon butter
¼ teaspoon nutmeg
¼ teaspoon salt
¼ teaspoon pepper
1 tablespoon chopped mint
pinch mixed herbs
2 tablespoons milk
2 shallots, finely cut
½ cup sliced fresh mushrooms

Peach Sauce

1 cup cranberry sauce
½ cup diced peaches
2 tablespoons sweet vermouth
 or sherry

Time: 39 minutes. Serves 4–6

Combine all ingredients for seasoning. Place seasoning on boned lamb. Roll up. Tie firmly with string or fasten with bamboo sate sticks. Place onto roasting rack, fat side down. Cook 36 minutes on high, turning halfway through cooking time. Wrap in foil and stand for 15 minutes before carving.

Combine ingredients for Peach Sauce and cook 3 minutes on high to heat.

Pork Chops with Mustard and Apple Sauce

6 pork chops, fat removed
salt and pepper to taste
1 tablespoon oil

Mustard and Apple Sauce

1 tablespoon wholegrain
 mustard
1 small green apple, peeled,
 cored and chopped
1 tablespoon freshly chopped
 parsley
2 teaspoons white wine

Time: 22 minutes. Serves 6

Preheat browning dish on high 6 minutes. Add oil and cook chops, 3 at a time, on high 6 minutes, turning once. Repeat with remaining chops. Arrange on serving dish.

Combine sauce ingredients in a bowl, cover and cook on high 3–4 minutes. Stir and serve over chops.

100

Beef Olives

500 g very thinly sliced rump
 steak
1 rasher bacon, diced
1 small onion, chopped
¼ cup breadcrumbs
1 tablespoon chopped parsley
1 teaspoon grated lemon rind
1 small carrot, grated
black pepper
¼ teaspoon salt
1 egg
seasoned flour
30 g butter
150 mL brown stock
150 mL red wine
3 teaspoons arrowroot
1 tablespoon cold water
parsley for garnish

Time: 30 minutes. Serves 3–4

Cut steak into 10 cm squares. Pound with meat mallet. Place bacon and onion into bowl, cook 3 minutes. Add breadcrumbs, parsley, lemon rind, carrot, pepper, salt, and egg. Blend together. Spread filling over meat slices. Roll up and tie with string. Coat meat with seasoned flour. Preheat browning skillet 6 minutes. Add butter to melt. Add beef rolls, cook 3 minutes on high on each side. Add stock, wine and cook covered 12 minutes medium.

Remove string from rolls, transfer to serving plate. Reserve juices and add 3 teaspoons arrowroot blended with 1 tablespoon cold water to skillet juices. Cook on high 2–3 minutes to form sauce. Mask rolls with sauce. Sprinkle with cut parsley.

Pepper Steak

4 thin slices fillet steak
2 tablespoons ground black
 pepper
2 tablespoons oil
2 cloves garlic, finely chopped
2 tablespoons brandy
¼ cup white wine

Time: 17 minutes. Serves 4

Cover steaks with ground pepper and pound with mallet. Heat browning skillet 6 minutes on high. Add oil and garlic. Heat for 3 minutes. Press steak into pan, cook 3 minutes on each side. Add brandy and wine, cook 2 minutes.

Guard of Honour

2 racks of lamb, each with 8
    cutlets

Stuffing

60 g butter
1 small onion, finely chopped
2 cups fresh breadcrumbs
1 tablespoon chopped parsley
pinch dry mixed herbs
1 egg, beaten
1 teaspoon grated lemon or
    orange rind
garlic slivers

Time: 23 minutes. Serves 4-6

Place butter into bowl for 15-20 seconds to melt. Add
onion and cook 2-3 minutes on high. Combine with remaining ingredients.

Interlace cutlet bones to form an arch. Stud with garlic
slivers and season lightly. Place seasoning in centre of cutlet racks, and fasten with bamboo sate sticks to retain
shape. Cook 20 minutes on high. Cover with foil and allow
to stand 10-15 minutes. Top cutlet bones with frills. Serve
with minted Potato Balls, Glazed Carrots and a green vegetable (see Vegetables).

Potato Pie

2 tablespoons butter
1 small onion, finely chopped
500 g cold roast lamb, minced
2 tablespoons chopped parsley
250 g peas, cooked
250 g cooked carrots, sliced
250 g fresh mushrooms, sliced
1 teaspoon curry powder
1 × 165 g can mushroom soup
salt and pepper
2 cups hot mashed potato
nutmeg and paprika

Time: 12 minutes. Serves 4-6

Melt butter in casserole dish for 15 seconds. Add onion and
cook 3 minutes on high. Fold in lamb, parsley, peas, carrots, mushrooms, curry powder, soup, salt and pepper.
Pipe potatoes over top of mixture. Sprinkle with nutmeg
and paprika. Cook 9 minutes.

Garlic Brains

500 g calves' or lambs' brains
1 tablespoon white wine
45 g butter
4 cloves garlic
juice of ½ lemon
chopped parsley
seasoning salt

Time: 16 minutes. Serves 2-4

Trim and rinse brains. Place in flat dish and add 1 tablespoon of dry white wine. Cover with plastic food wrap and
cook 4 minutes on high. Turn over after 2 minutes. Cool
and cut into thick slices. Heat browning skillet for 6 minutes. Add butter and chopped garlic. Cook 2 minutes. Add
sliced brains and cook 2 minutes on each side. Add lemon
juice, chopped parsley, seasoning salt.

Vienna Schnitzel

500 g fillets of veal
¼ cup lemon juice
seasoned flour
1 egg, beaten
2 tablespoons milk
1 teaspoon soy sauce
1 cup breadcrumbs
1 cup oil
lemon wedges

Time: 15 minutes. Serves 2-3

Pound veal fillets with meat mallet until thin. Marinate in
lemon juice for 20 minutes. Dust with seasoned flour.
Combine egg, milk and soy sauce. Dip veal fillets into egg
mixture, and coat with breadcrumbs. Preheat browning
skillet for 8 minutes on high. Add oil and heat for 3 minutes. Add schnitzels, cook 2 minutes on each side. Serve
with lemon wedges.

Glazed Ham Steaks

750 g ham steaks
¼ cup maple syrup
¼ cup brown sugar
pinch ground cloves

Time: 17½ minutes. Serves 6

Combine maple syrup, brown sugar and ground cloves in
small basin. Cook on high 1½ minutes, stir to dissolve
sugar.

Heat browning dish on high 8 minutes. Add ham steaks.
Pour over half glaze, cover and cook on high 4 minutes,
turn steaks after 2 minutes and pour over remaining glaze.
Cook on medium 4 minutes uncovered.

Lamb Stew

750 g lean lamb
3 tablespoons flour
salt and pepper
oregano
pinch of thyme
60 g butter
1 large onion, finely chopped
2 carrots, sliced
250 g potato balls
½ red capsicum, diced
bouquet garni
1½ cups beef stock

Time: 52 minutes. Serves 4

Cut lamb into even sized pieces. Combine flour, salt, pepper, oregano and thyme. Roll lamb in seasoned flour. Heat browning skillet for 8 minutes. Add butter to melt. Add lamb pieces, cook 2 minutes on each side. Add all vegetables and bouquet garni, cook covered 5 minutes on high, stirring once during cooking. Add stock, cook covered on medium for 35 minutes. Let stand 10-15 minutes before serving.

Roast Leg of Lamb

1 × 2.5 kg leg of lamb
3 cloves garlic, peeled
lemon-flavoured black pepper
1 teaspoon powdered ginger
variety of vegetables
1 can drained pears
1 jar mint jelly

Time: 53 minutes. Serves 8

Trim excess fat from lamb. Cut garlic in slivers and stud lamb. Sprinkle with lemon-flavoured black pepper and rub lightly with ginger. Place lamb, fat side down, on a roasting rack in an oblong casserole dish or just place into casserole dish. Cover with a sheet of white kitchen paper and cook 25 minutes on high. Turn leg over and baste with pan drippings. Cook a further 15 minutes. Wrap in foil, allow to stand for 15 minutes before carving.

During this time vegetables can be cooked in the baking dish. Suggested vegetables: whole onions, sweet potato, pumpkin, potatoes. Place vegetables into pan and baste with drippings. Cook 5 minutes on high. Turn over to cook a further 5 minutes or until tender. Fill pears with mint jelly and heat 3 minutes.

Beef Stroganoff

2 tablespoons oil
500 g rump steak
½ teaspoon salt
½ teaspoon pepper
2 tablespoons flour
2 onions, sliced
1 clove garlic, cut finely
250 g fresh mushrooms, sliced
150 mL red wine
150 mL beef stock
1 tablespoon tomato paste
1 carton sour cream

Time: 25 minutes. Serves 4-6

Preheat browning skillet for 8 minutes on high. Add oil and heat for 2 minutes. Combine salt, pepper and flour. Cut meat into very thin slices, across grain. Roll in seasoned flour. Add to pan and cook 3-4 minutes, stirring frequently to brown meat. Add onions, garlic and cook 3 minutes. Add mushrooms, wine, stock, tomato paste and cook 6 minutes on medium. Blend in sour cream, cook to reheat 2 minutes. Serve with rice or buttered noodles.

Sauerbraten

1 × 1.5-1.75 kg piece boneless
  sirloin

Marinade

1¾ cups cold water
½ cup red wine vinegar
1 medium onion, sliced
1 stalk celery, sliced
2 teaspoons salt
6 whole cloves
6 whole peppercorns
2 large bay leaves

Sauce (reserved marinade)

¼ cup seaoned flour
1 tablespoon brown sugar
10 gingernut biscuits, crushed

Time: 64 minutes. Serves 8-10

Mix marinade ingredients together in large casserole. Add sirloin, cover and marinate in refrigerator 24 hours, turning several times. Strain marinade.

Place beef and 1 cup of the marinade into a 1.5L casserole. Cover and cook on medium 60-75 minutes or until fork tender, turning halfway through cooking. Let stand, covered, while making sauce.

Place reserved marinade, flour and sugar into a 1 litre jug and blend well. Cook on high 2-3 minutes, stirring every minute. Place roast on warm serving platter. Stir sauce into meat drippings. Add gingernut biscuits and cook 1-2 minutes on high until boiling, stirring once.

Note: For long slow cooking of beef, cook on low 105-120 minutes.

Roast Pork Ribs

750 g pork spareribs

Marinade

1 medium onion, chopped
2 tablespoons dark soy sauce
3 tablespoons honey
2 tablespoons lemon juice
1 clove garlic, crushed
¼ teaspoon salt
pinch pepper
½ teaspoon curry powder
¼ teaspoon chilli powder
½ teaspoon ground ginger
¼ cup oil

Time: 20 minutes. Serves 4

Combine marinade ingredients. Remove rind and excess fat from ribs. Prick with skewer and place in marinade for 2 hours. Place ribs onto a roasting rack and cook 20 minutes on high, turning after 10 minutes. Spare ribs may also be cooked in an oven bag.

Note: Chicken wings can be cooked in this method.

Roast Pork Ribs

Lamb Curry

750 g boneless leg of lamb
30 g butter
250 g onions, chopped
1 clove garlic, chopped
2 tablespoons curry powder
1 tablespoon flour
1 tablespoon chutney
2 teaspoons coconut
1 tablespoon sultanas
60 g chopped apple
2 tablespoons tomato paste
1 cup beef stock
salt

Time: 36 minutes. Serves 4–6

Trim lamb and cut into even sized pieces. Preheat browning skillet 6 minutes on high. Add butter and heat for 2 minutes. Cook lamb pieces 3 minutes on each side with onion and garlic. Drain off any fat, add curry powder and flour. Mix well and cook 2 minutes. Add chutney, coconut, sultanas, apples, tomato paste and stock. Cook covered 20 minutes on high, stirring occasionally. Serve with plain boiled rice and cucumber sambal.

Corned Silverside

4 cups boiling water
1.5 kg corned silverside
3 cloves
1 small onion, chopped
1 cinnamon stick
¼ teaspoon nutmeg
1 tablespoon brown sugar
1 bay leaf
1 tablespoon vinegar

Defrost Cooking Cycle Method
Place water, meat and remaining ingredients into a covered casserole dish and cook on defrost cycle 1¾–2 hours, or until tender when pierced with a fork. Allow to stand 10 minutes before carving.

Oven Bag Method

Time: 1–2 hours (see instructions). Serves 6–8

Soak beef in 2 changes of cold water for 2 hours. Place meat into an oven bag with remaining ingredients and 1½ cups of cold water. Tie bag. Place in large pyrex bowl. Pierce bag once or twice. Cook 30 minutes on high, turn meat over and cook 30 minutes on medium. Allow to stand 10 minutes before carving.

Veal Marsala

500 g veal steak
seasoned flour
3 tablespoons butter
½ cup Marsala

Time: 14 minutes. Serves 4

Pound veal with mallet to flatten. Dust with seasoned flour. Heat browning skillet 6 minutes on high. Add butter to melt. Add veal and cook 2 minutes on each side. Add Marsala and cook 3–4 minutes to form a sauce with pan drippings.

Veal Cordon Bleu

4 × 125 g slices veal
2 slices Gruyere cheese
2 slices lean ham
seasoned flour
1 beaten egg
1 tablespoon milk
1 teaspoon soy sauce
1 cup seasoned breadcrumbs

Time: 19 minutes. Serves 2

Pound veal slices with mallet until thin. Place 1 slice each of cheese and ham on 2 veal slices. Top with remaining veal. Seal outer edges of veal by tapping with meat mallet.

Combine egg, milk and soy sauce. Dust veal with seasoned flour, dip into egg mixture and coat with breadcrumbs. Preheat browning skillet 8 minutes on high. Add oil and heat for 3 minutes. Cook veal for 4 minutes on each side.

Stuffed Butterfly Pork Chops

4 butterfly pork chops
1 cup peeled chopped apple
¼ cup raisins
2 teaspoons orange zest
1/8 teaspoon cinnamon
1 tablespoon butter
½ cup dry breadcrumbs
2 teaspoons brown sugar

Time: 24 minutes. Serves 4

Combine apple, raisins, orange zest, cinnamon and butter in bowl and cook on high 3 minutes. Stir in ¼ cup breadcrumbs and all brown sugar. Pack filling into each chop and press edges together. Coat chops with remaining breadcrumbs and arrange on the outer edge of roasting rack in baking dish.

Cook chops on high 5 minutes. Reduce power to medium and cook 16 minutes or until meat is no longer pink.

Veal Cordon Bleu

Roast Pork

2.5 kg leg or loin of pork in one
  piece
3 tablespoons oil
1 teaspoon salt
1 teaspoon five spice powder
juice of half a lemon
apple and pineapple slices for
  garnish
apricot jam for glaze

Time: 45 minutes. Serves 6

Score rind of pork. Brush with oil. Rub salt and five spice powder into the skin and allow to stand for 15 minutes. Pour lemon juice over. Place on roasting rack in casserole dish and cook 40–45 minutes on high. (It is not necessary to turn pork over during cooking.) Wrap in foil and allow to stand 20 minutes before carving. During last 4 minutes of cooking, place slices of apple and pineapple around pork. Glaze slices with apricot jam.

Braised Pork Chops

4 shoulder pork chops
seasoned flour
2 tablespoons oil
1 onion, sliced
3 large mushrooms, sliced
2 tomatoes, peeled and sliced
½ cup chicken stock
½ cup port wine
2 cloves
salt and pepper

Time: 23 minutes. Serves 4

Coat chops with seasoned flour. Heat browning skillet 6 minutes on high. Add oil and heat for 3 minutes. Press chops into skillet and cook 3 minutes on each side to brown. Add onion, mushrooms, tomato, stock, port, cloves, salt and pepper. Cover and cook for 8 minutes. Allow to stand 5 minutes before serving. Sauce may be thickened lightly with cornflour.

Polynesian Kebabs

750 g lean boneless pork cut
  into 2.5 cm cubes
1 cup pineapple pieces
1 cup red or green capsicum,
  diced or 1 onion, diced

Time: 20 minutes. Serves 6–8

Marinade

1 clove garlic, chopped
½ cup pineapple juice
1 cup soy sauce
¼ cup dry sherry
3 teaspoons brown sugar

Combine marinade ingredients in basin and add pork cubes. Toss to coat. Cover and marinate 2 hours or overnight. Thread pork cubes onto long sate sticks alternating with pieces of capsicum, or onion and pineapple.

Heat browning dish on high 8 minutes and lightly oil. Arrange kebabs and cook on high 12 minutes turning and basting frequently.

Meat Loaf

2 bread slices, 1 cm thick
500 g minced topside
60 g onion, chopped finely
60 g green capsicum, chopped
  finely
60 g celery, chopped finely
½ cup grated tasty cheese
1 tablespoon chopped parsley
125 mL tomato juice
2 eggs
¾ teaspoon salt
dash of pepper and nutmeg
2 tablespoons Worcestershire
  sauce
60 g tomato sauce

Time: 25 minutes. Serves 4–6

Soak bread slices in water until soft. Squeeze out water thoroughly. Mix mince, bread, onion, green capsicum, celery, cheese, parsley and tomato juice in a bowl. Stir well. Add eggs, salt, pepper and nutmeg. Stir well again. Shape meat into a loaf and place in dish. Cook 20 minutes on high. Blend Worcestershire sauce and tomato sauce. Drizzle liquid over top of loaf. Cook 5 minutes.

Note: Fruit chutney and extra grated cheese can be spread on top of meat loaf during last 5 minutes of cooking.

Tongue a la King

750 g cooked tongue, diced into
  2 cm pieces
1 tablespoon butter
90 g red capsicum, diced into 2
  cm pieces
180 g button mushrooms, sliced
1½ tablespoons sherry
1½ tablespoons butter
1½ tablespoons plain flour
1 cup chicken stock
1 cup milk
⅛ teaspoon salt
⅛ teaspoon white pepper
2–3 tablespoons cream

Time: 14 minutes

Combine butter, capsicum and mushrooms in a 2 litre casserole and cook on high 2 minutes, stirring after 1 minute. Drain off any liquid. Add tongue and sherry.

Place butter into a 1 litre jug and cook on high 1 minute. Stir in flour and cook on high 2 minutes. Blend in milk and stock. Cook on high 5–6 minutes or until boiling, stirring twice during cooking. Add salt, pepper and cream.

Fold into vegetable mixture and cook on high 2–3 minutes or until heated through. Serve with rice (p.00).

Roast Pork

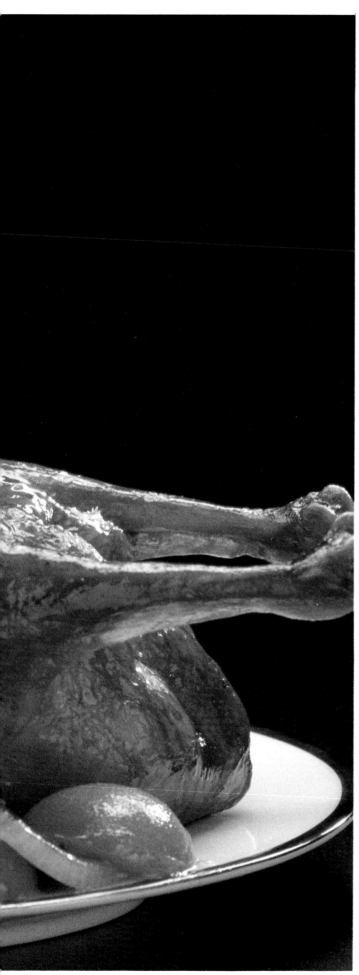

Poultry

Chicken is one of the most economical sources of protein available and when cooked in a microwave oven none of the natural tenderness and juiciness of the chicken is lost. As chicken will not brown in a microwave, baste the chicken during cooking with a mixture of barbecue or soy sauce and butter.

To roast a whole chicken place uncovered on a rack and allow 11–13 minutes cooking time for each 500 g. Complete the first 10 minutes of cooking on high, then finish with the microwave set to medium. Baste and turn the chicken during cooking and when cooked the internal temperature should be 190°C. Try not to prick the chicken with a fork as the loss of natural juice can dry out the flesh.

For casseroles remove the skin from the breast, thighs and drumsticks.

Ducks render a great deal of fat and therefore the roasting dish should be emptied a number of times during cooking. Allow 8–9 minutes cooking time for each 500 g and complete the first 10 minutes on high and finish on medium. After the first 10 minutes the duck can be removed from the oven and the cavity filled with a prepared stuffing. Secure the neck with a bamboo skewer. Turn halfway through cooking and before carving allow the duck to stand for 5 minutes. For both duck and turkey commence cooking breast side down.

When buying a turkey for cooking in a microwave oven make sure that there will be at least 7.5 cm between the turkey and the oven walls and at least 5 cm between the turkey and the oven roof.

To prevent drying out, wings, drumsticks, neck and cavity can be wrapped in thin strips of foil. Allow 10–15 minutes cooking time for each 500 g. Cook in the same fashion as chicken and duck.

Finish cooking breast side up and remove any foil half way through cooking. When the turkey is done the internal temperature should be 185°C and the juices should run clear. Stand turkey for 20 minutes before carving.

For cooking rolled turkey breast (boned or deboned, stuffed or plain) allow 12–15 minutes for each 500 g. Cook on high, with the breast side down, for the first 5 minutes and finish cooking on medium. Turn breast halfway through cooking time and baste. When cooked internal temperature should be 170°C. Stand for 10–15 minutes before carving.

Follow these guidelines for other turkey portions. Wings and drumsticks can be roasted, grilled or casseroled. Allow 12–16 minutes cooking time for each 500 g, cook for the first 5 minutes on high and finish cooking on medium. Allow 16 minutes for each 500 g when cooking hindquarters and cook on high for the first 10 minutes and finish on medium. For turkey breast steaks allow 15 minutes cooking for each 500 g and cook on medium.

Roast Apricot Duck

Turkey Divan

750 g cooked turkey, diced
    into 2 cm pieces
1 cup chicken stock
500 g broccoli heads, washed
1 tablespoon water
1/8 teaspoon salt
1 tablespoon melted butter
3 tablespoons dry sherry
60 g grated cheese
2 1/2 cups béchamel sauce
1 quantity hollandaise sauce
    (see recipe Eggs Benedict)
2 tablespoons dry sherry
60 g grated tasty or Parmesan
    cheese
strip of pimiento or blanched
    red capsicum strips
chopped parsley

Time: 24 minutes. Serves 6–8

Place turkey and stock in a casserole, cover and cook on high 3 minutes, stirring after 2 minutes. Set aside.

Place broccoli, water and salt in a 3 litre casserole dish. Cover and cook on high 6 minutes. Drain. Sprinkle with melted butter, 3 tablespoons sherry and cheese.

Drain turkey cubes and arrange over broccoli. Fold béchamel *(see recipe following)* and hollandaise sauce together, blend in remaining sherry and spoon over turkey. Sprinkle with remaining cheese.

Cook on medium 6–9 minutes until heated through and cheese melted. Garnish with pimiento strips and chopped parsley.

HINT: TURKEY IN THE MICROWAVE

The maximum size turkey suitable for cooking in a microwave oven is 6–7 kg. Larger birds should be roasted conventionally.

To test the oven for size, place turkey in oven and turn on all sides. There should be 7.5 cm space between turkey and oven walls and at least 5 cm between the top of the oven and the upper side of the turkey.

During cooking, baste the turkey occasionally. Check for areas that may be cooking too fast and shield these with small amounts of foil.

Cooking times remain the same whether the turkey is stuffed or unstuffed.

Turkey Chow Mein

2 boned turkey thighs, diced
    into 2 cm pieces
1–2 tablespoons cornflour
1/2 cup rich chicken stock
1 1/2 tablespoons soy sauce
1 cup thinly sliced celery
1 medium–sized onion, diced
1 × 440 g can Chinese mixed
    vegetables, drained
250 g fresh mushrooms, sliced
1 packet cooked chow mein
    noodles

Time: 18 minutes. Serves 8

Place turkey pieces in casserole. Cover and cook on high 6–8 minutes, stirring after 3 minutes.

Blend cornflour and stock and add to casserole. Stir in soy sauce and vegetables. Cover and cook on high 12 minutes, stirring after 6 minutes. Serve surrounded by chow mein noodles.

Roast Turkey with Pineapple Stuffing

1 × 6–7 kg turkey,
    completely defrosted

Pineapple Stuffing

1/4 cup chopped onion
1/4 cup butter
2 cups prepared poultry
    stuffing
2/3 cup hot water
1 × 440 g can crushed
    pineapple, well drained
1/2 teaspoon poultry seasoning

Time: 2 hours 36 minutes–3 hours 15 minutes.

Serves 10–12

Weigh turkey and estimate total cooking time. Allow 12–15 minutes cooking time on medium per 500 g.

In a 1 litre casserole cook onion and butter on high 3–4 minutes until onion is soft. Blend in remaining stuffing ingredients. Place stuffing into cavity of prepared turkey. Secure cavity and neck skin with bamboo saté sticks cut to required length.

Place turkey, breast side down, in baking dish. Divide cooking time into quarters. Cook on high for first 10 minutes. Reduce heat to medium and cook remaining part of first quarter of time. Shield wings, drumsticks, cavity and neck with foil strips if necessary. Turn turkey on side and cook for a further quarter of cooking time. Turn to other side. Baste with pan juices.

Turn breast side up and cook a further quarter of cooking time. Let stand 20–30 minutes (this can be done in microwave on warm setting) before carving. Turkey is cooked when the leg moves freely and is soft to touch. Pierce thigh with skewer; juices run clear when cooking is complete. A meat thermometer placed in the thigh can also be used to check it's ready — it should register 180°C.

Béchamel Sauce

2½ cups milk
60 g butter
60 g flour
salt
white pepper
pinch nutmeg
4 tablespoons cream

Time: 8½ minutes. Makes 2-3 cups

Place butter in a bowl and cook on high 1 minute. Stir in flour and cook 1 minute. Blend in milk. Cook on high 6½ minutes or until boiling, stirring twice during cooking. Season with salt, pepper and nutmeg. Fold in cream.

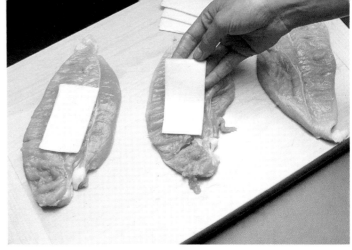

Step 1 Chicken Roulade. Place cheese slice on each chicken fillet

Chicken Roulade with Almond and Broccoli Stuffing

4 large chicken breast fillets,
    skin removed
2 slices sandwich cheese slices
300 g frozen broccoli,
    defrosted and chopped
60 g almonds or cashews,
    chopped
1 cup milk
1 tablespoon flour
1 tablespoon white wine
2 teaspoons chopped parsley
¼ teaspoon salt
¼ teaspoon pepper
1 tablespoon grated cheese

Time: 12 minutes. Serves 4

Cut each slice of cheese in half. Pound chicken fillets to flatten. Place a piece of cheese onto each fillet and divide broccoli and almonds between the four chicken fillets. Roll up fillets around broccoli and secure with cocktail sticks. Place rolls seam side down in 20 cm square baking dish. Cover with white kitchen paper and cook on high 8 minutes, turning twice during cooking. Drain and set aside.

Blend milk, flour, wine, parsley, salt and pepper in a jug. Cook on high 2-3 minutes until thickened, stirring twice during cooking. Blend in grated cheese. Pour sauce over roulade and cook on high 1 minute to reheat.

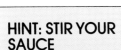

HINT: STIR YOUR SAUCE
Stirring sauce during cooking ensures an even distribution of the cooked sauce and ensures a thoroughly tasty meal.

Chicken Roulade with Almond and Broccoli Stuffing

Step 2   Divide broccoli and almonds between fillets

Step 3   Roll up fillets and secure with cocktail sticks

Chicken Schnitzel with Asparagus Cream Sauce

4 large chicken breast fillets,
    skin removed
2 tablespoons butter
1 cup breadcrumbs
2 tablespoons grated
    Parmesan cheese
1 tablespoon dried parsley
    flakes
1 teaspoon paprika
2 tablespoons flour
2 tablespoons butter
¼ teaspoon salt
⅛ teaspoon white pepper
1¼ cups milk
2 tablespoons sherry
1 cup green asparagus tips
½ cup grated cheese
pinch nutmeg

Time: 22 minutes. Serves 4

Place butter in pie plate and heat on high 1 minute. In another plate combine breadcrumbs, Parmesan cheese, parsley and paprika. Dip each fillet in butter then coat with crumb mixture. Place in a single layer in baking dish and cook on high 12–14 minutes or until tender. Rearrange fillets half way through cooking. Let stand, covered.

Place 2 tablespoons butter in jug and cook on high 45 seconds. Stir in flour, salt and pepper and cook a further minute. Blend in milk and sherry. Cook on high 4 minutes or until thickened. Blend in asparagus, cheese and nutmeg. Cook on medium 2 minutes until cheese melts. Pour over chicken to serve.

> **HINT: TESTING IF CHICKEN IS COOKED**
> Pierce thigh with cocktail stick. If liquid runs clear the chicken is cooked. Should the natural juice have a slight pink colour — this may occur if chicken was frozen — the chicken requires longer cooking.

Coq au Vin

1.5 kg chicken thighs
4 slices bacon, diced into 2 cm
    pieces
⅓ cup flour
½ cup red wine
½ cup chicken stock
2 tablespoons brandy
2 teaspoons chopped parsley
1 teaspoon salt
1 clove garlic, finely chopped
1 bay leaf
¼ teaspoon thyme
¼ teaspoon pepper
¼ teaspoon chicken seasoning
250 g mushrooms, sliced
1 large onion, sliced

Time: 35 minutes. Serves 6

Place bacon in a 3 litre casserole dish. Cover and cook on high 4 minutes. Drain, leaving 1 tablespoon bacon fat in casserole. Blend in flour. Stir in liquids and seasonings.

Add mushrooms, onion and chicken. Cover and cook on high 15 minutes. Stir and rearrange chicken. Cook 11 minutes or until chicken is tender. Let stand, covered, 5 minutes before serving.

Five Spice Chicken

1 × 1.5 kg fresh chicken
2 cloves garlic
4 tablespoons soy sauce
2 tablespoons peanut oil
½ teaspoon Chinese five spice
    powder
½ teaspoon salt
1 teaspoon sugar
¼ teaspoon pepper

Time: 20–30 minutes. Serves 4–6

Weigh chicken and allow 8–9 minutes cooking time on high for 500 g.

Chop garlic finely and sprinkle with salt. Mash together with side of a knife into a creamy paste. Combine with remaining ingredients in a large bowl. Place chicken into bowl and baste with marinade. Let chicken marinate 1 hour, basting and turning every 15 minutes.

Drain chicken and place breast side down on roasting rack in baking dish. Cook on high for half the required cooking time. Turn chicken breast side up. Baste with remaining marinade. Continue cooking on high for rest of time. Carve chicken or chop up Chinese style to serve.

Coq au Vin

Crab Stuffed Chicken

1 × 1.5 kg fresh chicken
150 g crabmeat
½ cup chopped green
   capsicum
1 teaspoon lemon juice
¼ teaspoon pepper
2 slices bread cut in 1 cm
   cubes

Glaze

2 teaspoons soy sauce
1 tablespoon white wine
2½ tablespoons water
1 teaspoon cornflour
⅛ teaspoon garlic salt

Time: 20-30 minutes. Serves 4-6

Weigh chicken and allow 8-9 minutes cooking time on high per 500 g. Combine stuffing ingredients in bowl. Place inside cavity of chicken and truss with white kitchen string.

To make glaze: Blend all glaze ingredients together in a bowl and cook on high 2 minutes, stirring after 1 minute.

Place chicken on roasting rack, breast side down. Brush with prepared glaze. Cook on high for half required time. Turn chicken breast side up and baste with remaining glaze. Cook on high for remainder of time.

Chicken with Avocado

6 chicken breast fillets, skin
   removed
3 tablespoons butter
2 teaspoons soy sauce
½ cup pineapple juice
1 teaspoon chopped ginger
   root
1 small clove garlic, chopped
⅛ teaspoon paprika
1 large avocado, thickly sliced
1 teaspoon arrowroot

Time: 19 minutes. Serves 6

Place butter into baking dish and cook on high 1 minute. Arrange chicken breasts in butter. Blend soy sauce, ginger and garlic with ¼ cup pineapple juice, coating each breast evenly with liquid. Sprinkle with paprika and cook on high 12 minutes.

Place thick slices of avocado on fillets and cook a further 4 minutes. Mix arrowroot with remaining pineapple juice. Cook liquid on high 1½-2 minutes until thickened. Strain sauce over chicken and avocado to serve.

Step 1   Crab Stuffed Chicken. Combine stuffing ingredients

Step 2   Place stuffing in chicken

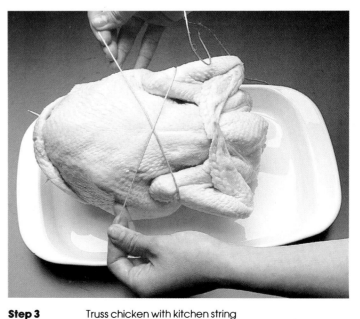

Step 3   Truss chicken with kitchen string

Crab Stuffed Chicken

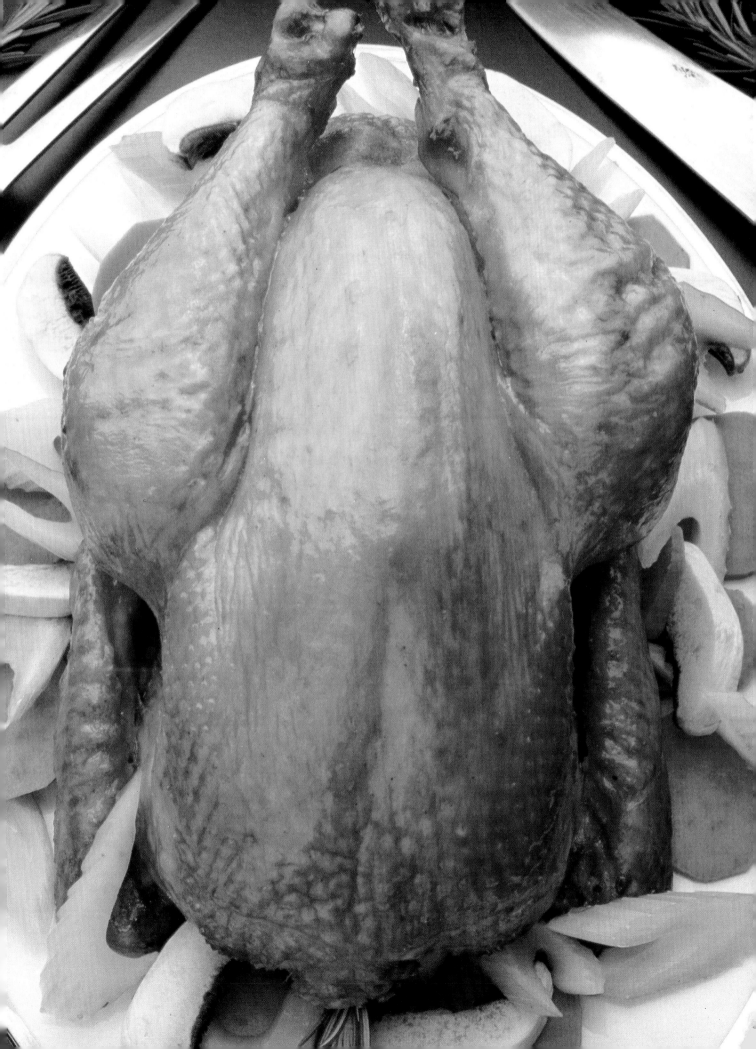

Chicken Catalan

8 large chicken breast fillets,
  skin removed
300 g stuffed olives
250 g fresh mushrooms, sliced
2 slices bacon, diced in 2 cm
  pieces
1 tablespoon flour
¾ cup red wine
½ teaspoon salt

Time: 20 minutes. Serves 8

In a baking dish layer olives, mushrooms and chicken fillets. Set aside.

Place bacon in pie plate and cook on high 3 minutes. Remove bacon with slotted spoon. Blend flour into bacon drippings and stir in wine and salt. Cook on high 2–3 minutes to form sauce, stirring during cooking. Add bacon and pour over chicken.

Cover and cook on high 10–11 minutes. Rearrange chicken after 5 minutes. Let stand 5 minutes before serving.

Barbecued Drumsticks

10 chicken drumsticks, skin
  removed
¼ cup finely chopped onion
2 tablespoons finely chopped
  celery
½ teaspoon sugar
½ teaspoon dry mustard
1 teaspoon Worcestershire
  sauce
1 tablespoon vinegar
1 tablespoon barbecue sauce
¾ cup tomato sauce
⅛ teaspoon freshly ground
  black pepper
water

Time: 33 minutes. Serves 5

Combine all ingredients except drumsticks in jug. Cook on high 3 minutes or until hot, stirring once. Reduce to medium and cook 12 minutes, stirring every 3 minutes.

Arrange drumsticks in roasting dish. Brush with one-third of sauce and cover. Cook on high 7 minutes. Turn over and rearrange drumsticks and brush with one-third of sauce. Cover and cook on high 7 minutes. Brush with remaining sauce. Cover and cook on high 4 minutes.

HINT: REMOVING SKIN FROM FILLETS
Removing skin from chicken fillets enables the flavour of seasoning and other ingredients to penetrate the meat.

Orange Pecan Drumsticks

1.5–2 kg chicken drumsticks,
  skin removed
180 mL concentrated orange
  juice
½ cup water
1 teaspoon poultry seasoning
½ teaspoon salt
¼ cup water
2 tablespoons cornflour or
  arrowroot
½ cup finely chopped shallots
½ cup pecan nuts

Time: 23 minutes. Serves 4–6

Combine orange juice, water, poultry seasoning and salt in jug. Arrange drumsticks in roasting dish with the meaty ends arranged around the edge. Pour sauce over chicken, cover and cook on high 20 minutes until tender.

Combine ¼ cup water with cornflour or arrowroot in medium-sized bowl. Remove drumsticks to serving platter. Blend arrowroot into sauce. Add shallots and pecan nuts. Cook on high 2–3 minutes, stirring after 1 minute. Pour sauce over drumsticks. Serve with rice.

Roast Apricot Duck

1 × 2.5 kg duck
1 × 500 g can apricot or
  mango halves with juice
2 teaspoons arrowroot
2 tablespoons orange juice
1 tablespoon brown sugar
½ teaspoon French mustard
¼ teaspoon salt
⅛ teaspoon curry paste
1 onion, quartered
1 stalk celery, cut in 2.5 cm
  lengths

Time: 45 minutes. Serves 4

To make glaze: combine ½ cup apricot juice from can with arrowroot or cornflour in 1 litre jug. Blend in remaining ingredients except apricot halves, onion and celery. Cook on high 3–4 minutes until thick, stirring until smooth. Coarsely chop apricots and stir into glaze.

Weigh duck and allow 8–9 minutes cooking time on high per 500 g. Place prepared duck breast side down on roasting rack and cook on high 10 minutes. Drain well. Fasten neck skin to back with bamboo saté stick. Place onion and celery into cavity and return duckling to rack breast side down. Reduce heat to medium. Cook for remaining first half of cooking time.

Drain fat from dish, turn duck breastside up and spoon over half the apricot glaze. Cook on medium for remaining cooking time. Drain off fat and add remaining glaze. Let stand covered for 5 minutes.

Braised Lemon Chicken

2 tablespoons dark soy sauce
1 tablespoon dry sherry
1 cup lemon juice
2 teaspoons sugar
1 kg chicken breasts, cut into
    serving pieces
3 tablespoons oil
2 thin slices of green ginger
1 clove garlic, peeled and
    crushed
¾ cup water
1 tablespoon cornflour
salt
2–3 tablespoons water

Time: 52 minutes. Serves 4–6

Mix soy sauce, sherry, lemon juice, sugar in a bowl. Add chicken pieces and marinate for 20 minutes. Preheat browning skillet for 6 minutes. Add oil and heat for 2 minutes. Add ginger, garlic, chicken pieces and cook on high 3 minutes on each side.

Place chicken, garlic and ginger in casserole dish. Add remaining marinade and water. Cook covered 15–18 minutes, stirring twice during cooking. Add blended cornflour, cook 2 minutes. Season. Serve with plain boiled rice.

Spanish Chicken

1 kg chicken breasts, cut into
    pieces
seasoned flour, salt and pepper
4 tablespoons oil
2 onions, chopped
1 clove garlic, crushed
2 tablespoons chopped parsley
2 tablespoons chopped shallots
4 tomatoes, sliced
1 green capsicum, chopped
125 g button mushrooms
1¼ cups red wine
1 teaspoon red chilli, finely
    chopped
salt
pepper
1 cup frozen lima beans,
    cooked

Time: 36 minutes. Serves 4–6

Toss chicken pieces in seasoned flour. Preheat browning skillet for 6 minutes on high. Add 2 tablespoons oil and heat a further 2 minutes. Place chicken pieces in skillet and cook 3 minutes on each side. Place chicken pieces into a 2 litre casserole dish.

Reheat browning skillet for 2 minutes, add onions, garlic, remaining oil and cook for 2 minutes. Remove and add to chicken. Add parsley, shallots, tomatoes, capsicum, mushrooms, wine, chilli, salt and pepper. Cover casserole and cook 15 minutes. Add cooked beans and cook a further 3 minutes. Serve with boiled rice.

Mexican Chicken

1 large chicken, jointed, or
    chicken pieces
seasoned flour
4 tablespoons oil
3 large onions, sliced
2 cloves garlic, crushed
1 red capsicum, diced
1 tablespoon sesame seeds
½ teaspoon oregano
¾ cup dry red wine
1 cup blanched almonds
1 cup sliced stuffed olives
½–1 teaspoon chilli powder (to
    taste)
1 cup chicken stock
1 cup whole kernel corn

Time: 35 minutes. Serves 4–6

Dust chicken pieces lightly with seasoned flour. Preheat browning skillet for 6 minutes on high. Add oil, heat for 2 minutes. Add chicken pieces and cook for 3 minutes on each side. Remove chicken and place into a 2 litre casserole dish.

Place onions, garlic, capsicum, into browning skillet and cook 3 minutes, stirring after 2 minutes. Add sesame seeds, oregano, wine and pour over chicken pieces. Add almonds, olives, chilli powder, stock, and cook covered 15 minutes. Fold in corn kernels and cook 3 minutes longer.

Honeyed Chicken Liver Kebabs

500 g chicken livers
2 tablespoons honey
1 teaspoon black pepper
2 teaspoons soy sauce
2 medium onions, cut into
    sixths
bamboo sate sticks

Time: 19 minutes. Serves 6

Marinate chicken livers with honey, pepper and soy sauce for 20 minutes. Drain. Arrange chicken livers and onion wedges on bamboo sate sticks to cover 6–8 cm of the point end of each stick.

The kebabs may be cooked on a browner grill preheated on high for 8 minutes or arranged in a roasting dish. Cook on high 2 minutes. Reduce power to medium and cook 7–8 minutes or until livers are tender.

Baste with marinade and turn kebabs twice during cooking.

Apricot Chicken Casserole

3 tablespoons oil
1 kg chicken breasts, cut into
    serving pieces
2 tablespoons butter
1 large onion, diced
1 green capsicum, diced
2 tablespoons plain flour
1½ cups apricot nectar
salt and pepper
pinch oregano
2 teaspoons chopped parsley,
3 large tomatoes, peeled and
    sliced

Time: 37 minutes. Serves 4–6

Preheat browning skillet for 6 minutes. Add oil and heat for 2 minutes. Add chicken pieces and cook for 3 minutes on high on each side. Melt butter in a 2 litre casserole for 15 seconds. Add onion, capsicum and cook for 3 minutes. Stir in flour and cook for 2 minutes. Stir in apricot nectar to form a sauce. Add browned chicken pieces and remaining seasonings. Cover with tomato slices. Cook covered 18 minutes. Serve with buttered, boiled macaroni, which has been sprinkled with toasted sesame seeds.

Chicken in Red Wine

1 chicken, cut in serving pieces
60 g seasoned flour
3 tablespoons oil
120 g bacon, diced
1 clove garlic, chopped
6 small onions
2 cups red wine
120 g button mushrooms
salt and pepper

Time: 39 minutes. Serves 4–6

Coat chicken pieces lightly with seasoned flour. Preheat browning skillet for 6 minutes. Add oil and heat for 2 minutes. Place in chicken pieces pressing down on all sides to seal and colour. Cook 3 minutes on high on each side.

Remove chicken from pan and place in 2 litre casserole dish. Reheat browning skillet for 4 minutes, add bacon, garlic and onions, cover with kitchen paper and cook for 3 minutes. Add this mixture to chicken. Gradually blend in wine with remaining flour to form a smooth paste. Add mushrooms and cook covered 15–18 minutes on high, stirring twice during cooking.

Gourmet Chicken

2 whole chicken breasts
seasoned flour
3 tablespoons oil
¼ cup blanched slivered
    almonds
1 small onion, diced
1 clove garlic, minced
1 cup celery, diced
2 tablespoons parsley, minced
¾ cup dry sherry
1 cup button mushrooms
1 tablespoon cornflour
    (optional)
parsley sprigs and almonds for
    garnish

Time: 38 minutes. Serves 4

Cut chicken breasts into serving pieces and dust lightly with seasoned flour. Preheat browning skillet for 6 minutes on high. Add oil and heat for 2 minutes. Add almonds, brown slightly, set aside for garnish. Reheat skillet for 2 minutes, add chicken pieces and cook 3 minutes on each side on high. Remove chicken and place into a 2 litre casserole dish.

Place onion, garlic, celery, parsley into browning skillet and cook 2 minutes. Add sherry, mushrooms and stir well. Pour mixture over chicken pieces and cook covered 15–18 minutes. Thicken slightly with cornflour if necessary and cook 2 minutes longer. Serve garnished with almonds and parsley sprigs.

Golden Chicken

1.5 kg chicken breasts, cut into
    serving pieces
2 tablespoons curry powder
½ teaspoon salt
½ cup honey
2 tablespoons French mustard
2 cloves garlic, finely chopped
½ teaspoon ground cardamon

Time: 46 minutes. Serves 8–10

Preheat browning dish for 6 minutes. Remove skin from chicken portions and place bone side down in casserole dish. Sprinkle with curry powder and salt. Combine honey, mustard, garlic and cardamon. Cook on high 2 minutes then brush or spoon over chicken portions.

Cover chicken and cook on high 10 minutes. Turn portions over and baste with honey mixture. Cook on medium 20 minutes. Rearrange pieces from outer edge to centre halfway through cooking.

Test for doneness. If underdone, cook on medium a further 8 minutes or until juices run clear. Let stand 8–10 minutes before serving. Standing time can take place in a conventional oven heated to 100°C to keep chicken warm. Standing time: 8–10 minutes.

Crumbed Chicken Drumsticks

8 drumsticks
2 cups cooking oil
1 clove garlic, peeled and
    crushed
4 tablespoons flour
salt and pepper to taste
pinch oregano
½ level teaspoon five spice
    powder
1 egg
¼ cup milk
1½ cups dry breadcrumbs
¼ cup sesame seeds

Combine flour, salt, pepper, oregano and five spice powder. Beat egg and milk together. Combine breadcrumbs and sesame seeds.

Heat oil in pan on top of range. Add garlic, brown and remove. Roll drumsticks in seasoned flour. Coat with egg mixture, then with breadcrumb mixture. Fry drumsticks until a rich golden colour. Remove and drain.

Arrange on a glass platter with the thickest part of the drumstick to the outside edge. Cover with white kitchen paper. Cook for 8 minutes on high, turn over after 5 minutes of cooking. Serve with fried rice (*see recipe*).

Note: This method combines the crispness of pan frying with the moist cooking of the microwave oven.

Crumbed Chicken Drumsticks

Red Roast Chicken

1 whole chicken
1 slice ginger
1 clove garlic, crushed

Marinade

¾ cup Chinese barbecue sauce
pinch red food colouring
    powder
½ cup dry sherry

Time: 25 minutes. Serves 4–6

Place ginger and crushed garlic into cavity of chicken. Combine marinade ingredients. Coat chicken with marinade and allow to stand for 2 hours. Place chicken into an oven bag. Tie loosely with string. Prick bag once or twice. Place in casserole dish and cook on high 15 minutes. Turn over and cook a further 10 minutes. Allow to stand 10 minutes before carving. Serve hot or cold with salads.

Sweet and Sour Chicken

750 g fresh chicken breasts
3 tablespoons oil
1 clove garlic, chopped finely
1 thin slice ginger, chopped
    finely

Sauce

½ cup sugar
½ cup vinegar
¾ cup pineapple juice or water
1–2 tablespoons dark soy sauce
2 tablespoons oil
1 clove garlic, chopped finely
½ red capsicum, diced
½ green capsicum, diced
¼ cup Chinese pickles, diced
¼ cup mushrooms, sliced
¼ cup bamboo shoots, sliced
3 shallots, cut into 2 cm lengths
2 tablespoons cornflour
    blended with ½ cup water

Time: 34 minutes. Serves 4–6

Remove flesh from bone and cut into 2 cm dice. Preheat browning skillet for 8 minutes. Add oil and heat for 3 minutes. Add garlic, ginger and cook 1 minute. Add chicken pieces and stir to coat with oil. Cook on high 5 minutes, stir and cook a further 5 minutes.

Combine sugar, vinegar, pineapple juice, and soy sauce. Heat oil in casserole dish for 2 minutes. Add garlic, vegetables and cook for 3 minutes uncovered on high. Add vinegar mixture. Cook for 3 minutes. Blend cornflour and water to a paste. Add to other ingredients and cook for 2 minutes. Add chicken pieces. Reheat for 2 minutes. Serve with plain or fried rice (see recipe).

Chilli Chicken

2 whole chicken breasts, cut
    into serving pieces
4 red chillies, seeds removed
    and chopped finely
2 slices green ginger, chopped
    finely
2 cloves garlic, chopped finely
1 medium onion, chopped finely
2 teaspoons lemon or lime juice
1 teaspoon turmeric
1 teaspoon sugar
salt

Time: 20 minutes. Serves 4

Salt chicken pieces lightly. Combine all other ingredients in a bowl. Add chicken pieces and allow to stand 15–20 minutes. Place chicken and marinade in an oven bag. Tie bag loosely with string or elastic band. Cook 10 minutes on high, then turn bag over and continue cooking a further 10 minutes.

Note: The chicken in the oven bag must be in one layer, not bunched up.

Chicken Curry

1.5 kg chicken pieces
2 tablespoons butter
1 clove garlic, chopped
250 g onions, chopped
2 tablespoons curry paste or
    powder
1 tablespoon flour
1 tablespoon tomato paste
1 tablespoon sultanas
1 cup coconut milk (see recipe
    following)
1 tablespoon chutney
60 g chopped mango or
    pineapple

Time: 43 minutes. Serves 6

Preheat browning casserole dish on high 6 minutes. Add butter and cook 2 minutes. Place chicken pieces skin side down in casserole. Add onion and garlic. Cook on high 8 minutes, turning chicken over after 4 minutes. Add curry paste and flour and stir. Cook on high 2 minutes.

Mix in tomato paste, coconut milk, chutney, sultanas and mango. Reduce heat to medium and cook 25–30 minutes or until chicken is tender. Stir and rearrange pieces twice during cooking.

Coconut Milk

1 cup desiccated coconut
1 cup milk or half milk, half
    water

Place coconut and milk into basin. Cook on high 3 minutes. Allow to cool. Strain mixture through white cloth. Squeeze to extract milk. This process can be repeated with a second quantity of milk. This will yield a thinner milk which can be used for vegetable cookery.

Roast Chicken

1 large chicken, size 16,
    washed and dried

Stuffing

1 small onion, chopped finely
1 cup white breadcrumbs
pinch of mixed herbs
1 tablespoon butter
¼ teaspoon salt
pinch pepper
1 tablespoon chopped parsley

Basting Sauce

1–2 tablespoons melted butter
1 teaspoon soy sauce

Time: 33 minutes. Serves 4–6

Saute onion in butter, 3 minutes on high. Add remaining ingredients. Place stuffing into cavity. Truss chicken to a neat shape. Baste with 2 tablespoons melted butter mixed with 1 teaspoon soy sauce. Place into an oven bag. Tie loosely with string and prick bag once or twice. Cook 15 minutes on high, breast side down. Turn over and cook a further 15 minutes. Let stand in bag for 10 minutes before carving.

Note: Baked rabbit can also be cooked in this way.

Chicken Sate

500 g chicken breasts
1 cup pineapple pieces
1 cup button mushrooms
1 cup red capsicum diced same
    size as pineapple

Marinade

3 tablespoons soy sauce
1 tablespoon dry sherry
1 tablespoon brown sugar
½ teaspoon powdered ginger
2 teaspoons grated onion

Sauce

1 cup pineapple juice
1 tablespoon cornflour

Time: 16 minutes. Serves 4–6

Debone chicken. Cut into 2 cm cubes. Combine marinade ingredients, add chicken pieces and marinate for 1 hour. Arrange chicken pieces, pineapple and vegetables on bamboo skewers. Preheat browning skillet for 8 minutes. Add 2 tablespoons oil and heat for 2 minutes. Arrange skewers in oil and cook 3 minutes on high, turn and cook a further 3 minutes. Place on serving platter. Heat pineapple juice and cornflour to form a sauce. Spoon over chicken sate and serve.

Roast Orange Duck

1 × 2 kg duck
1 clove garlic
2 tablespoons butter, melted
    and mixed with 2 teaspoons
    soy sauce
1 onion, peeled and cut into
    quarters
1 orange, unpeeled, cut into
    quarters
¼ cup dry sherry
½ cup orange juice
½ teaspoon ground ginger
1 teaspoon salt
parsley
1 tablespoon cornflour
2 tablespoons water

Time: 33 minutes. Serves 4

Wipe duck inside and out with a damp cloth. Cut garlic in half and rub skin with it. Brush with butter and soy mixture. Place onion and orange into cavity and fasten with a bamboo skewer. Place duck in shallow glass baking dish. Cover loosely with plastic food wrap and cook 15 minutes on high. Pour sherry, orange juice, ginger and salt over duck. Re-cover and cook a further 15 minutes. Allow to stand 10 minutes. Remove orange and onion.

Blend 1 tablespoon cornflour with a little water and add to pan drippings. Cook a further 3 minutes. Carve duck and garnish with orange segments and parsley. Mask with thickened orange sauce.

Note: The duck can also be cooked in an oven bag.

HINT: POULTRY
To avoid overcooking poultry the bird must be raised from the base of the dish by a rack or upturned plate. Proper trussing is also important to avoid drying out protruding legs and wings.

Roast Orange Duck

Roast Turkey with Apple Dressing

1 turkey, approximately 5 kg

Time: 80 minutes. Serves 8–10

Clean and prepare turkey for cooking. Place turkey, breast side down in a glass baking dish. Put apple dressing (see recipe) inside cavity of turkey. Cover bottom half of wings and legs with small pieces of aluminium foil. Secure legs and wings close to body with string. Cover turkey lightly with plastic food wrap — this keeps the inside tender and juicy.

Cook turkey for 40 minutes on high then remove foil, turn turkey over, cover and cook a further 40 minutes. When cooking time is up, rest turkey 15–20 minutes before carving.

Note: If turkey cavity is filled with apple dressing, add 2 minutes per kilo to cooking time.

Apple Dressing

1 cup butter
1½ cups finely chopped celery
¾ cup onion, finely chopped
1 teaspoon salt
1 teaspoon sage
½–¾ cup water
5 cups dry breadcrumbs, more
*   if needed*
3 cups peeled and chopped
*   apple*

Time: 3 minutes.

Melt butter in a large casserole, saute celery and onion 2–3 minutes on high, stirring after every minute. Mix salt, sage, and water together. Pour over breadcrumbs and toss lightly. Add breadcrumbs to vegetables, and stir in apples. Stuff turkey just before roasting.

Alternative Stuffings for Turkey

Stuffing for Cavity

125 g butter
60 g onion, finely chopped
125 g fresh white breadcrumbs
fresh or dry mixed herbs
1 tablespoon chopped parsley
turkey liver, chopped
salt and pepper

Time: 4 minutes

Place butter and onion into casserole dish or bowl. Cook 4 minutes on high, add remaining ingredients, mix well and place into cavity. Truss turkey firmly. A small amount of foil may be placed on the wings and drumsticks for half of the cooking time to prevent drying out. Cover the whole turkey with plastic wrap to retain natural juices.

Stuffing for Neck Cavity

500 g sausage mince
125 g water chestnuts, diced
salt and pepper

Combine ingredients and place into neck cavity. Fasten with bamboo skewer.

HINT: EASY ROASTING
Average sized birds require basting and turning to ensure even cooking. Larger birds like turkey take longer to cook and often baste themselves in the process. Special oven bags can be bought to speed up cooking time and prevent loss of juices. Poultry pieces should be prepared with the larger parts angled out to allow even cooking

Roast Turkey

Seafood

Seafood cooked in a microwave oven takes on new dimensions of flavour, appearance and texture. The entire range of shellfish, whole fish and fillets can be cooked with minimum fuss and handling.

Fresh shellfish can be opened easily with the aid of a microwave oven, then cooked in their own shells and juices. Always prick oysters, mussels, scallops and fish eyes (when whole fish are being cooked) as this allows steam to escape and prevents bursting.

Frozen fish can be thawed on a defrost setting, but if time permits it is preferable to use a warm setting. Defrost and cook fillets with the thickest portion of the fish at the outer edge of the dish. Cook covered and in a single layer.

Coconut Prawn Cutlets

8 green prawns
seasoned flour
1 egg, beaten
1 tablespoon milk
1 cup shredded coconut
1 slice green ginger
1 cup peanut oil

Time: 20 minutes. Serves 2

Peel prawns, leaving tail intact. Split prawns down the back and remove intestinal tract. Continue to cut ⅔ through the prawn and press prawns to form a cutlet shape. Beat egg and milk together. Dip each prawn in flour, egg and milk. Coat with shredded coconut.

Heat browning casserole dish on high 8 minutes. Add oil and ginger and heat on high 3 minutes. Add cutlets and cook 4–5 minutes until tail turns pink. Drain on paper towel.

Serve with curry sauce (see recipe following) and lemon slices.

Curry Sauce

1 tablespoon butter
1 finely diced onion
1 teaspoon curry powder
1 finely chopped small, red chilli
1 tablespoon flour
1 cup chicken stock
1½ teaspoons fruit chutney
1 tablespoon thickened cream

Time: 5 minutes. Makes 1 cup

Melt butter in a jug. Cook on high 40 seconds. Stir in onion and cook on high 30 seconds. Blend in curry powder and heat for 30 seconds on high. Add chilli and stir in flour. Heat on high 40 seconds.

Add chutney, blend in stock and cook on high 4 minutes, stirring twice. Stir in cream.

Serve hot or cold.

Garlic Scallops

500 g prepared scallops
2 shallots, finely chopped
4 cloves garlic, finely chopped
1 fresh hot chilli, finely chopped
½ teaspoon chilli powder
4 tablespoons peanut oil

Time: 15 minutes. Serves 4–6

Combine shallots, garlic, chilli and oil in casserole dish. Add scallops and toss to coat. Leave to marinate 10 minutes. Cover and cook on high 5 minutes. Rearrange scallops halfway through cooking to ensure they are evenly done. Serve with lemon rice (see recipe Lemon Rice).

> **HINT: PREPARING SCALLOPS AND OPENING MOLLUSC SHELLS**
> To prepare scallops remove the beard, which is brownish coloured and usually found near the coral. The intestinal tract should also be removed. Split large scallops in half before cooking.
>
> Fresh scallops, clams and oysters in the shell may be opened in the microwave oven. First clean the shells and soak in cold water for 10 minutes. Place 6 shells at a time around edge of pie plate, cover with lid or plastic wrap and cook on high for 45 seconds or until shells have just opened. Continue to heat any unopened shells, checking every 15 seconds. Insert knife between shells to open.

Coconut Prawn Cutlets

Curried Smoked Cod Supreme

500 g smoked cod
1 tablespoon butter
250 g onions, sliced
2 teaspoons curry powder
2 tablespoons butter
2 tablespoons flour
2 cups milk
½ teaspoon salt
¼ teaspoon pepper
¼ cup white wine
2 tablespoons mayonnaise
½ cup grated cheese
½ teaspoon paprika

Time: 25 minutes. Serves 6

Place cod fillets into plastic bag or baking dish. Cook on high 5 minutes. Remove any bones and skin, flake fish with a fork and set aside.

Melt butter in a bowl on high for 1 minute. Add onions and cook 4–5 minutes, covered, on high. Stir twice during cooking. Add curry powder, cook 1 minute on high and set aside.

Melt 2 tablespoons butter in jug on high 1 minute. Stir in flour and cook 2 minutes on high. Stir in milk and cook on high 5–6 minutes until boiling, stirring twice during cooking. Add salt, pepper, wine and mayonnaise.

Place a layer of sauce in a 20 × 20 cm casserole dish. Cover with onions and the flaked cod. Cover evenly with remaining sauce. Sprinkle with grated cheese and paprika and cook on medium 6 minutes. Let stand 3 minutes before serving.

Swiss Style Mussels

12 mussels on shell
2 tablespoons butter
3 tablespoons Gruyère cheese
1 tablespoon finely diced red
    pimiento
pinch cayenne pepper
3 tablespoons Parmesan
    cheese

Time: 3 minutes. Serves 2

Place butter in a medium–sized bowl. Heat in microwave on high 1 minute. Fold in cheese, pimiento and cayenne.

Arrange mussels around outer edge of plate and prick each with a toothpick. Spoon over Gruyère butter, sprinkle with Parmesan and cook on medium 2–3 minutes.

HINT: USING PLASTIC BAGS

Plastic bags may be secured with an elastic band. Prick once or twice to allow hot air to escape during cooking.

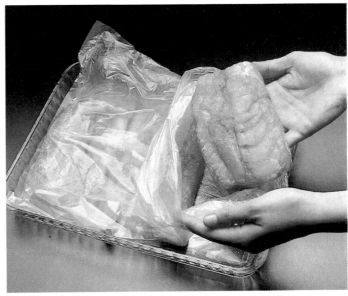

Step 1   Curried Smoked Cod Supreme. Cook cod fillets in plastic bag

Step 2   Add curry powder to cooked onions

Step 3   Cover onions and flaked cod with sauce

134

Prawn Creole

500 g green prawns, shelled
  and deveined
1 × 500 g can tomato pieces
1 medium-sized onion, diced
  in 1 cm pieces
1 green capsicum, diced in
  1 cm pieces
½ teaspoon salt
½ teaspoon white pepper
½ teaspoon chilli powder
1 bay leaf

Time: 13 minutes. Serves 4-6

Combine all ingredients except prawns in a 1.5 litre casserole dish. Cover and cook on high 9 minutes, stirring once. Stir in prawns, cover and cook on high 4-5 minutes, stirring twice during cooking.

Avoid overcooking as this toughens prawns. Remove bay leaf before serving.

Lobster Newburg

1 cooked lobster tail
2 tablespoons butter
2 tablespoons flour
½ cup cream
2 tablespoons dry vermouth or
  Riesling
1 cup sliced fresh mushrooms
½ teaspoon salt
⅛ teaspoon onion salt
⅛ teaspoon cayenne pepper
⅛ teaspoon nutmeg
2 egg yolks
⅛ teaspoon paprika
1 teaspoon chopped parsley
lemon wedges

Time: 8 minutes. Serves 2-4

Remove meat from lobster tail, split in half lengthwise and remove intestinal tract. Cut meat into 2 cm cubes.

Place butter in a 2 litre casserole dish. Cook on high 1 minute. Stir in flour and cook an extra minute on high.

Add cream, vermouth (or Riesling), mushrooms and seasoning. Cook on high 5 minutes, stirring twice during cooking.

Beat egg yolks in a small bowl. Add 1 tablespoon of the sauce and whisk. Stir yolks into remaining sauce.

Fold in lobster and cook on high 1-2 minutes until hot. Spoon into lobster shell or ramekins. Sprinkle lightly with paprika and garnish with parsley and lemon wedges to serve.

Salmon Burgers with Parsley Sauce

1 × 500 g can salmon,
  drained
2 cups white breadcrumbs
2 tablespoons butter, melted
1 onion, finely chopped
1 egg, beaten
¼ cup cream
2 tablespoons lemon juice,
  strained
3 teaspoons chopped parsley
1 teaspoon chopped dill
salt
lemon pepper
1½ cups dry breadcrumbs
½ cup toasted sesame seeds

Time: 15 minutes. Makes 12

Place butter and onion in a medium-sized basin. Cook on high 3 minutes. Cool. Blend in salmon, breadcrumbs, egg, cream, juice, herbs, salt and pepper.

Use an ice cream scoop to form the mixture into even portions. Combine dry breadcrumbs and seeds and roll each portion in crumbs to coat evenly. Shape into patties.

Preheat browning grill for 7 minutes, then cook burgers 2½ minutes on each side.

Serve on toasted buns with parsley sauce (see recipe following) or with a vegetable platter.

Parsley Sauce

250 mL warm milk
1 bay leaf
3 peppercorns
⅛ peeled onion
1 tablespoon butter
1 tablespoon flour
¼ teaspoon onion salt
⅛ teaspoon white pepper
1 tablespoon finely chopped
  parsley

Time: 9½ minutes. Makes about 3 cups

Place milk, bay leaf, peppercorns and onion into a jug. Cook on medium-low 5 minutes to infuse flavours. Melt butter in a medium-sized bowl on high 1 minute. Stir in flour and cook on high 1 minute. Blend in strained milk, salt and pepper. Cook on high 2½ minutes or until boiling, stirring every minute. Fold in parsley.

> **HINT: TOASTING SESAME SEEDS**
> 1 tablespoon butter
> 3 tablespoons sesame
>   seeds
> Place butter in pie plate and cook on high 30 seconds. Stir in sesame seeds and cook on high 3-4 minutes, stirring every minute until golden. Drain on white paper towel.

Prawn Creole

Crab Stuffed Flounder Fillets

8 thin, evenly sized, flounder
   fillets
300 g flaked crab meat
1 tablespoon butter
½ cup chopped onion
½ cup chopped capsicum
4 tablespoons breadcrumbs
1 teaspoon parsley
½ teaspoon salt
½ teaspoon lemon pepper
¾ cup tomato juice
½ teaspoon chopped basil
   leaves
1 teaspoon lemon juice
4 lemon slices

Time: 22 minutes. Serves 4

Combine butter, onion and capsicum in a bowl and cook on high 4 minutes, stirring once during cooking. Stir in crab meat, breadcrumbs, parsley, salt and lemon pepper.

Arrange 4 flounder fillets in a roasting dish, cover each evenly with stuffing mixture then place a second fillet on top.

Combine tomato juice, basil and lemon juice in a bowl and cook on high 2 minutes. Spoon sauce over fillets and top with lemon slices. Cook on medium 16 minutes or until fish flakes easily.

Garlic Oysters

12 oysters on shell
2 tablespoons butter
1 clove garlic, finely chopped
1 teaspoon finely chopped red
   chilli
⅛ teaspoon lemon pepper
1 tablespoon finely chopped
   parsley
2 tablespoons toasted
   breadcrumbs

Time: 4 minutes. Serves 2

Heat butter on high 1 minute. Add garlic, chilli and lemon pepper. Heat on medium 1 minute.

Prick oysters with a cocktail stick. Spoon a little garlic butter onto each oyster. Sprinkle with parsley and breadcrumbs.

Arrange oysters around the outer edge of a plate and cook on medium 2–3 minutes.

Step 1 Crab Stuffed Flounder Fillets. Combine butter, onion and capsicum

Step 2 Stir in crabmeat and breadcrumbs

Step 3 Cover each fillet with stuffing and place another fillet on top

138

Crab Stuffed Flounder Fillets

Fillets of Bream Caprice

4 bream fillets
2 bananas, peeled and halved
*   lengthwise*
seasoned flour
125 g butter, melted
dry breadcrumbs
1½ cups peanut oil
1 slice green ginger

Time: 15 minutes. Serves 4

Coat bream fillets with seasoned flour, dip in melted butter then coat with breadcrumbs. Lightly coat banana halves with seasoned flour.

Preheat browning casserole dish on high 6 minutes. Add oil and green ginger. Cook on high 6 minutes until ginger is brown. Remove ginger.

Place fillets into oil and cook 3 minutes. Turn over and add banana pieces. Cook on high 2 minutes. Remove and drain on white paper towel.

Place half a banana on each portion of fish and serve with orange cream *(see recipe following)*.

Orange Cream

1 cup sour cream
4 tablespoons mayonnaise
2 teaspoons Dijon mustard
½ teaspoon finely grated
*   orange zest*
2 teaspoons orange juice or
*   Grand Marnier*
2 tablespoons chopped
*   shallots or chives*

Beat sour cream until smooth. Stir in mayonnaise and mustard. Add orange zest, orange juice or Grand Marnier. Garnish with shallots or chives and serve with fish.

> **HINT: PREPARING OYSTERS AND MUSSELS**
> Always prick each oyster and mussel about 4 times with a cocktail stick before cooking in microwave oven. This allows steam to escape and prevents them from splitting.

Oysters Kilpatrick

12 oysters on the shell
4 rashers bacon, diced without
    rind
2–3 tablespoons
    Worcestershire sauce
salt and pepper to taste

Time: 5 minutes. Serves 1–2

Wash oysters and shell to remove any grit. Dry with a clean cloth. Place diced bacon on white kitchen paper. Cover with a second piece of paper. Cook 3 minutes on high. Pierce oysters with toothpick. Top with bacon. Sprinkle with sauce. Season to taste. Cook 1–2 minutes.

Oysters Mornay

12 oysters on the shell. Pierce
    oysters with toothpick before
    cooking.

Sauce

2 tablespoons butter
2 tablespoons flour
1⅓ cups milk
¼ cup Parmesan grated cheese
¼ cup Swiss grated cheese

Time: 6 minutes. Serves 1–2

Put butter into small ovenproof dish and cook 15 seconds to melt. Stir in flour, then milk. Cook 3 minutes on high or until mixture boils. Stir sauce after 1 minute. Stir in cheese. Cover and cook until cheese melts. Spoon sauce over each oyster on the shell. Dust lightly with paprika, or a little extra grated cheese. Cook 1–2 minutes and serve with lemon wedges.

Garlic Prawns

4–6 tablespoons peanut oil
4 cloves garlic, finely cut
2 shallots, finely cut
1 fresh hot red chilli, sliced
    without seeds, or ½ teaspoon
    chilli powder
500 g shelled green prawns

Time: 4 minutes. Serves 4

Combine oil, garlic, shallots and chilli in microwave oven dish. Add prawns and toss to coat with oil. Allow to stand 10 minutes. Cook 2 minutes on high. Stir and cook until they turn pink, another 2 minutes.

Fillets of Flounder with Pernod Sauce

20 g butter
6 fillets of flounder
fish seasoning
juice of half a lemon
2 tablespoons Pernod
⅓ cup cream
sprinkling of dry basil
chopped chives for garnish

Time: 9 minutes. Serves 4–6

Melt butter in an oblong dish for 15 seconds. Sprinkle fillets lightly with seasoning and place in butter. Pour over lemon juice and Pernod. Cook covered 6–7 minutes on high. Remove to plate, reheat liquids, add cream, basil and cook 1½ minutes. Spoon over fillets. Sprinkle with chopped chives and serve.

Salmon Ring

1 × 500 g can red salmon
½ cup chopped onion
¼ cup salad oil
⅓ cup dry breadcrumbs
2 eggs, beaten
1 teaspoon dry mustard
½ teaspoon salt

Time: 9 minutes. Serves 6

Drain salmon, reserving ⅓ cup liquid. Cook onion in oil for 2½ minutes. Combine onion, dry breadcrumbs, salmon liquid, eggs, mustard, salt and flaked salmon in a basin and mix well. Place into a microwave ring pan and cook for 6 minutes on high. Give pan a quarter of a turn after 3 minutes. Let stand for 5 minutes before serving.
    Note: Tuna may be used instead of salmon.

Oysters Kilpatrick

Smoked Salmon Quiche

180 g smoked salmon, thinly
    sliced

Pastry

2 cups flour
1¼ cups butter
½ teaspoon salt
¼ cup cold water

Custard

1 cup cream
4 egg yolks
2 shallots, finely chopped
salt, cayenne pepper, and
    nutmeg to taste

Time: 31 minutes. Serves 6

Sift dry ingredients in bowl. Rub in butter and mix to a firm dough with water. Knead lightly and roll out to fit a 21 cm pie plate. Chill for 15 minutes. Cook for 6 minutes on high.

Blend together custard ingredients, pour into cool pastry shell and carefully float salmon slices on the surface. With a teaspoon, carefully lift some of the custard over the top of the salmon. Bake on the defrost cycle for 25 minutes until centre is set. Stand 3 minutes before serving.

Salmon Stuffed Mushrooms

12 medium to large mushrooms
6 tablespoons flaked red
    salmon
6 tablespoons soft breadcrumbs
2 teaspoons finely chopped
    shallots
2 teaspoons finely chopped
    parsley
2 teaspoons lemon juice
2 tablespoons butter, melted
grated Parmesan cheese

Time: 5 minutes. Serves 6

Remove stems from mushrooms. Chop stems finely. Combine salmon, breadcrumbs, stems, shallots, parsley, lemon juice and butter. Fill caps with mixture. Sprinkle with cheese. Arrange mushrooms in a circle on the outer edge of a glass platter. Cook 5 minutes on high.

Whole Fish with Black Bean Sauce

1 whole fish, approximately
    750 g, or fish fillets
fish seasoning (optional)

Sauce

1 tablespoon oil
1 slice green ginger, cut finely
1 clove garlic, cut finely
1 tablespoon black beans
½ teaspoon dry sherry
½ teaspoon sugar
2 teaspoons soy sauce
1 cup fish stock or water
1 tablespoon cornflour
water
3 shallots, cut finely
red capsicum for garnish

Time: 11 minutes. Serves 4–6

Trim off fins and tail with a pair of scissors. Remove the eyes. Check that all scales have been removed. Wash well and dry with kitchen paper. A small amount of fish seasoning may be sprinkled into cavity. Place fish onto a plate and cover with plastic food wrap. Cook approximately 6–8 minutes on high or until flesh flakes easily.

Heat oil in a bowl for 2 minutes. Add ginger, garlic, beans, and stir. Cook for 1 minute on high. Add sherry, sugar, soy sauce and stock. Cook 1 minute. Blend cornflour and water, stir into mixture. Cook a further 2 minutes. Stir in shallots. Spoon over fish. Serve garnished with shredded red capsicum.

Melba Toast with Curried Salmon

125 g canned red salmon,
    drained
3 tablespoons mayonnaise
3 tablespoons finely chopped
    peanuts
3 tablespoons canned crushed
    pineapple, drained
½ teaspoon curry paste
Melba toast (see recipe)

Time: 1 minute. Serves 6

Combine all ingredients in a bowl and spoon onto rounds of Melba toast.

Arrange on a plate lined with paper towel and cook on high 1 minute.

Baked Orange Fish

1 large orange
1 small clove garlic
1 tablespoon butter
1 small onion, finely cut
1 tablespoon finely chopped
    parsley
salt and pepper
1 cup fresh bean sprouts, roots
    removed
¾ cup orange juice
1 whole fish (750 g–1 kg)

Time: 9½ minutes. Serves 4

Peel orange and cut into segments. Cut garlic into small pieces and half the orange segments into dice. Place butter, onion, garlic, orange segments, parsley, salt and pepper into a microwave oven dish and cook covered on high for 2 minutes. Add bean sprouts.

After trimming fins and tail, place fish on a baking dish, removing eyes and checking for any scales which may have been missed. If the fish is large it may be scored 2 or 3 times on each side to ensure even cooking. Season cavity with salt and pepper. Stuff cavity with onion and orange mixture. Cover fish with plastic wrap and cook 5 minutes on high. Pour juice over fish and arrange remaining segments over fish neatly. Continue cooking 2½ minutes until flesh flakes easily.

Note: Allow 5 minutes per 500 g cooking time.

Whole Fish with Chinese Pickle Sauce

1 whole fish, approximately
    750 g

Chinese Pickle Sauce

2 teaspoons tomato sauce
½ teaspoon salt
2 teaspoons soy sauce
2 cups pineapple juice
½ cup diced Chinese mixed
    pickle
1 slice pineapple, diced
2 tablespoons vinegar
3 tablespoons brown sugar
small piece capsicum, diced
1–2 tablespoons cornflour

Time: 15 minutes. Serves 4–6

Prepare and cook the fish in the same way as Whole Fish with Black Bean Sauce (see recipe).

Combine all ingredients in a bowl except cornflour. Cook 4–5 minutes on high until boiling. Stir after 3 minutes. Thicken with blended cornflour. Cook 2 minutes, serve over fish.

Note: Allow 5 minutes per 500 g cooking time.

Scallops in Oyster Sauce

1½ tablespoons oil
1 slice green ginger, cut finely
1 clove garlic, cut finely
500 g scallops
1 tablespoon dry sherry
2 teaspoons soy sauce
½ cup fish stock
2 tablespoons oyster sauce
1 teaspoon sugar
3 teaspoons cornflour
2 shallots, cut into 2 cm lengths
½ teaspoon salt

Time: 7 minutes. Serves 4

Heat oil in an ovenproof dish for 1 minute. Add ginger, garlic and scallops. Cook for 3 minutes on high. Add sherry, soy sauce and cook 1 minute. Blend the stock, oyster sauce, sugar and cornflour. Add to dish, stir to blend and cook 2 minutes until boiling. Fold in shallots, salt and serve with plain boiled rice.

Scallops with Barbecue Sauce

500 g prepared scallops
1 egg white, lightly beaten
2 teaspoons seasoned cornflour
2 tablespoons peanut oil
1 slice green ginger, finely
    chopped
1 clove garlic, finely chopped
½ onion, cut in 2 cm pieces
½ red capsicum, cut in 2 cm
    pieces
½ green capsicum, cut in 2 cm
    pieces
2 tablespoons Chinese
    barbecue sauce
1 tablespoon dry sherry
2 shallots, cut in 2 cm pieces

Time: 12 minutes. Serves 6

Combine scallops, egg white and cornflour in a medium-sized bowl. Preheat browning casserole dish on high 5 minutes. Add oil, ginger, garlic, onion and capsicum and cook on high 3 minutes, covered.

Add scallops, barbecue sauce and sherry. Cook on high 4–5 minutes, stirring twice during cooking. Add shallots.

Serve in a parsley rice (see recipe Parsley Rice Ring) ring (p.00).

Coquilles St. Jacques

4 tablespoons butter
1 small onion, finely chopped
250 g scallops
2 teaspoons lemon juice
½ teaspoon salt
marjoram
dash paprika
6 tablespoons white wine
2 tablespoons flour
½ cup cream
60 g mushrooms, sliced thinly
fresh white breadcrumbs
1 teaspoon chopped parsley

Time: 9½ minutes. Serves 4

Combine 1 tablespoon butter and onion in a medium sized casserole dish. Cook uncovered 1 minute. Stir in scallops, lemon juice, seasoning and wine. Cook, covered 3 minutes on high. Drain liquid and reserve. Melt 3 tablespoons butter for 30 seconds. Blend in flour then stir in reserved liquid and cream. Heat, uncovered, 2 minutes or until sauce thickens. Add scallop mixture, mushrooms and spoon into 4 individual ramekins, or scallop shells. Sprinkle with breadcrumbs and parsley and heat uncovered 3 minutes.

Fresh Trout with Asparagus Sauce

2 whole trout, approximately
    250 g each
2 small branches of fresh dill
fish seasoning
1 shallot, cut finely
1 tablespoon dry vermouth
4 tablespoons fish stock or
    white wine
1 lemon, peeled and sliced
butter

Time: 7 minutes. Serves 2

Wash and dry trout, remove eyes. Place fresh dill into cavities and season. Place in a glass dish, sprinkle with shallots, vermouth, fish stock and cover with slices of lemon. Dot lightly with butter. Cover with plastic food wrap and cook 6-7 minutes on high.

Asparagus Sauce

1 (340 g) can green asparagus
    spears
8 tablespoons chicken stock
salt and pepper to taste
1 tablespoon fresh cream

Time: 2 minutes. Serves 2

Combine asparagus with stock, salt, pepper and cream. Puree in a blender until smooth. Correct seasonings. Pour into glass jug. Cook 2 minutes on high. Mask trout with sauce.

Curried Prawns

2 tablespoons butter
¼ cup minced onion
1 tablespoon fresh ginger,
    grated
¼ cup plain flour
1 tablespoon curry powder
1 cup milk
1 cup coconut milk
2 teaspoons lemon juice
500 g green prawns

Time: 13 minutes. Serves 4-6

Place butter, ginger and onion in 2 litre casserole and cook 2 minutes on high. Stir in flour and curry powder. Stir to a smooth paste. Add both milks and cook 5 minutes, stirring every minute. Blend in remaining ingredients. Mix well and cook 6 minutes, stirring after 2 minutes. Serve with plain boiled rice, toasted coconut and mango chutney.

Simple Fish and Vegetable Pie

500 g white fish: barramundi,
    jewfish, etc.
125 g fresh peas
125 g diced carrot
1 onion, finely diced
freshly ground black pepper
salt to taste
2 tablespoons chopped parsley
2 tablespoons butter
2 tablespoons cornflour
2 cups milk
½ teaspoon mixed herbs
paprika
¼ cup grated Cheddar cheese

Time: 35-40 minutes. Serves 8-10

Place fish in shallow dish. Cover and cook on medium 15 minutes. Stand covered 5 minutes.

Combine peas, carrots and onion in small bowl. Cover and cook on high 8 minutes. Stand covered 5 minutes.

Combine pepper, salt, parsley and butter. Cook on high 45 seconds. Blend in cornflour milk and mixed herbs. Cook on high 3-5 minutes. Stir and cook on high further 1-2 minutes. Stir

Flake fish and add to vegetables and sauce. Pour mixture into shallow dish, top with paprika and grated cheese. Cook on high 2-3 minutes to melt cheese. Serve hot. Standing time: 10 minutes.

Fresh Trout with Asparagus Sauce

146

Desserts

Without doubt the crowning glory of any meal is dessert and with the microwave on your side the variety of desserts you can prepare is endless. Even better for the host or hostess is the advantage of being able to prepare desserts well in advance of the guests arriving.

Keep these hints in mind when preparing your sweet dinner finale: fruit pies can be started in the microwave and finished on the convection setting; flan cases can be pre-baked, frozen and then quickly thawed on the defrost setting; and a whole range of imaginative dessert sauces can be prepared and frozen in containers till you need them.

Fruit Pizza

2 cups self-raising flour
1–2 tablespoons sugar
½ teaspoon salt
1½ tablespoons butter
¾ cup milk

Topping

250 g cream cheese, softened
¼ cup sugar
1 teaspoon grated lemon zest
6 cups sliced fresh fruit (kiwi
*   fruit, strawberries, mango,*
*   peeled grapes, etc.)*
⅔ cup apple or orange juice
2 teaspoons arrowroot or ⅔
*   cup fruit gel*

Time: 12–15 minutes. Serves 12

Sift flour into a bowl and add sugar and salt. Cut butter into small cubes and rub into flour. Add milk, blending mixture with a table knife.

Turn dough onto floured board and knead lightly. Roll dough into a 30 cm circle and place onto a lightly greased round pyrex plate.

Set convection oven to 220°C and bake pizza base 12-15 minutes until well browned. Allow to cool.

Place softened cream cheese into bowl and beat in sugar until dissolved. Add lemon zest and spread mixture evenly over pizza crust. Arrange sliced fruits on top.

Combine juice and arrowroot in small bowl. Cook on high 2–2½ minutes until thickened and clear, stirring after each minute. Cool until warm. Spoon over fruit and chill until set.

Fruit Pizza

148

Strawberry Cheese Cake

1½ tablespoons butter
125 g biscuit crumbs
500 g cream cheese, softened
½ cup caster sugar
2 egg yolks
1 teaspoon grated lemon zest
1 tablespoon lemon juice,
    strained
2 stiffly beaten egg whites

Topping

1 cup sour cream
1 tablespoon sugar
1 teaspoon vanilla essence
1 punnet strawberries
1 jar fruit gel

Time: 23 minutes. Serves 8–12

Place butter in bowl and soften on high 1 minute. Stir in biscuit crumbs and cook on high 2 minutes. Press crumb mixture into base of flan dish.

In a large bowl beat cream cheese, sugar, egg yolks, zest and juice until creamy. Avoid overbeating. Fold in stiffly beaten egg whites, using a metal spoon. Pour into prepared dish and cook on defrost 20 minutes. Allow to cool.

In a small bowl beat sour cream, sugar and vanilla until sugar dissolves. Spread over cheese cake. Wash and dry strawberries, place upright on cheese cake and coat evenly with fruit gel. Chill several hours before serving.

Custard Sauce

375 mL milk
3 tablespoons sugar
2 tablespoons custard powder
2 egg yolks
1 teaspoon vanilla
cinnamon sugar

Time: 6–7 minutes. Makes about 4 cups

Combine milk, sugar and custard powder in jug and cook on high 4 minutes until sauce thickens, stirring after 2 minutes.

Beat egg yolks in basin with whisk. Blend in 2 tablespoons of custard mixture and whisk egg mixture into remaining custard. Cook on defrost cycle for 1–2 minutes. Blend in vanilla.

Sprinkle surface of custard with a little cinnamon sugar to prevent skin forming.

Step 1   Strawberry Cheese Cake. Press biscuit mixture into base of flan dish

Step 2   Use a metal spoon to fold in egg whites

Step 3   Pour mixture into biscuit base

Rhubarb Pie

750 g rhubarb, cut into
   2.5 cm lengths
½–¾ cup sugar
2 tablespoons custard powder
pinch salt
1 teaspoon mixed spice
60 g raisins

Pastry

1½ cups flour
1 teaspoon baking powder
½ teaspoon salt
½ cup butter, cut in small
   cubes
2 teaspoons sugar
3–4 tablespoons cold water
1 tablespoon sugar

Time: 17–20 minutes. Serves 6–8

Combine rhubarb, sugar, custard powder, salt, mixed spice and raisins in a bowl.

Sift flour, baking powder and salt and place in food processor. Add butter and 2 teaspoons sugar and blend to a crumb texture, adding water gradually until dough forms a ball. Chill pastry 15–20 minutes.

Roll out two-thirds of pastry, line 22.5 cm pie plate and place rhubarb mixture onto pastry, piling centre high. Roll out remaining pastry and brush edge of pastry in pie plate with cold water. Place remaining pastry over rhubarb and seal edges. Cut air vents in top, brush with water and sprinkle with 1 tablespoon sugar.

Cook on high 8 minutes, then convection at 200°C for 7–10 minutes until pastry is well browned. Serve with cream or custard sauce (see recipe Custard Sauce).

Orange Sponge Pudding

2 tablespoons butter
2 tablespoons sugar
1 egg
¾ cup self-raising flour
¼ cup milk
1 tablespoon orange juice or
   Grand Marnier
1 tablespoon grated orange
   zest
orange sauce (see recipe
   following)

Time: 4–5 minutes. Serves 4–6

Cream butter and sugar; beat in egg. Fold in flour, milk, orange juice and zest. Lightly grease china pudding basin and place a small circle of greaseproof paper in the bottom. Top with sponge mixture and cook on high 4–5 minutes. Turn out onto serving plate. Mask with sauce.

Orange Sauce

2 tablespoons sugar
1 tablespoon cornflour
⅔ cup strained orange juice
⅓ cup water
1 tablespoon Grand Marnier
2 tablespoons butter
1 tablespoon grated orange
   zest
2 teaspoons strained lemon
   juice

Time: 2½ minutes

Blend sugar, cornflour and orange juice in jug and cook on high 2–2½ minutes, stirring twice during cooking. Mix in remaining ingredients and serve warm over pudding.

Pears with Chocolate Sauce

6 firm pears
1 tablespoon lemon juice,
   strained
¼ cup sugar
2 tablespoons dry sherry
2 tablespoons Grand Marnier
180 g cooking chocolate
   pieces
40 g butter

Time: 14 minutes. Serves 6

Peel pears, leaving stems intact. De-core from the base by cutting a circle with paring knife. Brush with lemon juice to prevent discolouring.

In a 1 litre casserole combine sugar, sherry and Grand Marnier. Place pears on sides with the thicker ends towards the outside. Add remaining lemon juice and cover. Cook on high for 6 minutes. Turn pears over and baste. Cover and cook a further 6 minutes or until tender. Remove pears. Reserve poaching liquid.

Measure ½ cup poaching liquid and return to casserole. Add cooking chocolate pieces and cook on high 2 minutes. Add butter and whisk till smooth.

Fill each pear with custard sauce (see recipe Egg Custard). Place upright on serving dish. Pour remaining custard around pears and spoon chocolate sauce over top.

> **HINT: MELTING CHOCOLATE**
> When melting chocolate test it with a skewer to confirm that it has in fact melted, and not just softened. When reheating melted or softened chocolate be careful to avoid burning.

Egg Custard

3 tablespoons sugar
1 tablespoon flour
½ cup milk
½ cup cream
6 egg yolks
1 teaspoon Grand Marnier
1–2 teaspoons caster sugar

Time: 3 minutes. Makes about 2 cups

Combine sugar and flour in a bowl and beat in milk and cream. Cook on high 2 minutes, stirring every 30 seconds. Beat egg yolks, add to milk and cream sauce.

Cook on high 30–45 seconds, stirring after each 15 seconds. Beat in Grand Marnier. Sprinkle lightly with a little caster sugar to prevent a skin forming on the sauce.

Pavlova Roll

2 teaspoons melted butter
2 teaspoons cornflour
6 egg whites
1½ cups caster sugar
¾ teaspoon vanilla essence
1 teaspoon white vinegar
½ cup toasted almond slivers
1 tablespoon cinnamon sugar
2 cups fresh strawberries
300 mL whipped cream

Time: 3 minutes. Serves 6–8

Place butter in small bowl and cook on high 15 seconds to melt. Lightly grease tray and line base with greaseproof paper. Regrease and dust lightly with cornflour and shake off excess.

Beat egg whites until firm peaks form. Add sugar, one tablespoon at a time, beating until dissolved. Blend in vanilla and vinegar.

Spread meringue evenly into prepared 30 × 30 cm tray and sprinkle with toasted almonds. Cook on high 3 minutes and allow to cool.

Sprinkle a large sheet of greaseproof paper with cinnamon sugar and turn pavlova onto it. Slice 1½ cups of strawberries and fold into whipped cream. Spread cream over two-thirds of the pavlova.

Roll up as for a Swiss roll. Pipe rosettes of cream on top and garnish with remaining strawberries, cut into fans. Chill before serving.

> ## HINT: MAKING STRAWBERRY FANS
> Wash and hull strawberries and with a sharp, thin-bladed knife make 5–6 cuts into each strawberry. These cuts should extend only ⅔ into the strawberry from the top. Carefully separate slices till the strawberry takes on a fan-shape.

Step 1   Pavlova Roll. Spread meringue evenly into tray

Pavlova Roll

Step 2   Sprinkle with roasted almonds

Step 3   Roll up pavlova with greaseproof paper

Grasshopper Torte

⅓ cup butter
1 packet chocolate flavoured
　　plain biscuits, crumbed
4 cups white marshmallows,
　　diced
¾ cup milk
¼ cup green creme de menthe
2 tablespoons white creme de
　　cacao
2 teaspoons gelatine
2 tablespoons cold water
1 cup stiffly beaten cream

Time: 3 minutes. Serves 8

Place butter in glass bowl and cook for 45 seconds on high. Stir in biscuit crumbs. Put half the mixture into a 23 cm round glass dish. Chill. Place marshmallows and milk into a large bowl. Cook 1½–2 minutes to melt marshmallows. Stir in creme de menthe and creme de cacao.

　　Blend gelatine and water in small bowl. Heat 15 seconds on high. Blend into mixture. Cool. Fold in whipped cream. Pour into crumb-lined dish. Top with remaining crumbs. Chill until firm. Cut into wedges and pipe with whipped cream.

Pineapple Meringue Pie

Pastry

125 g butter
⅓ cup sugar
2 cups plain flour, sifted
3 drops vanilla
2 teaspoons water
1 egg yolk

Filling

1 × 500 g can crushed pineapple
1 egg yolk
2 tablespoons custard powder
1 tablespoon arrowroot
¼ cup orange juice

Meringue

3 egg whites
½ cup caster sugar

Time: 13 minutes. Serves 8

Rub butter into sugar and flour. Add vanilla, water and egg yolk. Knead lightly and let rest 15 minutes. Roll out pastry and line a 23 cm pie plate. Prick well and cook for 4 minutes on high. Allow to cool.

　　Place pineapple into a casserole dish and cook 4 minutes until boiling. Beat egg yolk, add custard powder, arrowroot and orange juice. Mix into hot pineapple and cook for 2 minutes on high. Cool and spoon into pastry case.

　　Beat egg whites, adding sugar, 1 tablespoon at a time, until soft peaks form. Pipe or spread over pineapple filling and cook to set for 2–3 minutes. Place under grill for a few minutes if a light golden colour is required.

Savarin

60 g butter
105 g caster sugar
3 eggs
125 g self-raising flour
2 tablespoons milk or cream

Syrup

225 mL water
250 g sugar
5 tablespoons Grand Marnier

Time: 6 minutes. Serves 8

Beat softened butter and sugar to a cream. Add eggs, one at a time. Add flour, all at once. Fold in milk or cream. Grease and line base of micro-ring dish. Grease again. Pour in mixture and cook 5–6 minutes on high. Turn out on a cooking rack.

　　Boil water and sugar to form a syrup. Add Grand Marnier. Spoon warm syrup over cake until all is absorbed. Place on serving platter. Fill centre with fresh fruit salad. Decorate with whipped cream and extra fruit.

Apricot Upside Down Cake

Base

60 g butter
⅓ cup brown sugar
14 apricot halves
7 glace cherries, halved

Cake

80 g butter
½ cup sugar
1 egg
½ cup golden syrup
⅓ cup milk
1½ cups flour
1 teaspoon bicarbonate of soda
1 teaspoon ground ginger
1 teaspoon ground cinnamon
pinch salt

Serving Suggestion

rum-flavoured whipped cream
chopped pecans

Time: 12 minutes. Serves 14

Cream butter and brown sugar. Lightly grease a 25 cm ring mould with melted butter and line base with greaseproof paper.

　　Spread butter mixture over base. Place one cherry half into hollow of each apricot centre and lie them, cut side down, on batter mixture.

　　For cake, cream butter and sugar, add egg, golden syrup and milk. Sift dry ingredients together and blend into mixture. Spread carefully over apricot layer. Cook uncovered on high 10–12 minutes.

　　Serve with rum flavoured whipped cream sprinkled with chopped pecans.

Baba au Rhum

Fruit

1 tablespoon raisins
1 tablespoon currants
1 tablespoon sultanas
1 tablespoon rum

Baba Batter

60 g butter
105 g caster sugar
3 eggs
125 g self-raising flour
2 tablespoons milk

Syrup

½ cup sugar
1 cinnamon stick
1 cup syrup from tinned
  apricots
2 tablespoons lemon juice
4 tablespoons rum

Time: 11 minutes. Serves 8

Combine fruit and rum and set aside. Cream butter and sugar. Add eggs, one at a time. Add flour all at once and fold in milk and fruit. Place batter in greased and lined glass Baba mould. Cook 5-6 minutes on high. Turn out on a serving platter.

Combine sugar, cinnamon stick and syrup together and cook 5 minutes on high. Add lemon juice and rum. Cool.

Spoon syrup over Baba. Serve decorated with whipped cream, apricots and glace cherries.

Apple Crumble

6 cooking apples, peeled and
  sliced
½ cup water
½ cup sugar
½ teaspoon cinnamon
60 g soft butter
¼ cup flour
½ cup coconut
½ cup brown sugar

Time: 9 minutes. Serves 6-8

Place apples, water, sugar and cinnamon into a 1 litre casserole dish, cover and cook 5 minutes on high. Rub butter into flour, coconut, brown sugar and sprinkle over apples. Top with extra cinnamon and cook 3-4 minutes. Serve with Custard Sauce (see recipe).

Pineapple Ginger Cake

60 g butter
⅓ cup brown sugar
6 small slices of canned
  pineapple
6 maraschino cherries

Cake

80 g butter
½ cup white sugar
1 egg
½ cup golden syrup
⅓ cup milk
1½ cups flour
1 teaspoon bicarbonate of soda
1 teaspoon ground ginger
1 teaspoon ground cinnamon
pinch salt

Time: 10 minutes. Serves 8

Cream 60 g butter and brown sugar together and spread into the bottom of a baking dish. Place pineapple rings into mixture with a cherry in the centre of each ring.

Cream together 80 g butter and white sugar, add egg, golden syrup and milk. Sift dry ingredients together. Blend all into a creamy mixture. Spread over pineapple slices. Cook uncovered 10 minutes on high.

Note: Other fruits may be used: sliced mangoes, peaches or apricots.

Pineapple Coconut Cake

60 g butter
¾ cup sugar
vanilla
1 egg
½ cup milk
1 cup well-drained crushed
  pineapple
½ cup coconut
1½ cups flour
1 teaspoon baking powder
½ teaspoon salt

Time: 6-9 minutes.

Cream butter, sugar and vanilla until light and fluffy. Beat in egg and fold in milk, crushed pineapple, coconut and sifted dry ingredients. Grease and line micro-baking dish. Pour mixture into dish and cook 6 minutes on high or 9 minutes on medium.

Baked Bread and Butter Custard

30 g butter
2 cups milk
5 eggs
¼ cup raw sugar
1 teaspoon vanilla
4 slices white bread, crusts
   removed, then buttered
nutmeg
2 tablespoons sultanas

Time: 62 minutes. Serves 6

Place butter into milk and heat for 2 minutes. Beat eggs, sugar and vanilla, add milk and butter mixture. Sprinkle buttered bread lightly with nutmeg, cut into cubes, and place into a greased baking ring with sultanas. Pour custard over bread and cook uncovered 60 minutes on defrost.

Rice Custard

Time: 22 minutes

Note: 1 cup of precooked rice can be used in place of the buttered bread.

Queen Pudding

4 slices of buttered, stale plain
   cake
5 eggs
2 tablespoons sugar
2 cups warm milk
vanilla
strawberry jam

Time: 63 minutes. Serves 6

Cut cake into cubes. Place into well-buttered baking ring. Beat eggs, sugar and vanilla, add warm milk. Pour over cake cubes and cook 60 minutes on defrost.

Spread top of custard with strawberry jam. Top with piped meringue (*see recipe Pineapple Meringue Pie*) and cook 2-3 minutes on high. Sprinkle with sugar lightly coloured with a few drops of pink food colouring.

Caramel Tart

1 precooked pastry case (see
   recipe Pineapple Meringue
   Pie)
2 tablespoons butter
1 cup brown sugar
4 egg yolks
3 drops vanilla
pinch salt
2 tablespoons flour
2 cups milk
1 quantity meringue (see recipe
   Pineapple Meringue Pie)

Time: 8 minutes. Serves 8

Beat butter and sugar until fluffy. Beat in egg yolks. Add vanilla, salt, fold in sifted flour, stir in milk. Cook 4-5 minutes on high, stirring every minute until mixture thickens. Spoon into pastry case. Top with meringue and cook 2-3 minutes on high.

Chocolate Souffle

6 teaspoons gelatine
¾ cup sugar
3 eggs, separated
1 cup milk
60 g melted cooking chocolate
   (chop or grate chocolate, and
   cook ¾-1 minute to melt)
1 cup whipped cream

Time: 7½ minutes. Serves 6

In a large bowl combine gelatine with ½ cup sugar. Stir in egg yolks and beat in the milk. Heat on defrost for 6½-7½ minutes or until gelatine dissolves, stirring occasionally. Stir in chocolate and chill, stirring occasionally until mixture mounds slightly.

Beat egg whites until soft peaks form, gradually add remaining sugar and beat until stiff. Fold in the chocolate mixture with whipped cream. Pour into souffle dish with a collar. Chill. To serve, garnish with extra whipped cream and almond slivers.

Chocolate Souffle

160

Strawberry Marshmallow

4 egg whites
1 cup caster sugar
½ teaspoon vanilla
¾ teaspoon white vinegar
3 teaspoons butter, melted
cornflour

Filling

½ cup strawberry jam
2 teaspoons brandy
1 punnet strawberries, hulled,
    washed and dried
whipped cream

Time: 4 minutes. Serves 8

Beat egg whites until soft peaks form. Add ⅓ cup sugar, beat until dissolved. Gradually add remaining sugar. When dissolved, add vanilla and vinegar, beating 1 minute.

Grease a 23 cm pie plate with melted butter, dust well with cornflour and shake off any excess. Spoon egg whites into pie plate leaving outside edge higher than the centre. Cook 3 minutes on high. Place under preheated grill until pale golden if desired.

Heat jam to melting point, 1 minute on high, then sieve. Blend in brandy. Cut strawberries in halves, coat lightly with jam. Spread top of filling with cream, pile strawberries on top of cream. Pipe rosettes of cream around outside edge.

Strawberry Cream Dessert

2 punnets ripe red strawberries
4 eggs, separated
1 tablespoon gelatine
8 tablespoons sugar
1 carton whipped cream

Time: 7 minutes. Serves 6–8

Wash and hull strawberries. Place 1½ punnets into a blender and puree. Blend puree, egg yolks, gelatine and sugar. Place into a glass bowl and cook on defrost 7 minutes until gelatine dissolves, stirring constantly. Chill until slightly set.

Beat cream to form stiff peaks. Fold into strawberry puree and beaten egg whites. Pour into individual glass sweet dishes to set. Decorate with whipped cream and remaining strawberries.

Peaches Flambe

30 g butter
1 can drained peach halves
5 tablespoons Grand Marnier
30 g sugar

Time: 5½ minutes. Serves 4

Heat butter in glass serving dish for 1–2 minutes. Add peach halves and 2 tablespoons Grand Marnier. Sprinkle with sugar and cook 3 minutes on high. Heat 3 tablespoons Grand Marnier in glass jug for 25 seconds, flame and pour over peaches. Serve with vanilla ice cream.

Lemon Meringue Pie

1 precooked pastry case (see
    recipe Pineapple Meringue
    Pie)
1 quantity meringue (see recipe
    Pineapple Meringue Pie)

Filling

½ cup cornflour
½ cup sugar
¾ cup water
⅓ cup lemon juice
⅓ cup butter
3 egg yolks
grated rind of 1 lemon

Time: 7 minutes. Serves 8

Combine cornflour, sugar, water, juice of lemon and butter in a casserole dish and cook 2 minutes on high, stir and cook a further 2 minutes. Cool. Beat in yolks and lemon rind. Place in pastry case. Top with meringue, cook 2–3 minutes. Cool.

Strawberry Pavlova

Baked Honey Pears

4 firm pears
4 tablespoons chopped dates
2 tablespoons chopped walnuts
3 tablespoons honey
¼ teaspoon cinnamon

Time: 8 minutes. Serves 4

Peel pears. Cut off caps 2.5 cm from top. Core each pear without cutting right through. Remove seeds. Combine dates, walnuts, honey and cinnamon. Fill pear centres with date mixture, replace caps. Arrange in a circle on a glass plate and cook 6–8 minutes on high. Pears can be served whole: remove cap and top with whipped cream, or cut in half, served with a rosette of whipped cream.

Apple Tea Cake

60 g butter
¾ cup sugar
vanilla
1 egg
¾ cup milk
1½ cups flour
2 teaspoons baking powder
½ teaspoon salt
1 green apple, peeled, cored
   and sliced thinly
2 teaspoons brown sugar
2 teaspoons cinnamon

Time: 6–9 minutes

Cream butter, sugar and vanilla until light and fluffy. Beat in egg and fold in milk and sifted dry ingredients except the apple, brown sugar and cinnamon. Prepare the micro-baking dish, grease it first, then line it with greaseproof paper and grease it again. Arrange thinly sliced apples and lightly dust with mixture of brown sugar and cinnamon. Pour batter on top of apples. Cook 6 minutes on high or 9 minutes on medium.

HINT: FRUITFUL VITAMINS
To retain the natural goodness of fruit, it must be cooked with care. Most fruits can be simply prepared to taste delicious and provide a healthy vitamin supplement.

Apple and Raisin Strudel

2 tablespoons butter
4 sheets filo pastry
4 tablespoons ground almonds
   or cake crumbs
4 large cooking apples
¼ cup raisins
¼ cup sugar
1 teaspoon cinnamon
2 teaspoons grated lemon zest
1 beaten egg

Time: 6 minutes. Serves 6-8

Place butter into bowl. Cook on high 1 minute or until melted. Brush 1 sheet of filo pastry lightly with butter and sprinkle with 1 teaspoon ground almonds. Place another sheet of filo pastry on top and repeat, brushing with butter and sprinkling with ground almonds until all pastry is used. Reserve some almonds for filling.

   Peel, core and thinly slice apples and place in a bowl. Add raisins, sugar, cinnamon, zest and remaining ground almonds and blend together.

   Cover two-thirds of pastry with apple mixture. Brush uncovered pastry with beaten egg and roll up. Brush with remaining butter and sprinkle with extra cinnamon.

   Cook in roasting dish on high 6–8 minutes or on preheated browning grill 6 minutes on high. Cook strudel 3–4 minutes on each side. Transfer to serving plate and dust with icing sugar mixture.

Ginger Puff Sponge

2 eggs
60 g sugar
1 teaspoon golden syrup
30 g cornflour
30 g flour
2 level teaspoons ground ginger
1 level teaspoon cinnamon
1 level teaspoon cocoa
¼ level teaspoon bi-carbonate
   of soda
½ level teaspoon cream of
   tartar

Time: 2½ minutes

Beat eggs until thick and creamy, gradually adding sugar, beating until dissolved. Add golden syrup and beat until well mixed. Fold in sifted dry ingredients. Place into a well-greased micro-baking ring and cook for 2½ minutes on high, turning every minute. When cold, split and fill with cream.

Baked Honey Pears

Meringue-topped Chocolate Cheese Cake

Base

1 cup biscuit crumbs
½ cup melted margarine (to
    melt margarine put in oven
    ¾–1 minute)

Filling

375 g cream cheese (to soften
    cheese, cut up and place in
    oven on defrost 1 minute)
2 eggs
½ cup caster sugar
1 teaspoon vanilla
60 g melted chocolate (to melt
    chocolate, cut up and place
    in oven and cook 1 minute)

Topping

2 egg whites
5 tablespoons caster sugar
⅓ cup coconut
2 teaspoons cornflour

Time: 9 minutes

Combine base ingredients and press evenly into a 20 cm pyrex pie plate. Chill until firm.

To make filling, beat cream cheese using an electric mixer until smooth. Add eggs one at a time. Add sugar, vanilla, and beat until creamy smooth. Pour into crumb crust. Swirl in melted chocolate to give a marble effect. Cook 3 minutes.

Whip egg whites until stiff, using an electric beater, gradually adding sugar, beating to dissolve. Fold in coconut (can be lightly toasted if desired) and cornflour. Pipe onto cheese cake and cook 3 minutes. Serve cold.

Banana Cake

60 g butter, melted
¼ cup milk
1 egg, beaten
½ cup mashed banana
½ cup brown sugar
1 cup self-raising flour
½ cup chopped nuts

Topping

¼ cup brown sugar
¼ cup chopped nuts
1 tablespoon plain flour
2 tablespoons coconut
pinch cinnamon
15 g softened butter

Time: 10½ minutes

Combine butter, milk, egg, banana, and brown sugar in a basin. Mix well. Fold in flour and nuts. Pour into a greased and lined round 21 cm pyrex souffle dish. Combine topping ingredients and sprinkle in souffle dish. Cook on medium 10½–11½ minutes. Let stand 5 minutes before turning out

Marble Cake

60 g butter
¾ cup sugar
vanilla
1 egg
¾ cup milk
1½ cups plain flour
2 teaspoons baking powder
½ teaspoon salt

Time: 6–9 minutes

Cream butter, sugar and vanilla until light and fluffy. Beat in egg, fold in milk and sifted dry ingredients alternately. Divide the mixture into 3 separate bowls:
    Leave one plain.
    Add a few drops of red food colouring to the second one.
    Add 2 tablespoons cocoa, pinch of bi-carbonate and 1 tablespoon milk to the third.
Drop into greased, lined micro-baking ring in alternate colours. Lightly mix with a metal skewer to blend colours. Cook 6 minutes on high or 9 minutes medium.

HINT: CAKE CONTAINERS
Cake mixtures should not fill the container more than half way or they will spill over. Cooking in a microwave makes rising agents more active.

Marble Cake

166

Carrot Cake

½ cup butter or margarine
½ cup firmly packed brown
   sugar
1 egg
1 cup firmly packed fresh
   grated carrot
1 dessertspoon crystallised
   ginger
½ cup seeded raisins
½ cup sultanas
1½ cups double sifted flour
1 teaspoon baking powder
½ teaspoon soda
½ teaspoon cinnamon
½ teaspoon nutmeg
¾ cup milk

Frosting

250 g icing sugar mixture
90 g cream cheese
3 tablespoons butter
1 teaspoon vanilla
1 teaspoon sherry

Time: 9 minutes

Cream butter or margarine and brown sugar. Beat in egg until well blended. Stir in carrots, ginger, raisins and sultanas. Sift together flour, baking powder, soda, cinnamon and nutmeg. Stir into the mixture with milk. Blend well. Turn into a well greased micro-ring dish and cook in oven 6 minutes high then 3 minutes medium. Serve cold with lemon frosting or hot with lemon sauce.

Beat all frosting ingredients until fluffy — spread over cake. Decorate with mandarin quarters or small marzipan carrots.

Orange Tea Ring

60 g butter
¾ cup sugar
vanilla
1 egg
3 tablespoons orange juice
3 tablespoons milk
2 teaspoons grated orange rind
1½ cups flour
2 teaspoons baking powder
½ teaspoon salt

Time: 6–9 minutes

Cream butter, sugar and vanilla until light and fluffy. Beat in egg and fold in orange juice, milk, orange rind and dry ingredients alternately. Drop into a greased, lined and greased micro-baking ring. Cook for 6 minutes on high or 9 minutes on medium. Cool and top with orange frosting.

Date Loaf

2 tablespoons butter or
   margarine
½ cup raw sugar
1 egg
⅔ cup milk
½ cup dates
½ cup chopped walnuts
1½ cups self-raising flour
pinch salt
½ teaspoon cinnamon
½ teaspoon ginger
1 teaspoon mixed spice

Time: 6–9 minutes

Beat butter and sugar to a cream. Add well-beaten egg. Add milk gradually. Add chopped dates and nuts. Stir in lightly the sifted flour, salt, and spices. Spoon mixture into prepared micro-baking dish. Cook 6 minutes on high or 9 minutes on medium.

Date and Cherry Slice

250 g chopped dates
60 g chopped glace cherries
125 g butter
30 g crystallised ginger,
   chopped
45 g brown sugar
60 g pecan nuts, roughly
   chopped
3 cups Rice Bubbles
200 g cooking chocolate
1 tablespoon butter

Time: 6–6½ minutes. Makes 25

Place dates, butter, cherries, ginger, sugar and pecan nuts in a medium-sized bowl. Cook on medium for 5 minutes. Stir in Rice Bubbles, press mixture into a lightly greased 20 × 20 cm dish and chill until firm.

Chop chocolate into cubes and place in a basin with butter. Cook on high 1–1½ minutes until soft. Stir until smooth. Spread chocolate over slice and chill until set. Cut into small serving pieces.

Black Forest Cherry Cake

1 packet chocolate cake mix

Filling

1 can stoned black cherries
⅓ cup Kirsch
2 tablespoons arrowroot
3 tablespoons cherry syrup
300 mL cream
grated dark chocolate
red cherries

Time: 12 minutes

Make cake as directed on packet. Grease and line a microwave baking ring. Pour cake mix into prepared dish. Cook in oven 5½–6 minutes on high. Turn onto a cake cooler and cover before cake is cold.

Place cherries, 2 tablespoons of Kirsch and syrup from cherries into a bowl to cover. Cook 4 minutes on high or until boiling. Blend arrowroot with 3 tablespoons syrup. Stir into cherry mixture, cook 2 minutes and allow to cool.

Split cake into 3 layers. Spread cherry mixture over base, top with second layer. Whip cream with remaining Kirsch. Spread half over second layer, top with third piece of cake. Spread top and outside edges lightly with cream. Mark top into serves. Dust top and sides with grated chocolate. Pipe a rosette of cream on edge of each marked portion and top with a whole red cherry.

Black Forest Cherry Cake

Lemon Sponge Roll

4 egg yolks
1 cup sugar
¼ cup water
juice and rind 1 lemon
1 cup flour
4 egg whites
½ teaspoon cream of tartar
pinch salt
sifted icing sugar
¼ cup lemon spread jam

Time: 6–7 minutes. Serves 6–8

Beat egg yolks with ½ cup sugar, water and lemon juice and rind. Fold in sifted flour. Set aside.

Whisk egg whites till stiff. Beat in remaining ½ cup sugar, cream of tartar and salt. Fold egg white mixture with egg yolk mix. Pour mixture into greased and lined oblong dish. Cook on medium 5 minutes, then a further 1–2 minutes on high.

Turn cake immediately onto sheet of plastic wrap. Sprinkle with icing sugar. Remove paper lining. Roll up cake with plastic wrap. Cook on cake rack for ½ hour.

Carefully unroll, spread cake with lemon, reroll without plastic wrap. Dust surface with icing sugar and serve.

Chocolate Bars

1 cup Cornflakes
1 cup sifted self-raising flour
1 cup coconut
¾ cup sugar
2 heaped teaspoons cocoa
pinch salt
180 g butter, melted

Chocolate Icing

2 tablespoons butter
2 tablespoons cocoa
6 tablespoons icing sugar
⅛ teaspoon vanilla essence

Time: 8 minutes. Makes 25

Blend all ingredients together in bowl. Press into greased 20 × 20 cm square casserole and cook on medium-high 8 minutes.

Combine chocolate icing ingredients in basin and beat with electric hand mixer until smooth. Spread evenly over biscuits while still warm. When set, cut into squares.

Apricot and Almond Balls

1 cup chopped dried apricots
1 cup chopped, toasted
  almonds
½ cup butter
1 cup sugar
⅓ cup flour
½ teaspoon salt
2 eggs
3 cups Weet-Bix, finely crushed
1 teaspoon vanilla essence
½ cup icing sugar

Time: 6 minutes. Makes 50

Place butter into a mixing bowl and soften on high for 1 minute or until melted. Blend in sugar, flour, salt and eggs. Stir in apricots and cook on high 5 minutes or until very thick, stirring every 2 minutes. Cook for 5 minutes.

In a large bowl, combine Weet-Bix flakes and almonds. Stir in apricot mixture and vanilla until well blended. Shape into 2.5 cm balls. Roll balls in icing sugar to coat and chill until firm.

HINT: TOASTING NUTS

Almonds take 3–4 minutes on high, stirring once or twice to allow even toasting. Smaller nuts will take half the time.

Sauces and Jams

Sauces are very quick and easy to make in the microwave. And they are delicious served with meats, vegetables and desserts. Be sure to stir frequently. You can even leave the wooden spoon in the bowl in the oven to make this a very simple operation. Use a large glass-type container when making sauces to prevent boiling over. When thickening a sauce, remember that arrowroot will make a more transparent sauce than cornflour.

There's just nothing like homemade jams and fruit butters. With a microwave oven, jam-making is so quick and easy. But remember to stir for even cooking.

Basic White Sauce I

1 small onion, peeled
6 whole cloves
600 mL milk
1 bay leaf
60 g butter
60 g flour
salt and pepper

Time: 10½ minutes. Makes about 2 cups

Stud onion with cloves. Pour milk into a glass jug, add onion and bay leaf. Cook on high for 4½ minutes to heat and infuse flavours.

Place butter into a glass jug or casserole and cook 1 minute to melt. Add flour and stir with wooden spoon. Cook 1 minute.

Stir in milk to blend. Cook for 4 minutes, stirring after 2 minutes. Remove onion and bay leaf. Season with salt and pepper.

Parsley Sauce

2 tablespoons chopped parsley
1 quantity Basic White Sauce I

Time: Fold 2 tablespoons of parsley into Basic White Sauce I.
Serve with seafood, vegetables, or corned meats.

Onion Sauce

Basic White Sauce I ingredients
60 g onion, diced

Melt butter in Basic White Sauce I recipe. Add onion and cook 3–4 minutes before adding the flour.
Add milk and cook as above.
Serve with roast mutton, corned beef, or corned ox tongue.

Egg Sauce

2 hard-boiled eggs
1 quantity Basic White Sauce I

Dice eggs finely. Fold into Basic White Sauce I. A little finely cut parsley may also be added.

Cheese Sauce I

1 quantity Basic White Sauce I
60 g grated tasty cheese
1 egg yolk, beaten

Add 2 tablespoons of Basic White Sauce I to egg yolk and beat quickly. Return to remainder of sauce, along with cheese. Reheat for 2 minutes if necessary. Do not allow to boil.
Serve with seafood or vegetables.

Basic White Sauce II

2 tablespoons butter
2 tablespoons flour
½ teaspoon salt
little white pepper
250 mL milk

Time: 4 minutes. Makes about 1 cup

Place butter in a glass bowl. Cook for 45 seconds or until melted. Stir in flour, salt and pepper. Add milk and cook on high approximately 3 minutes until boiling, stirring from time to time.
Note: Use a wooden spoon when stirring.

Mushroom Sauce (see recipe this section)

Cheese Sauce II

Time 4 minutes. Makes about 1 cup

Ingredients are the same as Basic White Sauce II except that you add ¼ teaspoon dry mustard with the flour. After sauce has cooked, stir in ½ to 1 cup shredded cheese until melted.

Hollandaise Sauce

⅓ cup butter
2 tablespoons lemon juice
2 egg yolks
¼ teaspoon salt

Time: 1 minute 45 seconds

Place butter into a small bowl, heat for 45 seconds on high. Stir in lemon juice and egg yolks, beat with whisk until well mixed. Cook 60 seconds, whisking every 15 seconds. Stir in salt halfway through.

Basic Brown Sauce

30 g butter
60 g carrot, diced
60 g onion, diced
30 g celery, diced
45 g pre-browned flour
1 tablespoon tomato paste
1 bayleaf
600 mL brown stock

Time: 12 minutes

Place butter into a casserole, cook 1 minute to melt. Add carrots, onion and celery, cook 4 minutes on high. Blend in flour and cook 1 minute. Add tomato paste, bay leaf, blend in stock and cook 3 minutes, stir well and cook another 3 minutes. If slower cooking is required, cook sauce on defrost 15–20 minutes, stirring from time to time. Strain.
    Serve with roast meats or as a base for other sauces.

Demi Glace Sauce

300 mL Brown Sauce (see
    recipe)
250 mL brown stock
50 mL Madeira

Time: 6 minutes

Combine ingredients in a jug. Cook 4–6 minutes on high, stirring twice during cooking time.

174

Chasseur Sauce

30 g butter
1 shallot, cut finely
60 g mushrooms, sliced
50 mL dry white wine
125 g tomatoes, chopped,
    deseeded
300 mL Demi Glace Sauce (see
    recipe)
parsley, chopped
salt and pepper to taste

Time: 13 minutes

Cook butter in a casserole for 1 minute. Add shallots and cook 2 minutes on high. Add mushrooms and cook covered 2 minutes. Drain off butter. Add wine and cook 2–3 minutes until boiling and reduced to half. Add tomatoes, Demi Glace Sauce and cook 5 minutes. Add parsley, salt and pepper.
    Serve with steaks, chicken, barbecued food or lamb.

Port Wine Sauce

300 mL Demi Glace Sauce (see
    recipe)
3 tablespoons port wine
30 g butter

Time: 6 minutes

Cook Demi Glace Sauce in jug for 3–4 minutes on high. Add port wine and cook 2 minutes. Blend in the butter.
    Serve with roast or barbecued meats.

Curry Sauce

30 g butter
1 clové garlic, chopped
60 g chopped onion
1 tablespoon curry powder
30 g flour
2 teaspoons tomato paste
450 mL chicken stock or fish
    stock for seafood
60 g apple, chopped
1 tablespoon fruit chutney
1 tablespoon sultanas
1 tablespoon chopped almonds
salt and pepper

Time: 11 minutes

Cook butter in casserole 1 minute to melt. Add garlic, onion and curry powder. Cook 3 minutes on high, blend in flour and cook 1 minute. Add tomato paste and stock, blend with wooden spoon. Add remaining ingredients and cook 4–6 minutes, stirring after 2 minutes.
    Serve with seafood, poultry, hard-boiled eggs or vegetables.

Mint Sauce

250 g sugar
60 g arrowroot
dash salt
500 mL warm water
2–3 drops green food colouring
1 teaspoon finely chopped mint
2 drops peppermint essence

Time: 9 minutes

Combine sugar, arrowroot and salt in a 4 cup glass measure. Stir well, add water. Cook for 6 minutes on high, stirring after first 2 minutes and then after every minute. Bring to boil. Add food colouring, chopped mint, and essence. Heat for 30 seconds.

Apple Sauce

500 g cooking apples
3 tablespoons water
30 g butter
30 g sugar
¼ teaspoon cinnamon or
  nutmeg

Time: 12 minutes

Peel, core and slice apples. Place into a casserole with sugar, butter and water. Cook covered for 12 minutes on high or until a puree is formed. Stir twice during cooking. Strain, stir in nutmeg or cinnamon.
  Serve with roast pork or poultry.

Fresh Tomato Sauce

1 medium onion, chopped
1 large clove garlic
500 g fresh tomatoes, peeled
  and chopped
2 bay leaves
2 teaspoons sugar
½ teaspoon dry basil
2 tablespoons tomato paste
1 tablespoon butter
1 cup stock
salt
pepper

Time: 14 minutes

Melt butter in pyrex dish 30 seconds. Add onion, garlic. Cook 4 minutes on high. Add remaining ingredients. Cook on high 10 minutes, remove bay leaves. Puree mixture.

> **HINT: SAUCE TALK**
> Sauces are simple in a microwave. You can usually make them in the jug you want to serve them in and they do not need the constant attention required when using your conventional oven. Occasional stirring of milk-based sauces is essential to avoid spillage.

175

Veloute Sauce

This is a basic sauce, a little darker in colour. Chicken, fish or veal stock is used in place of milk.

60 g butter
60 g flour
600 mL of stock (suitable for
 sauce required)
salt and pepper

Time: 11 minutes

Place stock into a glass jug and cook on high for 4 minutes. Place butter into a jug or casserole dish, cook 1 minute to melt. Stir in flour with wooden spoon. (A wooden spoon may be left in sauce during cooking for ease of stirring.) Cook 2 minutes. Blend in stock. Continue cooking for 4 minutes, stirring well after 2 minutes. Add seasonings.

Mushroom Sauce

Veloute Sauce ingredients (see
 recipe)
125 g sliced button mushrooms
 (canned mushrooms can be
 sliced and used if a mild
 flavour is required)
1 egg yolk, beaten
4 tablespoons fresh cream

Melt butter in a jug or casserole. Add mushrooms and cook for 1 minute on high. Blend in flour and cook a further 1 minute. Blend in warm stock (veal or chicken) and cook 4 minutes to thicken.

Stir after 2 minutes. Combine egg yolk and cream. Add 2 tablespoons of sauce, blend well and fold into remaining sauce. Season with salt and pepper.

Use with steak, veal or chicken.

Supreme Sauce

Veloute Sauce ingredients with
 chicken stock (see recipe)
30 g mushroom trimmings
1 egg yolk
75 mL fresh cream
squeeze lemon juice

Time: 8 minutes

Using basic veloute sauce ingredients, cook butter to melt and add mushrooms and cook 2 minutes on high. Blend in flour, cook a further 1 minute. Blend in stock and cook 4 minutes. Stir after 2 minutes. Add seasonings, stir well and strain. Blend cream and egg yolk. Add 2 tablespoons sauce, mix well and return to remaining sauce, add lemon juice.

Serve with hot, boiled chicken or as a basic sauce for pastry or bread cases.

176

Aurora Sauce

1 quantity supreme sauce (see
 recipe)
1 tablespoon tomato puree

Time: 8 minutes

Add puree to supreme sauce to enrich flavour and colour. Serve with chicken, poached eggs or pasta dishes.

Basic Custard Sauce

375 mL milk
3 tablespoons sugar
2 tablespoons custard powder
2 egg yolks
1 teaspoon vanilla

Time: 6 minutes

Combine custard powder and sugar with milk. Heat 4 minutes on high, until sauce thickens, stirring twice. With a wire whisk quickly beat in the egg yolks, heat for 1–2 minutes on defrost, then flavour with vanilla.

Chocolate Sauce

300 mL milk
15 g cocoa
15 g cornflour
75 g sugar
1 teaspoon butter

Time: 5 minutes

Blend cornflour, cocoa with 3 tablespoons of milk. Place remaining milk into a jug and cook 3 minutes on high to boil. Blend in cornflour mixture and cook 2 minutes. Blend in sugar and butter.

Chocolate Sauce

Jams

There is such a huge range of commercial sauces, jams and condiments now available that home production has largely fallen out of favour. In country areas where people still maintain vegetable gardens and fruit trees, the arts of jam- and pickle-making have survived. But even in the cities fruit in season suitable for jam or fruit chutney can often be bought in bulk very cheaply. Jam-making has a reputation for being tricky but this is not justified. If a few basic rules are observed it is really quite a simple procedure.

Fruit butters are traditional country fare, made with a fruit pulp (no butter) and cooked to a firm smooth texture. Tart fruit such as apples, quinces or cranberries may be used. Serve as jam, or with cold meats.

Bottling and Storing
Use jam jars or any clean, undamaged heatproof containers. Make sure that they are not chipped or cracked, and always wash and sterilize first. Warm the jars in a gentle oven before filling — this will prevent cracking. Store in a cool, airy cupboard or pantry.

Making Jam
Pectin content: The setting qualities of fruit vary according to their acidity and the amount of pectin they contain. Here is a guide to help you.

High pectin: blackcurrants; red and white currants; oranges; gooseberries; crab apples; lemons; grapefruit; plums and quinces.

Medium pectin: apricots; greengages; loganberries; raspberries and blackberries.

Low pectin: rhubarb; strawberries, cherries; figs; marrow; grapes; peaches; pears; melons.

If you are using fruit with a low or medium pectin content, you will have to add additional pectin. This is available commercially in liquid or powdered form. Or you can add some citric acid or lemon juice. The amount of pectin you add will vary according to the type of fruit but, as a general guide, you will need 50 mL–100 mL liquid pectin to 500 g fruit, or 30 mL lemon juice to 1 kg fruit.

Setting Tests
You will have to test the jam for setting after cooking it for the specified time. Be careful not to cook the jam beyond the setting point, or you are liable to spoil the flavour, colour and texture. Fruits vary slightly but, generally speaking, when the jam is boiled to a temperature of 105°C (221°F) the sugar concentration is about 65 per cent, and the jam will set and keep well. You can measure the temperature with a sugar thermometer, but it is always a good idea to test it as well. There are two methods.

Flake test: stir the jam with a wooden spoon, then remove and hold at right angles to the pan. Allow the jam clinging to the spoon to drip back into the pan. Setting point is reached when the drops collect at the spoon's edge and form large flakes.

Saucer test: drop a little jam on to a cold saucer and place in a refrigerator for about 1 minute. It should set and form a wrinkled skin on the surface when you draw a finger across.

Plum Jam

1 kg plums
crystal sugar
juice 3 medium lemons

Time: 32½ minutes

Cut plums into small pieces removing stones. Place into a dish and cook approximately 20 minutes on high until a pulp is formed. Allow 1 cup sugar for every cup pulp. Warm sugar in oven for 30 seconds. Add sugar and lemon juice to fruit pulp. Cook approximately 12 minutes until a gel is formed, stirring occasionally. Pour into sterilised jars. Cool slightly, label, date and seal.

Apple and Pear Jam

500 g apples, peeled and sliced
500 g pears, peeled and sliced
sugar
juice 3 lemons

Time: 32 minutes

Place peeled and sliced apples and pears into a dish and cook approximately 20 minutes on high until a pulp is formed. Allow 1 cup sugar for every 1 cup of pulp. Warm sugar in oven for 30 seconds. Add sugar and lemon juice to fruit pulp. Cook approximately 12 minutes, stirring occasionally until a gel is formed. Pour into sterilised jars. Cool, label, date and seal.

Strawberry Jam

500 g strawberries
1½ cups crystal sugar
juice small lemon

Time: 20 minutes

Chop strawberries roughly, place into oven with sugar and lemon juice. Cook approximately 20 minutes on high, stirring occasionally. Remove, pour into sterilised jars, label, date and seal.

Orange Marmalade

700 g oranges
1 lemon
3 cups sugar, heated

Time: 50 minutes

Wash and dry fruit. Cut in half, squeeze out the juice. Cut peel into very thin strips. Place peel into a large pyrex bowl. Make up the juice to 3 cups with water. Pour over fruit. Cover and cook on high 20 minutes. Add sugar to cooked peel. Cook on high for 30 minutes or until jam is at setting consistency. Bottle whilst hot.

Lemon Butter

Rind and juice of 1 large lemon
60 g butter
⅓ cup sugar
2 × 60 g eggs
pinch salt

Time: 8 minutes

Combine all ingredients in a medium sized bowl. Cook covered on defrost for 6–8 minutes, stirring occasionally until thickened. Store in hot, sterile jars, in a cool, dry place.

Breads, Muffins and Scones

Most yeast breads can be proven and baked in a microwave oven but as microwaves cook using moist heat, a baked loaf will not form a crisp, golden crust. But the clever cook can create a mock crust by sprinkling greased loaf dishes with oatmeal, crumbed crisp savoury biscuits, poppy seeds, toasted sesame seeds, rye or wholemeal flour, cracked wheat, crushed dried onions, wheat germ or seasoned breadcrumbs.

Dried or fresh yeast when mixed with warm water and sugar can be proven on a warm setting only (a defrost setting will kill the yeast) and usually takes 10–15 minutes for the mixture to double in bulk.

Breads made with baking powder should be cooked in lined and greased ring moulds, bar or loaf dishes.

Here's a couple of hints to make muffin and scone cooking easier and more successful: cook muffins in double thickness patty cake papers; and quick Sunday afternoon scones should be baked (only 1 minute per side) on a pre-heated browning dish.

Zucchini Loaf

1½ cups unpeeled, grated
    zucchini
1¼ cup self-raising flour
1 teaspoon baking soda
pinch salt
1½ teaspoons cinnamon
½ cup vegetable oil
2 eggs
1 teaspoon vanilla
2 tablespoons molasses
⅔ cup sugar
2 tablespoons wheat germ
    (optional)

Time: 6–9 minutes

Blend all ingredients in mixing bowl on low speed for 2 minutes. Beat on medium speed 1 minute. Spread mixture into lined loaf tin and sprinkle top with wheat germ.

Shield ends of loaf with 5 cm strips of foil covering 2.5 cm of batter. Cook on medium 6 minutes. Increase power to high and cook 2–3 minutes.

Mango Gingerbread

2 cups peeled, sliced fresh
    mango
1 packet commercial
    gingerbread mix
¼ cup butter
½ cup brown sugar
1 tablespoon milk

Time: 13–16 minutes

Cook butter on high 1–1½ minutes in 20 × 20 cm square dish. Blend in sugar and milk and cook on high 2 minutes, stirring twice. Arrange mango slices in rows on top. Prepare gingerbread as directed on package. Spoon batter evenly over fruit and cook on medium 6 minutes.

Increase power to high and cook 4–6 minutes until gingerbread springs back when touched. Cool 5 minutes. Loosen edges and turn out on platter. Cut into serving squares. If desired, top with whipped cream or ice cream to serve.

Pumpkin Pecan Bread

1 cup plain flour
¾ cup brown sugar
1 teaspoon baking powder
1 teaspoon baking soda
1 teaspoon salt
1 teaspoon mixed spice
1 teaspoon cinnamon
½ cup vegetable oil
2 eggs
½ cup chopped pecans
1 cup mashed, drained
    pumpkin

Time: 18 minutes

Blend all ingredients in mixing bowl on low speed 20 seconds; beat on medium for 1 minute.

Spread mixture into lined loaf dish. Shield ends of dish with 5 cm strip of foil covering 2.5 cm of mixture. Cook on medium 9 minutes. Remove foil. Cook on high 2–3 minutes. Let stand 5 minutes before turning out.

Mango Gingerbread and Zucchini Loaf

Soda Bread

2 tablespoons white
  breadcrumbs
2 cups flour
1 cup raisins
1 tablespoon sugar
2 teaspoons baking soda
½ teaspoon salt
2 tablespoons butter
⅔ cup buttermilk
1 beaten egg

Topping

1 tablespoon butter
2 tablespoons white
  breadcrumbs
1 tablespoon rolled oats
¼ teaspoon cinnamon

Time: 9½–10½ minutes

Lightly butter a 1 litre soufflé dish and coat inside with breadcrumbs. Blend flour, raisins, sugar, baking soda and salt in mixing bowl.

Place butter in small bowl and cook on high 45 seconds until melted. Stir butter, buttermilk and egg into flour mixture. Spread in soufflé dish.

Place butter in bowl and cook on high 45 seconds. Stir in breadcrumbs, rolled oats and cinnamon. Spread over top of bread. With a sharp knife cut a 2.5 cm 'X' on top of bread. Cook on medium–high 8–9 minutes until top springs back when touched. Let stand 5 minutes before serving.

Carrot and Bran Muffins

1 cup bran flakes
¾ cup milk
2 cups finely grated carrot
1 cup wholemeal flour
2 tablespoons brown sugar
2 tablespoons vegetable oil
1 tablespoon lemon juice
1 teaspoon baking powder
¼ teaspoon cinnamon
¼ teaspoon salt
1 egg, beaten

Time: 6–9 minutes. Makes 12–14

Combine bran, milk and carrot and let stand 5 minutes. Blend in remaining ingredients. Line muffin rings or cups with double paper liners. Half fill each with muffin mixture and cook on high. Takes 3–4½ minutes for each 6 muffins. Repeat with remaining mixture.

HINT: KEEPING FLOUR PRODUCTS FRESH

When bread, loaves and muffins are cooked and cool, wrap immediately in plastic wrap to retain moisture and prevent drying.

Step 1   Soda Bread. Coat buttered soufflé dish with breadcrumbs

Step 2   Stir buttermilk, egg and butter into flour mixture

Step 3   Cut a 2.5 cm cross on top of bread

Soda Bread

Savoury Scone Roll

2 cups self–raising flour
1/8 teaspoon cayenne pepper
1 teaspoon salt
60 g softened butter
60 g grated cheese
1 egg
3/4 cup milk
1 tablespoon milk
2 tablespoons poppy seeds

Filling

125 g ham, shredded
3 gherkins, grated
2 teaspoons butter
2 tablespoons finely chopped
   parsley
1 small onion, finely chopped
30 g grated cheese
1 tablespoon tomato sauce
salt and pepper to taste

Time: 6–7 minutes

Sift flour, cayenne pepper and salt into a bowl. Add butter, cheese, egg and 3/4 cup milk and blend together with a table knife to form a dough. Roll out on a lightly floured board to a rectangle 30 × 20 cm.

Combine filling ingredients in a bowl and spread over prepared scone leaving a 2 cm strip on one long edge. Brush edge with 1 tablespoon milk. Roll up and allow to rest on glazed edge to seal. Place rolled dough onto lightly floured round plate.

Join the two ends together to form a circle. Cut two-thirds of the way through roll at 3 cm intervals. Brush with milk and sprinkle with poppy seeds. Cook on high 6–7 minutes. Let stand 4 minutes before serving. Fill centre with vegetable sticks and parsley.

> ### HINT: DEFROSTING BREAD
> To defrost a 750 g loaf of bread. Remove metal tie from bread bag. Place wrapped bread into oven. Microwave on high 45 seconds. Turn loaf over. Microwave for a further 30 seconds. Let stand in bag for 6 minutes.

Microwave Cooking for One

Easy and Delicious Recipes for the Solo Cook

You get home, you are tired, in a hurry and starving. No time for messy pans. This section is designed for the person living alone who has a few of the basic culinary skills and a microwave. With a microwave you can even cook and eat off the same plate! It's as though this marvel of modern invention was specifically designed for the Solo Cook.

The recipes in this section have been devised by nutritionist Yvonne Webb as a culinary survival guide for the Solo Cook who wishes to spend the minimum time shopping, preparing and cooking a delicious and nutritious meal. The easy-to-prepare recipes will delight both the eye and the taste buds — so much so that the Solo Cook might even consider recipes for two.

All recipes in the 'Microwave Cooking for One' cooked on 'High' unless stated otherwise.

Mediterranean Lamb

Solo Snacks

Many of these recipes are substantial enough to serve as light meals.

When a cheese topping is called for do not cook for too long or the cheese will become rubbery and tough.

Curried Eggs

1 clove garlic, crushed
½ teaspoon curry powder
1 teaspoon ghee
2 tablespoons tomato purée
1 slice lemon
1 teaspoon apricot jam
2 eggs
¼ cup milk

Time: 8½ minutes

Combine garlic, curry powder and ghee in a cup and cook on high 30 seconds. Add tomato purée, lemon and jam. Mix well and cook 1 minute.

Beat together eggs and milk in a glass bowl. Stir in all other ingredients.

Cook on low for 5 minutes until egg is beginning to set. Stir with a fork to break up egg mass then cook 2 minutes on high.

Stuffed Mushrooms

4 large fresh mushrooms, washed
1 medium-sized dill pickle
2 shallots
3 tablespoons ricotta cheese

Time: 2 minutes

Wash mushrooms and remove stalks. Chop pickle, mushroom stalks and shallots and mix with ricotta cheese.

Stuff mixture into inverted mushroom caps and cook on high 2 minutes. Serve with sliced fresh fruit.

Variation: Finely diced ham and red capsicum may be added to the mushroom stuffing.

Winter Hearty

½ can peeled tomatoes
2 canned frankfurts, drained and
  chopped
½ can pea and ham soup

Time: 3 minutes

Stir tomatoes and frankfurts into soup. Cook in medium-sized glass bowl 3 minutes on high.

French Collation

½ red or green capsicum, seeded
  and cut into strips
1 hard-boiled egg
½ can anchovy fillets
mayonnaise
bread roll

Time: 1½ minutes

Chop egg and mix with anchovies, capsicum, and mayonnaise. Cook on high 1½ minutes. Cut roll in half. Scoop bread out of crust and fill with mixture.

Stuffed Mushrooms

Step 1 Wash mushrooms and remove stalks. Chop stalks, pickle and shallots

Step 2 Mix chopped ingredients with ricotta cheese

Step 3 Stuff mixture onto inverted mushroom caps

Stuffed Mushrooms

Empty Cupboard Surprise

1 can sweet corn
1 cup any cooked vegetable (a
    mixture is best)
½ cup any chopped, leftover
    meat (optional)
1 egg

Time: 3 minutes

Drain sweet corn and mix with vegetables and meat. Place in small glass bowl and break egg on top, piercing yolk with toothpick.

Cook 3 minutes on high or until egg is set. Cover and let stand 2 minutes before eating.

Prince's Pocket

1 small wholemeal pita (pocket
    or Lebanese) bread
1 small can mushrooms in
    butter sauce
small handful walnuts,
    chopped
1 tomato, thinly sliced
chicken leftovers

Time: 2–4 minutes

Mix mushrooms, chicken, tomato and walnuts and cook on high 2 minutes. Fill pita bread with mixture. Reheat on low 2 minutes (optional).

Asparagus Snack

1 egg
½ cup milk
1 teaspoon grated lemon rind
½ can asparagus spears,
    drained
2 slices bread

Time: 2½ minutes

Beat egg and milk together. Add lemon rind. Arrange bread on a dinner plate and place half the asparagus on each slice. Pour custard mixture over asparagus so it soaks into the bread. Cook on high 2½ minutes.

Penjas

3 thick slices liverwurst
    sausage
1 onion, chopped
1 can diced capsicum
½ cup cooked, diced vegetables
1 tomato
½ cup grated Parmesan cheese

Time: 2–3 minutes

Line base of ramekin or small soup plate with liverwurst sausage. Cover with chopped onion and dice capsicum, then vegetables, then thickly sliced tomato.

Sprinkle with Parmesan cheese and cook 2–3 minutes on high, or until cheese has begun to melt.

Pate

200 g liverwurst sausage
1 tablespoon unsalted butter
¼ teaspoon dried oregano
1 tablespoon cognac

Time: 2½ minutes

Mash sausage, butter and oregano together. Place in small glass bowl and cook 2½ minutes on high. Remove, pour Cognac over pate and let stand until cool.

Danish Delight

ham steak or 1 thick sliced,
    canned ham
1 onion, chopped
1 tablespoon vinegar
½ cup apricot nectar
1 teaspoon cooking oil

Time: 4½ minutes

Heat oil in a glass jar for 30 seconds. Add chopped onion, vinegar and apricot nectar. Cook on low 2 minutes. Let stand.

Arrange ham on serving plate. Cover with sauce and cook a further 2 minutes on high.

Polenta

½ cup yellow cornmeal or
    polenta
2 cups water
½ cup grated Parmesan cheese
pinch cayenne pepper

Time: 6½ minutes

Measure cornmeal into a large glass mixing bowl. Add water and stir well. Cook 4 minutes on high. Add cheese and pepper and cook 1½ minutes on high.

Let stand, covered, for 5 minutes. Wrap in greaseproof paper, refrigerate and cut into slices when required. To reheat, place slice on paper towel and heat for 50 seconds.

Jamaican Toast

2 slices wholemeal or kibble
 bread
sweet chutney
2 slices ham
1 banana
½ onion, chopped
1 dill pickle or gherkin, sliced
several slices mozzarella cheese
 or more if required
sour cream, paprika and dill
 for garnish

Time: 2–3 minutes

Spread each slice of bread with chutney and cover with ham. Arrange slices of banana on each, then onion and dill pickle. Cover with mozzarella cheese.

Cook 2–3 minutes on high until cheese has melted and is bubbling. Garnish with a dollop of sour cream sprinkled with paprika and a spray of dill.

White Elephant

2 slices rye bread
2 slices wholemeal or kibble
 bread
2 tablespoons pate (see recipe)
100 g ricotta cheese
1 can sweet corn, drained
1 medium-sized dill pickle,
 sliced
1 pickled or cocktail onion

Time: 6 minutes

Spread the 4 slices of bread with pate. Cover slices 1 and 3 with corn and dill pickle. Cover slice 2 with ricotta cheese and pickled onion cut in half.

Heat each slice for 2 minutes on high. Stack bread slices so that outer 2 layers of filling are corn and centre one is cheese.

Leftovers with Tomato

½ cup chopped, cooked leftover
 meat
½ cup chopped, cooked leftover
 vegetables
1 cup diced tomato
1 egg
½ cup grated Parmesan cheese

Time: 5 minutes

Combine meat, vegetables and tomato in glass bowl. Beat egg and pour over mixture. Cook on high 3 minutes.

Top with grated cheese and cook 2 minutes or until cheese has melted. Serve with rice for a hearty and nourishing meal.

Baked Beans

1 small can baked beans
1 small can diced capsicum
¼ teaspoon curry powder
1 tablespoon Tomato Magic

Time: 1½ minutes

Empty baked beans into mixing bowl. Drain capsicum, retaining liquid. Mix Tomato Magic with 2 tablespoons of this liquid until dissolved. Add curry powder.

Combine all ingredients, cover with greaseproof paper and heat 1½ minutes on high.

Jamaican Toast

Step 1 Spread chutney on bread and cover with ham

Step 2 Add banana, onion and dill pickle

Step 3 Cover with mozzarella cheese and cook until bubbling

The Virtue of Vegetables

The microwave oven performs best with vegetables. If cooked properly they retain flavour, colour and nutrients. Use the minimum of water in cooking. Instead of using salt try various herbs for extra flavour. Oregano and dill enhance tomatoes.

Sprinkle coriander on zucchini.

Try a meatless meal sometime. Simply dress up the vegetables for the main meal and add cheese or eggs for protein.

Herbed Tomato

1 large ripe tomato
pinch oregano
1 teaspoon dried dill

Time: 1½ minutes

Wash tomato and cut in half. Sprinkle halves with oregano and dill. Arrange on paper towel and cook on high 1½ minutes.

Winter Tomato Savoury

1 tomato
1 teaspoon Stilton or blue vein
  cheese
1 teaspoon chopped chives or
  parsley

Time: 1 minute

Cut tomato in half and place on flat serving plate. Cook on high 1 minute. Crumble cheese on top of tomato halves and cook on low 1 minute. Sprinkle with chopped chives before serving.

Willy Nilly

¼ cup diced broccoli stalks
¼ cup diced cauliflower stalks
1 onion, chopped
1 potato, peeled and diced
¼ cup (at least) diced, leftover
  meat
1 packet French onion soup
dash angostura bitters
1 cup water

Time: 5 minutes

Add water to French onion soup powder. Mix well to eliminate lumps. Add angostura bitters and mix. Add other ingredients.

Place in small glass bowl and cover with lid or greaseproof paper. Cook 5 minutes on high.

Artichoke Hearts

1 can artichoke hearts
2 tablespoons unsalted butter
1 tablespoon vinegar
1 teaspoon horseradish

Time: 2½ minutes

Heat butter with vinegar for 30 seconds in a glass jar. Add horseradish and mix well. Arrange artichoke hearts on serving plate. Pour sauce on each heart and cook 2 minutes on high.

Zucchini with Cheese

2 small zucchini (unpeeled)
1 tablespoon grated cheese
pinch coriander
Parmesan cheese
cracked black pepper

Time: 2 minutes

Cut zucchini lengthwise. Sprinkle with coriander, grated cheese and Parmesan cheese and pepper. Place on serving dish, cover and cook 2 minutes on high.

Corn on the Cob

1 fresh corn cob
1 tablespoon unsalted butter
pinch nutmeg

Time: 4 minutes

Remove silk from cob and place on serving dish. Dot corn with butter and cover with husks. Place on paper towel, double thickness. Cook 4 minutes on high. Allow to cool slightly before eating.

Zucchini with Cheese

Silver Beet Parcels

3 silver beet or spinach leaves
1 cup cooled mashed pumpkin
¼ cup chopped chives or
    parsley
1 egg

Time: 3 minutes

Wash and drain leaves and remove white stalks. (Keep stalks for soup or a leftover dish.) Arrange each leaf flat on a dinner plate and heat 30 seconds until tender.

Combine pumpkin, chives and egg. Mix well. Spoon pumpkin mixture onto centre of each leaf. Fold edges of silver beet over filling and roll up securely.

Arrange parcels on dinner plate and cook 2½ minutes on high or until heated through.

Easy Asparagus with Butter Sauce

1 can asparagus spears
½ cup unsalted butter
1 clove garlic, crushed
juice 1 small lemon
pinch cinnamon

Time: 2½ minutes

Choose a good brand of asparagus with thin green spears. Remove from can, drain and place on serving dish.

Melt butter in a cup for 30 seconds. Pour melted butter over asparagus. Pour over lemon juice and sprinkle with cinnamon. Cook 2 minutes on high.

Herbed Carrots

1 cup diced or sliced frozen
    carrot
½ cup canned cream of celery
    soup
½ cup canned cream of
    mushroom soup
pinch dried thyme
pinch dried marjoram or
    oregano
few button mushrooms
    (optional)
½ cup breadcrumbs
1 teaspoon unsalted butter
1 tablespoon chopped fresh
    parsley or basil
Parmesan cheese (optional)

Time: 6½ minutes

Mix first 5 ingredients and button mushrooms if used and place in a glass bowl or casserole dish. Melt butter in a cup for 30 seconds. Toss breadcrumbs into butter, stir and sprinkle over mixture.

Cook 6 minutes on high. Serve garnished with fresh parsley or basil and Parmesan cheese if liked.

Vegetable Soup

½ can celery soup
½ can water
1 stalk celery, chopped
½ cup frozen lima beans
½ cup frozen broccoli, broken
    into florets
1 zucchini, chopped
½ cup chopped white meat

Time: 2½ minutes

Combine all ingredients in a large bowl. Cover with greaseproof paper and cook 2½ minutes on high.

Herbed Carrots

Step 1 Combine carrot, soups and herbs in a glass bowl

Step 2 Toss breadcrumbs in melted butter, sprinkle over mixture and cook 6 minutes

Step 3 Garnish with herbs and Parmesan cheese

Herbed Carrots

194

Rice and Pasta

Rice cooks in the microwave in about two-thirds of the normal cooking time. Varieties such as Sun Gold Vita Rice will be fluffy and tender in five minutes — which makes rice the ideal basis for a meal for the Solo Cook.

If you decide to cook extra and freeze the leftovers, simply defrost in the microwave for two minutes. Cold rice is delicious as a salad served with a vinaigrette dressing or mayonnaise.

Easy Paella

½ cup cooked rice
½ onion, chopped
½ small can prawns or a few
  fresh green prawns, shelled
½ cup any cooked, diced fish
1 tomato
½ cup white wine
pinch oregano

Time: 3 minutes

Combine first 4 ingredients and place in a large glass mixing bowl. Pour over wine. Slice tomato and arrange on top of rice mixture. Sprinkle with oregano. Cook on low 3 minutes.

Variation: To give this dish the full Spanish treatment colour the rice with saffron and add some fresh peas.

Rice with Leftovers

1 cup cooked rice
½ can asparagus cuts, drained
1 cup cooked white meat pieces
1 small can whole mushrooms in
  butter sauce
1 can diced capsicum, drained
2 tablespoons fresh chopped basil
  (optional)

Time: 2½ minutes

Combine all ingredients in a mixing bowl and heat 1½ minutes on high. Mix and cook for 1 minute more. Serve with vegetables for a hearty meal.

Mediterranean Medley

⅓ cup Sun Gold Vita Rice
1 can tomatoes, drained
few olives (optional)
handful of raisins
1 clove garlic, crushed
½ cup grated Parmesan cheese
chopped fresh basil for garnish

Time: 5 minutes

Add equal quantity of boiling water to rice in bowl large enough to allow rice to swell. Put aside for 40 minutes. When rice is soft mix all ingredients together. Cook on low 5 minutes or until rice is tender. Garnish with basil.

196

Spinach Fettucine with Anchovies

200 g fettucine
1 small can sardines or
  anchovies
1 tablespoon grated Parmesan
  cheese
¼ red capsicum

Time: 10½ minutes

Place fettucine in glass mixing bowl and cover with hot water. Cook on high 10 minutes. Drain off water.

Empty can of sardines, including oil, into bowl. Mix well and heat for 30 seconds. Garnish with capsicum, sliced into thin strips and Parmesan cheese.

Step 1 Cover fettucine with hot water, cook 10 minutes and drain

Step 2 Mix anchovies through fettucine and heat on high 30 seconds

Simple Fried Rice

½ cup Sun Gold Vita Rice, pre-
  soaked
1 onion, chopped
1 small can mushrooms in butter
  sauce
1 small can prawns
¼ cup chopped almonds or
  toasted slivered almonds
1 egg
sliced shallots (optional)

Time: 5½ minutes

Combine onion, mushrooms, prawns and almonds in a large
glass bowl. Cover and cook 2½ minutes on high. Mix beaten
egg into rice and stir in prawn mixture. Cook, covered, 3 minutes. Let stand before serving. Garnish with shallots.

Fried Rice

Step 1 Combine onions, mushrooms,
       prawns and almonds in a large
       glass bowl, cover and cook
       2½ minutes
Step 2 Mix beaten egg into rice, stir in
       prawn mixture and cook,
       covered, 3 minutes

Main Meals in Moments

Meat, fish and chicken are still the most popular dishes for main meals — especially if the Solo Cook has only had a light luncheon. These recipes cooked in the microwave will provide a substantial and nourishing meal in half the time of conventional cooking.

As meat does not brown in the microwave to the same extent as in conventional ovens, fruits, sauces and vegetables come into their own both to mask and beautifully complement the flavour of the meat. Take care not to overcook meat, fish and chicken. Cooking times given are only approximate. Remember, it's best to undercook, check, then cook a little more if necessary.

Lemon Fish

1 frozen fish fillet
1 small onion, chopped
2 slices lemon

Time: 2–3 minutes

Place fish on serving plate. Sprinkle over onion and top with lemon slices. Cook on paper 2 minutes on high. Check. Depending on size, a minute more cooking time may be required.

Mackerel with Mushroom Sauce

1 can cream of mushroom soup
1 cup milk
½ teaspoon cumin
1 can mackerel
½ cup Weet-bix, Vita-brits, or
  Weeties crumbs

Time: 3 minutes

Mix soup with milk and cumin until smooth. Place mackerel in medium-sized glass bowl or casserole dish. Pour soup mixture over fish. Sprinkle crumbs on top to cover. Cook 3 minutes on high.

Prawns with Vegetables

200 g shelled, cooked prawns,
  fresh or frozen
½ cup chopped onion
2 cauliflower florets
2 broccoli florets
1 medium-sized carrot, thinly
  sliced
¼ cup coarsely chopped
  capsicum
½ can peeled tomatoes
½ can onion soup
1 tablespoon sherry

Time: 6 minutes

Combine prawns, onion, cauliflower, broccoli, carrot and capsicum. Place in a large glass bowl, cover with greaseproof paper and cook on high 3 minutes.

Meanwhile mix tomato, soup and sherry together and stir mixture into vegetables. Cook 3 minutes more. Let stand 2 minutes before serving.

This amount is enough for 2 meals. Refrigerate half. Before next serving, add 1 tablespoon water and reheat for 2 minutes.

Prawns with vegetables

Step 1 Place prawns, onion, cauliflower, broccoli, carrot and capsicums in bowl, cover and cook 3 minutes

Step 2 Mix together tomatoes, soup and sherry

Step 3 Stir into vegetable mixture and cook 3 minutes

Prawns with Vegetables

Fillet Steak with Piquant Sauce

1 piece eye fillet of beef
3–4 anchovy or sardine fillets
1 egg
1 teaspoon brandy
2 teaspoons Dijon mustard
½ onion, chopped
1 tablespoon chopped dill
    pickles
1 slice fresh or canned
    pineapple

Time: 3½ minutes

Cook steak on serving dish on high 2 minutes. Meanwhile make sauce by mashing sardines or anchovies in bowl with egg, brandy and mustard. Mix well. Add onion and pickles.

When meat is ready, remove from oven and cover completely with sauce. Return meat to oven and cook on low 1½ minutes. Let stand 1 minute before serving.

Serve with pineapple rings. Snow peas, mushrooms and cherry tomatoes make ideal accompaniments.

Beef and Vegetable Kebabs

1 tablespoon teriyaki sauce
1 tablespoon honey
½ clove garlic, crushed
1 tablespoon dry sherry
pinch ground ginger
1 beef steak, thickly cut
6 cherry tomatoes
4 shallots
½ capsicum
6 button mushrooms

Time: 1–2 minutes

Combine first 5 ingredients in a bowl. Cut steak into cubes and add to the mixture. Marinate 1 hour.

Wash and dry tomatoes. Trim shallots and cut capsicum into squares. Wash and trim mushrooms.

Thread beef and vegetables alternately on skewers. Cook on medium 1½ minutes. Brush kebabs with marinade and heat a further 20 seconds on high. Serve with a crisp salad or fried rice.

Beef in Red Wine

1 cup cooked beef, cut into thin
    strips
½ cup red wine
2 whole peppercorns
3 tablespoons vinegar
½ cup sultanas
½ cup walnuts
chopped shallots for garnish

Time: 4 minutes

In a medium-sized glass bowl mix wine and vinegar and add peppercorns and sultanas. Marinate beef in the mixture for 15 minutes. Stir in walnuts. Cook 2 minutes on high, stir and cook a further 2 minutes. Garnish with shallots and serve with any short pasta.

Pork and Bitters

1 pork chop or piece pork fillet
Dijon mustard
1 potato, peeled and sliced
2 medium-sized onions, sliced
¼ cup diced celery
½ can tomato puree
1 teaspoon angostura bitters
1 jar stewed apple baby food
cherry tomatoes for garnish

Time: 13½ minutes

Rub pork with mustard. Let stand. Arrange vegetables in layers in a glass bowl or casserole. Add tomato puree, and angostura bitters. Cook on low 10 minutes. Remove vegetables from oven, cover and let stand. Cook meat on serving dish 2½ minutes on high. Pork must be well cooked.

Arrange vegetables around pork and pour over apple. Heat 1 minute. Garnish with cherry tomatoes.

Beef in Red Wine

Step 1 Mix wine and vinegar in a medium-sized bowl and add peppercorns and sultanas

Step 2 Marinate beef in mixture for 15 minutes

Step 3 Add walnuts and cook 4 minutes stirring once during cooking

Fillet Steak with Piquant Sauce

Lamb with Mushrooms

2 lamb chops
1 can mushrooms in butter
sauce
1 can French onion soup
½ cup water

Time: about 3 minutes

Add water to soup and mix well. Stir in mushrooms. Place lamb chops on serving dish and cover with sauce. Cook 3 minutes on high or until well done.

Apricot Lamb

1 lamb chop
1 tablespoon apricot jam

Place lamb chop on serving dish and cover with apricot jam. Cook 2 minutes on high.

Mediterranean Lamb

1 cup diced, cooked lamb
½ cup Ratatouille (see recipe)
black olives and dill for garnish

Place lamb in small glass bowl and cook on low 3 minutes. Spoon Ratatouille over and cook on high a further 3 minutes. Garnish with black olives and dill.

Mustard Chicken

1 cooked chicken piece
1 tablespoon mustard powder

Time: 1½ minutes

Rub chicken over with mustard powder. Cook on serving dish on high 1½ minutes.

Chicken Tropicana

1 cup chopped cooked chicken
1 banana, peeled
1 can mango or 1 fresh mango,
peeled and sliced
1 can tomatoes
½ cup ginger wine or white
wine
1 clove garlic, crushed
1 small choko, peeled and
cored

Time: 4 minutes

Chop banana and choko into bite size chunks. Combine with chicken, mango, tomato and garlic and mix well. Place mixture into a large glass bowl. Cover with paper towel and cook on low 4 minutes.

Allow to stand for 3 minutes before eating to allow diffusion of flavour. Zucchini may be used instead of choko.

Chicken Curry

¼ teaspoon turmeric
¼ teaspoon powdered ginger
¼ teaspoon cayenne pepper
2 tablespoons sunflower oil
1 chicken breast

Time: 3 minutes

Combine spices with oil in a cup and heat 50 seconds. Let stand. Arrange chicken on dinner plate. Pour over curry mixture and cook on high 2 minutes. Serve with rice.

Chicken Medley

1 cup chopped cooked chicken
or 1 whole chicken breast,
chopped
1 can cream of chicken soup
1 tomato, chopped
¼ cup sliced, stuffed olives
1 jar stewed apple baby food
1 clove garlic, crushed
1 tablespoon sherry

Time: 3 minutes

Combine all ingredients and mix well. Place in a large glass bowl. Cover with greaseproof paper and cook 3 minutes on high.

Fruity Desserts

There's no need for the Solo Cook to stop at one course. Fruit is nature's sweet convenience food, both delicious and nutritiously high in vitamin C, some B group vitamins and carotene. These tempting recipes are for those evenings when a dessert is favoured over a piece of raw fruit.

Champagne Peaches

2 canned peach halves
1 cup champagne or white grape
    juice
1 clove

Time: 2½ minutes

Place all ingredients in a glass jar. Liquid should cover the peaches, if not, add extra liquid. Cook on high 2½ minutes. Cover with lid and refrigerate when cool. Will keep at least 48 hours.

Gingered Banana Ice Cream

1 serve ice cream
½ cup chopped unsalted walnuts
    or macadamia nuts
3 tablespoons honey
3 tablespoons water
1 teaspoon unsalted butter
1 tablespoon chopped ginger in
    syrup
1 banana, sliced

Time: 2 minutes

Place ice cream in a dessert plate and sprinkle with nuts. Put in freezer. Combine honey, water, butter, ginger and banana in glass jar and cook 2 minutes on high until mushy. Cool. Pour over ice cream and eat immediately.

Pears in Wine

2 whole pears
1 cup white wine
pinch cinnamon

Time: 7 minutes

Wash pears. Prick skin in a few places with a fork and place in small glass bowl. Add wine and cinnamon. Cook on low for 5 minutes. Turn pears over and cook 2 minutes on high.

Creme de Menthe Pears

2 canned pear halves
2 teaspoons lemon juice
2 tablespoons creme de menthe
1 serve ice cream
shreds of orange peel, blanched

Time: 1 minute

Drain pear halves, reserving syrup. Pour syrup into large glass jar. Add lemon juice and creme de menthe and heat on high 1 minute. Add pears to liquid in jar. Put on lid and invert so that liquid pours over fruit. Serve either hot or cold with ice cream. Rum and a pinch of nutmeg can be substituted for the creme de menthe. Garnish with orange peel shreds.

Remaining pears in can can be stored for 2–3 days in refrigerator and served as an accompaniment to lamb or pork.

Note: Whole, peeled, fresh pears may be substituted for canned pear halves.

Baked Pawpaw

1 small firm pawpaw, yellow
    but not quite ready for eating
2 tablespoons Cointreau
¼ cup chopped unsalted nuts
1 tablespoon honey

Time: 2 minutes

Split pawpaw in half and scoop out seeds. Do not peel. Spoon 1 tablespoon Cointreau into each cavity. Combine nuts with honey and pour into cavity.

Place on paper towel and cook 3 minutes on high. Let stand 2 minutes before serving.

Hot Apple Slice

Hot Apple Slice

1 bought apple slice
1 tablespoon honey
cinnamon

Time: 1 minute

Brush honey over top of apple slice and sprinkle cinnamon over sparingly. Heat 1 minute on high. Check that slice is heated through completely.

Hot Pineapple Rings

2 canned pineapple rings
½ cup pineapple juice
small pinch powdered ginger

Time: 2 minutes

Place rings side by side on serving plate. Stir ginger into juice in can. Mix well. Pour juice over rings and cook 2 minutes on high.

Spirited Nightcap

1 orange and cinnamon teabag
1 liqueur glass Grand Marnier
  or Chartreuse
1 slice orange

Time: 1 minute

Make 1 cup orange and cinnamon tea. Add liqueur and orange. Stir and reheat 1 minute.

Cherries in Kirsch

½ can pitted cherries
½ liqueur glass Kirsch
pinch cinnamon

Place cherries in glass jar and cover with juice. Cook until mixture just begins to boil then add cinnamon and Kirsch. Screw lid on tightly and leave for ½ hour until cherries are cool and flavours have diffused.

Mulled Wine

½ cup claret
½ cup port
1 tablespoon currants
¼ teaspoon cinnamon or 1
  cinnamon stick
strawberry and lemon garnish

Time: 2 minutes

Combine all ingredients in a measuring jug and heat on high 2 minutes. Serve in a tall glass with a strawberry and a lemon twist.

Venus Potion

1 rosehip teabag
1 liqueur glass Marsala
1 clove

Time: 2½ minutes

Make 1 cup rosehip tea and pour into measuring jug. Add Marsala and clove. Heat on low 2½ minutes. Let stand 5 minutes before removing clove. Reheat if required.

Mulled Wine

The Magic of Microwave Entertaining

The Magic of Microwave Entertaining compiled by Douglas Marsland and Jan Wunderlich shows just how simple it is to cook in stages and serve up an elegant dinner party for eight or a large buffet lunch for family and friends. Recipes and menus are included for all entertaining occasions. Try them. Then try out your own.

Dinner Parties

Entertaining friends and family with a superb dinner is something we all love to do. First come the decisions: Who? When? What to serve? Then there are the busy preparations. You can make your microwave your number one helper and throw a thoroughly modern dinner party by mastering the simple steps of sequential cooking. The recipes in this book are all perfect candidates for microwave sequential cooking and the selected menus with their preparation timetables will show you how to get the most out of your microwave.

Roasted Rosemary Leg of Lamb

The Ground Rules for Success

It's a trend, a revolution, a national craze. I'm not talking about aerobics or punk fashions — those fads are passé. I mean the expanding passion for gourmet cooking, and its concomitant — the dinner party. Unfortunately, another major trend of modern life is an ever-increasing lack of spare time. A particularly vicious circle? No.

Whipping up an elegant three course dinner in a few hours isn't just a fiction perpetrated by those prototypes of a superior form of humanity who inhabit television commercials. Ordinary mortals can accomplish such wonders, too. With a little bit of forward planning, the correct use of kitchen appliances, the microwave and organisation, good fast food can prove to be synonymous with good, sophisticated, and highly enjoyable food.

Giving a dinner party is a little like show business. There's a lot of behind-the-scenes action and sleight of hand. When you orchestrate a dinner party, keep it within your scope and abilities. Don't try to do too much, have too many courses. Three courses is all you should attempt, making one or preferably two of them dishes you can do ahead or put together at the last minute. Always make a shopping list before you start, and draw up a plan of action down to the last detail.

Planning makes perfect
Begin your planning by selecting the main dish, then plan other foods around it. Do think of colour. Consider a meal of lobster bisque, chicken in a creamed sauce and creme caramel. If there is anything good to say about it, well, it would be perfect for someone with a stomach ulcer.

Texture and taste are the next considerations. Something crunchy, something smooth. A crisp mignonette and watercress salad is a better partner for veal fillets with avocado and hollandaise sauce (*see recipe*) or veal zurichoise (a classic Swiss dish of veal strips, cream and mushrooms), than a vegetable salad breaststroking in mayonnaise.

Go for choices like suavely sauced turkey, venison (*see recipe*) or chicken breasts (*see recipe*) preceded by a basil-scented tagliatelle entree (*see recipe*). Hide a few surprises in some of your dishes. Fresh dill with fresh peas, grated carrot in rice, slivers of ham with broccoli, a dash or slurp of wine in a creamy fish dish. Roasts are perfectly sound choices for a dinner party, but they need an imaginative accompaniment. A successful menu is always provocative to the palate, never 'beige'.

It's old advice, but when preparing for a dinner party never attempt a dish for the first time. Murphy's Law bedevils the dinner party cook. Simple first courses, such as soup, pasta, flan, prosciutto and melon, salads and seafood, that can be made ahead of time are invaluable, because odds on the main course and accompaniments will take up the lion's share of your attention.

It's fast, it's efficient, it's microwave
The microwave oven has been the Australian kitchen success story of the past five years, and with good reason. It's fast, it's efficient, it's today. Unfortunately far too many people view the microwave as a thing apart, restricting its use to heating pre-cooked foods or 'doing' the vegetables. However, cooks that learn the techniques of sequential microwave cooking are more than seven steps ahead in throwing the thoroughly modern dinner party. Used alone or in conjunction with a conventional oven and range, the microwave can be your number one helper.

Microwave sequential cooking involves partially cooking one item while you prepare another, removing the first dish from the oven while you micro-cook its successor, and then returning the first dish to the oven to complete calculated cooking time. Meats, casseroles, potato and rice dishes are all perfect candidates for sequential cooking, as are recipes that can be divided into several steps. In short, do everything ahead, then simply heat when you want to serve.

A good example of a 'step' recipe is a vegetable accompanied by a sauce. The vegetable is cooked first, then the sauce is prepared, and finally the two are reheated together. As a general rule of thumb, you can sequence foods in the following order: desserts and foods that need to be pre-cooked; large cuts of meat, potatoes and small cuts of meat; and then foods that need to be reheated. For an average dinner party, plan a menu that includes two or three recipes cooked in the microwave.

Smooth, satiny microwave sauces

The making of sweet and savoury sauces is one of the areas where the microwave really comes into its own. Beautifully smooth and satiny, many can be measured, mixed and cooked in the same bowl or casserole. With no pots, pans or potential scorching and sticking involved, microwave owners are far more likely to create delicious sauces that make entertaining that much easier.

Perhaps the most versatile microwave sauce is the basic white sauce based on a roux. A good all-purpose sauce with myriad permutations, it can be made with fish, beef or chicken stock; milk or cream; or a mixture of white wine and milk. Chopped herbs such as dill, basil, chives and parsley, grated cheese, mustard, curry powder, chopped anchovies, prawns, and flaked crab are just a few of the additions you can make to this versatile sauce to serve with poultry, veal, fish and beef. Simply cooked meats become superlative with a good, well-flavoured sauce.

Sweet cornflour sauces, egg-based custards, chocolate and fruit sauces are also quick and easy to make in the microwave. Again, even the simplest fruit compote or pudding can be transformed into a knock-your-eye-out dessert with a well-made sweet sauce.

Fruits in season

Always take advantage of what the season has to offer. Melon, grapefruit and figs all make perfect first courses when combined with smoked chicken, baby mozzarella, ham or smoked beef. Fruits can also stand in as a quick, easy touch of glamour dessert. Envisage fresh strawberries with champagne, pineapple in kirsch or plums in marsala. Similarly vegetables of the moment can front up in simple entree soups, souffles, as crepe fillings, pureed, or tossed in butter and herbs.

Cheese makes a superbly simple last course, especially if you have planned an ambitious main course. Camembert, Brie and chevre are popular choices. Always allow cheese to mellow at room temperature for full enjoyment.

Setting the mood

Never let anyone tell you that great food tastes the same on Pyrex as on porcelain. Because the eye is partner to the palate, it usually tastes better on the latter. Pay attention to table setting. A white cloth is the ideal napery, setting off just about every pattern. You don't need to own heirloom china, just a set that suits food and matches.

Always polish cutlery first — there is nothing more off-putting than knives and forks carrying the legacies of your last dinner party. Polished glasses are another must. Offer people a choice of red or white wine and lay out two glasses right from the beginning. Flowers make superb centrepieces, but steer clear of highly scented ones. Fruit is also a top table decoration, with the added bonus that you can eat it afterwards.

Many a good meal has been spoiled by Tchaikovsky's 1812 Overture or Janis Ian's Seventeen. Choose background music carefully. Never play music with 'peaks' and 'troughs'. You don't want people's appetites blunted by crescendos and painful memories.

My final advice for a successful dinner party? Invite the people you like, not the ones you think you ought to ask.

EK

Food and Wine Chemistry

As Australian palates become more adventurous in the choice of food and wine the old rules, red if by turf and white if by surf, are becoming less trustworthy. What use are they in the face of exotic ethnic foods? What help do they give the poor benighted soul in a restaurant trying to order a bottle of wine when one person has ordered crab, another has decided on roast beef and yet a third has plumped for chicken?

Play it safe or take a risk?

The chief aim of wine is to accentuate the flavours of the food, and likewise food should always enhance the character of the wine. Such rigid formulas as red wine with red meat and game and white wine with white meat and fish will always be 'safe' choices, but they should never become, nor were they ever intended to be, rigid concepts. Anyone truly interested in food should be willing to experiment, take a few gastronomic risks with other more interesting combinations and even attempt a few apparently 'strange' ones. That said, let's take a look at the important parameters that still have to be borne in mind.

Wine and food partnerships

Champagne, dry vermouth, dry sherry and rose all make good opening wines for dinner, especially when the first course is smoked fish, an egg or vegetable dish or traditional type hors d'oeuvres. They are not sweet and therefore do the job of perking up the palate for what is to follow.

Depending on the richness of the ingredients, pates and terrines respond well to dry, fruity reds and whites and rose. The more strongly flavoured meat varieties obviously require stronger reds. Most pasta meals marry well with light reds and tangy whites, but if a heavy meat sauce or filling is involved a fuller bodied red is more suitable. Well-flavoured rice dishes such as paella and pastry main courses are also best matched with red wine.

As a general rule, light, slightly acid dry whites such as chablis, white burgundy and fumé blanc are the number one choices for fish, although a good rose is a solid selection for baked or highly seasoned fish dishes.

As chicken is to the cook what an empty canvas is to the painter, it can accommodate a great variety of wines depending on the cooking method and other ingredients involved. Light dry reds are good with highly seasoned or casseroled dishes, but in general slightly sweet white wines are the preferred choices. Turkey and duck have stronger tastes than chicken and easily merit a full-bodied white or light red.

Beef has always had an almost symbiotic relationship with full, dry reds but if a dish is highly seasoned, or you have used a budget cut, a really great wine would be wasted. The traditional wines with veal, pork and ham are rose or slightly sweet whites, but if you like spices with these meats, young fruity reds are a much better choice.

Dessert souffles, creams and mousses go well with champagne, sweet whites, and in some cases, cream sherry and madeira. Fresh fruit and fruit-based concoctions are beautiful with sauternes. Peaches are excellent with Barsac, apricots meld best with port. But take care with apple and orange desserts. Because of their acid/sugar ratio apples need a fruity white to achieve a good balance of taste. The citric acid in oranges is so dominant that only a low acid red can cope successfully.

Chart your own course
Fiery spices are well-known palate paralysers, therefore hot Asian curries and other highly spiced foods are infinitely better suited to beer or plain water. This should never be a blanket rule, however, as mild curries respond well to a good traminer.

Chinese food has also failed to 'demand' the right wine, and now that we are expanding our knowledge of one of the world's greatest cuisines beyond Australian-influenced Cantonese, the problem is even more difficult. For example, highly spiced Szechwan food needs beer, while milder Peking-style food can deal with a slightly sweet, fruity white. Gastronomcs exploring the different cuisines of China are still advised to chart their own course.

Champagne
You often hear the cry 'champagne goes with everything', but anyone who has ever washed down a chocolate dessert with it knows that this commonly held belief simply is not true. This is not to say that you cannot serve champagne throughout a meal, because if there is one wine which can claim to suit most things it is certainly champagne, but never let this deter you from making a superior wine selection. If you do want to give an air of profligacy to the whole meal, choose a rose champagne. Its fuller taste makes it the most suitable choice, especially for light meats such as chicken, veal and fish.

Suggestions of good wine and food partnerships should never be the death knell of spontaneity. Celestial unions such as Roquefort and sweet dessert wines, hot oyster dishes with light reds and dry sherry with seafood are just a few of the pleasures we owe to iconoclasts who went against conventional wisdom.   EK

Menu Number 1
Elegant Dinner Party for 4 or 6

Brie and Smoked Salmon Flan
Fillet of Beef with Oyster Sauce
Parsley French Potatoes
Broccoli and Carrot Saute
Pistachio Orange Souffle

This dinner menu is beautifully balanced at all levels — colour, texture, theme, and taste. The light familiar flan is given an unusual twist by the use of smoked salmon and is a perfect foil for the richer, more traditional main meal.

Brie and Smoked Salmon Flan (top); Broccoli and Carrot Saute;
Fillet of Beef with Oyster Sauce (centre); Pistachio Orange Souffle and
Parsley French Potatoes (bottom)

Preparation Timetable

Week ahead: Prepare and cook pastry crust for Brie and Smoked Salmon Flan. Allow to cool, then wrap securely in plastic. Freeze.

Day ahead: Take pastry crust from freezer. Remove wrap and thaw. Prepare and cook souffle. Spoon mixture into prepared souffle dishes and allow to set in refrigerator. Do not decorate until just before serving.

Prepare filling for flan and pour into crust. Cook. Allow flan to cool and then cover with plastic wrap. Do **not** refrigerate.

Place white wine into refrigerator to chill. Check table-cloth, serviettes, glassware, dinnerware and cutlery. Ensure that all are clean, polished and ready to use. Prepare any after-dinner chocolates and store in an airtight container.

3 hours before: Set table and arrange flowers. Prepare tray for pre-dinner drinks and hors d'oeuvres.

2 hours before: Prepare ingredients for Broccoli and Carrot Saute. Cook recipe for 5-6 minutes. Remove from microwave, cover and allow to stand.

1 hour before: Prepare Fillet of Beef. Cook steaks for 10-15 minutes. Remove from browning dish and place onto a microwave-safe platter. Cover and set aside. Cook Oyster Sauce omitting the oysters. Cover sauce with plastic wrap, ensuring that wrap rests on sauce to stop skin forming.

30 minutes before: Prepare and cook Parsley French Potatoes for 8 minutes. Uncover and drain. Add butter and sprinkle with parsley and celery salt. Cook on high 2 minutes. Remove from oven and set aside.

Open red wine to allow it to breathe.

15 minutes before: Cut flan into portions and place onto entree plates. Garnish with parsley and a lemon twist.

Time for dinner: Serve Brie and Smoked Salmon Flan.

Reheat covered Broccoli and Carrot Saute 2 minutes on high. Remove from oven and heat Oyster Sauce 2 minutes on high. Set aside. When reheated do not remove coverings from dishes.

Reheat uncovered Fillet of Beef on high 3 minutes. Remove from oven and cover with foil. Reheat Parsley French Potatoes on high 2 minutes. While potatoes are reheating, arrange Fillet of Beef and Broccoli and Carrot Saute onto dinner plates. Add oysters to sauce and pour over beef. Serve potatoes separately. Heat fresh bread rolls for 30 seconds. Enjoy your meal.

Garnish Pistachio Orange Souffle with orange slices and extra crushed pistachio nuts and serve.

The final touch: While your guests are resting after the superbly microwaved meal you may be able to tempt them with Irish coffee and chocolates.

HINT: COOKING IN BATCHES

To make entertaining easier, use your conventional oven as a warming drawer when cooking large quantities in batches in your microwave.

NOTE: RECIPE TIMES

Recipes in this book are timed for cooking in 600 or 650 watt ovens. If you are using a 500 watt oven add an extra minute or two to cooking times. For one of the larger 750 watt ovens, take off a minute or two.

Brie and Smoked Salmon Flan

Time: 23 minutes — Serves 6

Pastry
1½ cups flour
salt to taste
2 teaspoons ground black pepper
2 teaspoons mixed herbs
30 g butter
15 g lard
cold water

Filling
125 g smoked salmon
250 g Brie round, sliced
300 mL cream
3 eggs
2 tablespoons mixed herbs
1 teaspoon pepper
6 shallots, chopped
paprika

Combine flour, salt, black pepper and mixed herbs. Rub in butter and lard. Mix through enough water to form a soft dough. Knead dough lightly on a floured board, roll out and line individual pie dishes or a 22 cm pie plate. Trim edges and prick base of dough with fork. Cook pastry on high 6–8 minutes. Allow to cool slightly before filling.

Layer salmon then cheese on pastry base. Combine remaining filling ingredients, except paprika, and pour into crust. Sprinkle top lightly with paprika and cook on medium 10–15 minutes. JW

Fillet of Beef with Oyster Sauce

Time: 32 minutes — Serves 6

6 fillet steaks
1 tablespoon butter
1 clove garlic, crushed

Oyster Sauce
1 tablespoon oil
1 tablespoon cornflour
1 tablespoon parsley, chopped
salt and pepper
dash Worcestershire sauce
1 cup dry white wine
dash medium-sweet sherry
24 oysters

Preheat browning dish on high 7 minutes. Add butter and garlic. Cook 1 minute more then sear steaks. Cook steaks, 3 at a time, on high for 9 minutes, turning once.

Combine all ingredients for sauce and cook on high 3–5 minutes. Stir vigorously then add oysters.

Arrange steaks on a microwave-safe dish, reheat on high 30–60 seconds and serve with sauce. JW

Brie and Smoked Salmon Flan: **Step 1** Layer salmon and brie on pastry case

Step 2 Combine remaining filling ingredients

Step 3 Spoon egg mixture into crust

Parsley French Potatoes

Time: 11 minutes — Serves 4–6

4 medium-sized potatoes, peeled
1 tablespoon butter, melted
1 tablespoon freshly chopped parsley
celery salt

Cut potatoes into 0.5 cm thick slices and layer in shallow dish. Cover and cook on high 8 minutes. Uncover and drain. Pour over melted butter and sprinkle with parsley and celery salt. Cook on high 3 minutes and serve.   JW

Broccoli and Carrot Saute

Time: 8 minutes — Serves 4

500 g broccoli spears
3 carrots, peeled
2 tablespoons butter
freshly ground black pepper
1 tablespoon oregano
juice and rind of 1 lemon

Trim broccoli and cut into 2.5 cm spears. Cut carrots into 2.5 cm julienne strips.

Combine all ingredients in a shallow dish. Cover and cook on high 6–8 minutes. Allow to stand covered for 5 minutes.   JW

Pistachio Orange Souffle

Time: 5½ minutes — Serves 6

10 eggs, separated
2 cups sugar
½ cup orange juice
½ cup lime juice
grated rind 2 oranges
pinch salt
2 tablespoons gelatine
¼ cup water
2 cups cream
½ cup pistachio nuts, crushed

Garnish
orange slices
extra crushed pistachio nuts

Place egg yolks in mixing bowl and beat with electric mixer until fluffy. Add sugar and continue to beat till creamy. Cook on high 4 minutes, stirring occasionally. Add orange, lime juice and rind and blend thoroughly. Set aside.

Place gelatine and water into small bowl and cook on high 1½ minutes. Stir and set aside to cool. Whisk egg whites till stiff then add pinch salt. Whip cream.

Fold together gelatine, egg yolk mixture, egg whites and cream. Divide mixture between 6 individual 200 mL souffle dishes and chill for 2 hours.

Decorate with orange slices and crushed pistachio nuts.
JW

215

Menu Number 2

Dinner Party to Delight 4 or 6

Classic French Onion Soup
Parsley Veal Escalopes
Lemon Artichoke with Buttered Peas
Cauliflower with Almonds
French Cherry Tart

Our second dinner party menu is a well-rounded combination of the traditional and the inventive, is visually exciting, but simplicity to prepare. The onion soup entree is a tried and true winner, a stand-by of French cooking. The main meal combines flavours and textures that will delight and surprise your guests. The crunchy-topped veal is beautifully complemented by the vegetable dishes. For a rich but clean finish the cherry tart is perfection. Let the mellow mood of the evening slowly settle with coffee, liqueurs and chocolates.

French Cherry Tart (top right); Cauliflower with Almonds and Parsley Veal Escalopes (centre, left to right); Classic French Onion Soup (bottom)

Preparation Timetable

Week ahead: Prepare and cook pastry crust for French Cherry Tart. Allow to cool then wrap securely in plastic wrap. Freeze.

Day ahead: Take pastry crust from freezer. Unwrap and thaw. Prepare cherry filling for tart and set aside.

Prepare bouillon for Classic French Onion Soup. Allow to cool and then refrigerate.

Prepare artichokes. Trim and place lemon slices between leaves. Arrange in dish, pour over melted butter, cover and refrigerate.

Core cauliflower and place head on plate, cover and refrigerate.

Arrange cherries and pour filling into pastry base for French Cherry Tart. Cook then allow to cool. Do **not** refrigerate.

Place white wine in refrigerator to chill. Check table-cloth, serviettes, glassware, dinnerware and cutlery. Ensure that all are clean and polished. Prepare any after-dinner chocolates and store in an airtight container.

3 hours before: Set table. Arrange flowers or table decoration. Set up tray for pre-dinner drinks and hors d'oeuvres.

Cook onions for Classic French Onion Soup. Slice bread, grate cheese and set aside.

Prepare parsley and breadcrumb mix for Parsley Veal Escalopes. Coat veal and place ready to cook in shallow dish and cover. Cook cauliflower and set aside, keeping covered. Cook artichokes and peas. Toss together and set aside in serving bowl, covered.

1 hour before: Reheat bouillon, covered, on high 15 minutes and set aside.

30 minutes before: Uncork red wine and allow to breathe. Add onions to bouillon and cook on high 15 minutes, keep covered.

15 minutes before: Heat butter and almonds for cauliflower, pour over cauliflower. Cook Parsley Veal Escalopes for 6 minutes, Keep covered and set aside.

Place French Cherry Tart on serving dishes and whip cream.

Time for dinner: Reheat soup on high 5 minutes then top with bread and cheese, cook further 1–2 minutes on high and serve piping hot.

For the main course reheat veal uncovered on high 2 minutes then reheat artichoke and peas, covered, on high 2 minutes. Reheat Cauliflower and Almonds on high 2 minutes, covered. When all dishes have been reheated, arrange veal on platter and serve with uncovered artichokes and peas and cauliflower. Enjoy your dinner.

Serve French Cherry Tart for dessert with whipped cream, then tempt your guests with after-dinner chocolates, liqueurs and coffee.

Classic French Onion Soup

Time: 58 minutes — Serves 4–6

5 medium onions, peeled and sliced thinly
3 tablespoons butter
1 litre beef bouillon
½ teaspoon salt
freshly ground black pepper
6 slices French bread
¼ cup grated Gruyère cheese

Beef Bouillon
1 litre water
1 carrot, chopped
½ cup chopped turnip
2 leeks, chopped
1 bouquet garni
500 g soup beef with bone
1 teaspoon salt
freshly ground black pepper

To make bouillon: combine water, carrot, turnip, leeks, bouquet garni, beef and bone, salt and pepper in 4 litre casserole. Cover and cook on high 15 minutes, then a further 15 minutes on medium. Remove all vegetables, meat, bones and bouquet garni. Set stock aside.

Place onions and butter into 2 litre casserole dish. Cover and cook on high 5 minutes. Add bouillon, salt and pepper. Cover, cook on high 10 minutes, then a further 10 minutes on medium.

To serve: Uncover. Top soup with French bread and sprinkle over grated cheese. Cook on high 3 minutes and serve immediately.   JW

Parsley Veal Escalopes

Time: 10 minutes — Serves 4–6

freshly ground black pepper
60 g butter
4 tablespoons chopped parsley
2 cups soft wholegrain breadcrumbs
juice ½ lemon
1 egg, beaten
6 veal steaks

Combine pepper, butter, parsley, breadcrumbs, lemon juice and egg. Blend thoroughly.

Arrange veal steaks topped with parsley mix in a shallow dish. Cook covered on medium high 6–8 minutes, then a further 2 minutes on high uncovered.   JW

Lemon Artichoke with Buttered Peas

Time: 20 minutes — Serves 4–6

1 lemon, sliced
2 whole artichokes, trimmed
60 g butter, melted
freshly ground black pepper
500 g fresh peas, shelled
1 onion, finely chopped
2 tablespoons butter
juice ½ lemon

Cut lemon slices in half and place between artichoke leaves. Arrange artichokes in shallow dish, pour over melted butter, sprinkle with black pepper and cover with plastic wrap. Cook on high 6–8 minutes then allow to stand 5 minutes.

Place peas, onion and butter into shallow dish. Cover and cook on high 10–12 minutes. Stand 5 minutes.

Remove outer leaves from artichoke, cut artichoke hearts in quarters. Toss together artichoke leaves, hearts, peas and lemon juice and serve hot.   JW

Cauliflower with Almonds

Time: 16 minutes — Serves 6–8

1 whole head cauliflower
30 g butter
¼ cup almond flakes
freshly ground black pepper

Core cauliflower, keeping florets in shape of cauliflower. Place head on serving plate and cover in plastic wrap. Cook on high 12–14 minutes. Stand 5 minutes covered.

Place butter, almonds and pepper in shallow dish. Cook on high 1–2 minutes. Stir.

Uncover cauliflower, pour over butter, almonds and pepper mix and serve hot.   JW

French Cherry Tart

Time: 21 minutes — Serves 6

1 × 22 cm pastry crust (see recipe Hazelnut Pie)
2 eggs
½ cup caster sugar
4 tablespoons ground almonds
2 tablespoons sour cream
810 g can pitted black cherries, drained
½ teaspoon nutmeg
whipped cream

Beat together eggs, caster sugar, 2 tablespoons ground almonds and sour cream till fluffy.

Arrange cherries in a layer on base of pie crust. Pour over egg mixture. Sprinkle remaining almonds and nutmeg over pie. Cook on medium 15–20 minutes. Stand 5 minutes. Serve with whipped cream.   JW

French Cherry Tart: **Step 1** Beat together eggs, caster sugar, almonds and sour cream

Step 2 Arrange cherries in pie crust

Step 3 Pour egg mixture over cherries

Hors d'oeuvres

Hors d'oeuvres — tempting, bite-sized portions that stimulate both eye and appetite. Choose a single dish, simply served or offer a range with mouth-watering contrasts in colour, texture and flavour.

Crab Mousse

Time: 1 minute — Serves 8–10

1 tablespoon gelatine
2 tablespoons cold water
400 g crabmeat, flaked
2 teaspoons lemon juice
2 tablespoons white wine
⅔ cup mayonnaise
⅔ cup sour cream
¼ teaspoon cayenne pepper
pepper
1 packet toast squares
capers for garnish

Place gelatine and water in cup or small bowl and cook on high 1 minute. Stir and allow to cool slightly.

Combine crabmeat, lemon juice, wine, mayonnaise, sour cream and peppers. Gradually add gelatine mixture and blend. Spoon mixture into a prepared 4 cup mould. Chill for 2 to 3 hours. When firm, unmould. Slice thinly, place on toasts and garnish with capers.   JW

Crab Mousse: **Step 1** Combine crabmeat, lemon juice and wine

Step 2 Add mayonnaise and sour cream

Prawn and Curry Toasts

Time: 14 minutes — Serves 4

1 teaspoon cornflour
2 teaspoons curry powder
salt and pepper to taste
375 g green prawns, shelled, deveined and mashed
4 × 1 cm slices day-old wholegrain bread
1 egg white, lightly beaten
90 g pecan nuts, crushed
½ cup wholegrain breadcrumbs
¼ cup oil

Garnish

1 tablespoon fresh chopped parsley
½ lemon, finely sliced
extra prawns

Remove crusts from bread. Combine cornflour, curry powder, salt and pepper. Add mashed prawns, mix and spread over bread slices. Brush with egg white.

Mix together pecan nuts and breadcrumbs. Sprinkle evenly over prawn topping, pressing firmly into surface. Cut slices into quarters.

Preheat browning dish on high 6 minutes. Add oil and place squares 4 at a time on skillet, prawn side down. Cook 1 minute each side on high. Drain, cool and serve garnished with lemon twists, chopped parsley and extra prawns.   JW

Step 3 Gradually blend in gelatine mixture

Piri Piri Cashews

Time: 5½ minutes — Serves 4

2 teaspoons butter
185 g unsalted cashews
½ teaspoon cayenne pepper
½ teaspoon salt
dash nutmeg

Melt butter in mixing bowl on high for 30 seconds. Add cashews stirring until coated with butter. Cook 5 minutes on high. Drain.

Combine cayenne pepper, salt and nutmeg and sprinkle over cashews.   JW

Piri Piri Cashews (top left); Crab Mousse (centre) and Prawn and Curry Toasts (bottom)

Entrees

Today entrees or soup are most often served as the first course at a dinner party — or as an elegant light supper or luncheon dish. Attractively presented, they provide the magic that welcomes guests to the table.

Duck and Mushroom Pate Pots

Time: 12 minutes — Serves 6

Duck and Mushroom Pate

125 g rindless bacon, chopped
125 g veal, sliced thinly
125 g duck livers, cleaned and drained
60 g butter
1 leek, finely chopped
¼ cup port
salt and pepper to taste
¼ teaspoon thyme
1 egg
½ cup cream
6 small button mushrooms

Aspic

1 tablespoon gelatine
1 cup white wine
salt and pepper
½ tablespoon fresh dill, chopped

Serving Suggestion

celery sticks
carrot sticks
toast squares

Place bacon, veal, duck livers, butter, leek, port, salt, pepper and thyme in a shallow dish. Cover and cook on medium 10 minutes. Drain keeping 1 tablespoon of juice.

Transfer mixture to food processor bowl, add egg and cream and blend until smooth. Spoon into 6 pate pots. Thinly slice mushrooms and arrange slices on top of pate.

Combine aspic ingredients in small dish. Cook on high 2 minutes. Allow to cool without setting. Pour aspic over each pate and chill. Serve with toast squares, celery sticks or carrot sticks.   JW

Duck and Mushroom Pate Pots

Duck and Mushroom Pate Pots: **Step 1** Combine bacon, veal, livers, butter, leek, port and seasonings

Step 2 Transfer to food processor bowl, add egg and cream and blend

Step 3 Spoon pate into pots

Prawn and Scallop Brochettes with Saffron Rice

Time: 31 minutes — Serves 6

Prawn and Scallop Brochettes

18 green prawns, shelled and deveined
12 scallops
juice and rind of 1 lemon
6 shallots, chopped
freshly ground black pepper to taste
dash ground ginger
dash ground coriander
½ cup white wine
¼ cup sesame seeds
2 teaspoons oil

Saffron Rice

2 cups long-grain rice
3 cups water
pinch powdered saffron
salt and pepper to taste
1 tablespoon freshly chopped parsley

To make Prawn and Scallop Brochettes, thread 3 prawns and 2 scallops alternately on 6 wooden skewers and place into a shallow dish. Combine lemon juice, rind, shallots, pepper, ginger, coriander and white wine. Pour over brochettes, cover and marinate 1 hour. Drain and sprinkle with sesame seeds.

Preheat browning dish on high 5 minutes. Add oil and cook brochettes 4–6 minutes on high, turning once.

To prepare Saffron Rice, place ingredients in a 6 cup casserole. Cover and cook on high 15 minutes, then a further 5 minutes on medium. Allow to stand covered for 5 minutes.   JW

Chilled Borscht

Time: 20 minutes — Serves 4–6

1 litre rich beef stock or 2 cans consomme
125 mL sour cream or yoghurt
500 g beetroot
2 tablespoons lemon juice, strained
finely cut chives

Wash beetroot, remove stalks. Wrap each bulb in plastic wrap. Place in oven and cook on high 15–20 minutes. Turn beetroot over half way through cooking. Let stand, covered, 5 minutes.

When cooked, remove plastic wrap and peel and cut beetroot into small dice or grate.

Pour stock into serving bowl. Beat in cream or yoghurt until smooth. Add beetroot, lemon juice and chives. Refrigerate until chilled.

Top each serving with sour cream and garnish with a small piece of watercress or dill.

If preferred this soup may be pureed.   DM

The Main Course

It is usually the style and flavour of the main course which determines what comes before and after. So when designing dinner delights for your guests, always bear in mind, that it is the main meal which is paramount. In this section recipes are given for seafood, poultry, game and meat dishes. Among the traditional dinner recipes, like lobster and leg of lamb, there are some surprise recipes which will display your cooking talents and the range of the microwave oven to your guests.

Whole Baby Lobsters with Lemon Butter Sauce

Time: 15 minutes — Serves 2

Lobster
2 medium-sized lobsters, halved
salt and pepper to taste
½ teaspoon thyme
½ teaspoon oregano
2 tablespoons butter, melted
1 lemon, sliced

Lemon Butter
grated rind 1 lemon
200 g butter
salt and pepper to taste

Place lobster halves in shallow casserole dish. Season with salt, pepper, thyme, oregano and butter. Top with lemon slices. Cover and cook on medium for 15 minutes. Allow to stand covered.

Blend lemon rind, butter, salt and pepper till smooth. Serve lobster halves with lemon slices and lemon butter dotted on each tail.   JW

Whole Baby Lobsters with Lemon Butter Sauce

Whole Crumbed Whiting with Walnut Sauce

Time: 20 minutes — Serves 6

Crumbed Whiting

6 medium-sized whole whiting, washed and dried
2 eggs, beaten
2 tablespoons water
½ cup seasoned breadcrumbs
freshly ground black pepper
1 tablespoon freshly chopped parsley
½ teaspoon oregano
2 tablespoons oil

Walnut Sauce

½ cup crushed walnuts
¼ cup olive oil
¼ cup cream
salt and pepper to taste
dash nutmeg

Garnish

6 lemon wedges
freshly chopped parsley

Blend together egg and water. Combine breadcrumbs, pepper, parsley and oregano. Dip fish in egg mix and then coat with crumb mix. Refrigerate fish for 10 minutes.

Preheat browning dish on high 5 minutes. Add oil and cook fish, 3 at a time, 6–7 minutes on high, turning once.

Combine sauce ingredients in a bowl and cook 1 minute on high. Stir.

Serve fish with walnut sauce garnished with lemon wedges and parsley.   JW

Whole Fish with Cashew Nuts

Time: 14 minutes — Serves 8–10

1 × 1 kg silver bream
1 tablespoon lemon juice
2 shallots
2 slices green ginger, shredded finely
2–3 tablespoons peanut oil
2 tablespoons soy sauce
¼ cup finely chopped cashews
lemon slices for garnish

Prepare whole fish by trimming fins and tail. Remove or pierce eyes. Place three diagonal cuts on the thickest section of fish to ensure even cooking. Rub inside of fish lightly with salt and lemon juice, place on serving plate and cover with plastic wrap.

Trim and cut shallots into 5 cm sections, cut each section into 5 cm long strips and soak in cold water.

Cook fish on high 8–10 minutes. Place oil in basin. Cook on high 4 minutes.

Remove plastic wrap, pour soy sauce over fish and top with shallot strips and green ginger. Then pour over hot oil and add topping of chopped cashews. Serve hot with lemon garnish.   DM

Stuffed Trout

Time: 7 minutes — Serves 2

2 × 250 g whole trout
1 cup chopped, blanched broccoli
3 shallots, finely chopped
2 tablespoons butter
2 tablespoons roughly chopped cashews
60 g small shelled prawns
¼ teaspoon salt
¼ teaspoon lemon pepper
1 teaspoon lemon juice, strained

Place shallots and butter in a small bowl. Cook on high 1 minute. Add cashews, prawns, broccoli, salt and pepper.

Place trout in baking dish in single layer with the thickest part of the fish to the outside of the dish. Spoon prepared mixture into cavity of each fish. Arrange remaining mixture around trout and sprinkle with lemon juice.

Cover and cook on high 6 minutes or until fish flakes.
DM

Stuffed Trout: **Step 1** Mix shallots and butter together

Step 2 Add cashews, prawns, broccoli and seasonings

Step 3 Spoon stuffing into fish cavity

Jewfish Cutlets with Creamy Sauce

Jewfish Cutlets with Creamy Sauce

Time: 19½ minutes — Serves 6

6 medium jewfish cutlets	2 tablespoons lemon juice
1 tablespoon butter	150 mL cream
125 g mushrooms, sliced	1 tablespoon cornflour
60 g scallops, poached	1 teaspoon dill
6 shallots, finely chopped	pine nuts to garnish

Arrange jewfish cutlets in a shallow container in a single layer. Cover and cook on medium 10–15 minutes. Melt butter in a 1 litre casserole on high for 30 seconds. Add mushrooms, scallops, shallots and lemon juice. Cook on medium 2 minutes, stirring once.

Blend together cream, cornflour and dill. Add to mushroom mixture and stir. Cook on medium high 2 minutes. Stir.

Arrange jewfish cutlets on serving platter and pour over creamy sauce. Garnish with pine nuts.   JW

227

Whole Chicken Breasts, Florentine Style

Time: 9 minutes — Serves 4

¼ cup shredded carrot
¼ cup pine nuts
250 g frozen spinach, thawed, drained and chopped
2 cloves garlic, crushed
salt and pepper to taste
2 tablespoons freshly chopped parsley
4 whole chicken breasts, boned
1 egg, beaten
1 tablespoon water
dash nutmeg
1 cup seasoned breadcrumbs
1 tablespoon oil

Combine carrot, pine nuts, spinach, garlic, salt, pepper and parsley. Fill centre of chicken breasts with small portion of spinach mixture. Fold over and secure with wooden skewer or tie with string.

Blend egg and water. Combine nutmeg and breadcrumbs. Dip chicken breasts in egg mix and coat with breadcrumb mixture. Place on microwave roasting rack and cook on high 9 minutes, turning once during the cooking. Serve hot or cold.   JW

Potted Guinea Fowl with Cherry Sauce

Time: 75 minutes — Serves 6

6 small guinea fowl
juice and rind of 2 oranges
2 tablespoons butter, melted

Cherry Sauce
820 g can pitted black cherries
freshly ground black pepper
½ teaspoon marjoram

Combine orange juice, rind and butter and brush over guinea fowl. Place 3 guinea fowl on shallow roasting dish and cook on medium high 30 minutes or until fork tender. Transfer to individual pots, such as ramekins. Repeat for remaining guinea fowl.

Drain cherries, retaining 1 cup juice. Coarsely chop cherries. Combine sauce ingredients including cherry juice in a 2 litre mixing bowl. Cook on high 5 minutes.

Pour sauce over guinea fowl, cover pots and cook on high, 3 pots at a time 5–10 minutes to heat through. Serve in individual pots.   JW

Florentine Style Chicken Breasts served with pasta and salad

Roasted Rosemary Leg of Lamb

Time: 40 minutes — Serves 6-8

1.5–2 kg leg of lamb
2 tablespoons butter
2 cloves garlic, peeled and cut in slivers
2 sprigs fresh rosemary

Trim excess fat from lamb. Stud lamb with garlic slivers and sprigs of rosemary. Lightly coat with butter and place, fat side down, on a roasting rack in a shallow casserole dish.

Cover and cook for 35–40 minutes on high. Wrap in foil and allow to stand for 10 minutes before carving.   JW

Roast Venison with Green Peppercorn Sauce

Time: 76 minutes — Serves 6

1.5 kg leg of venison
2 cloves garlic, chopped
1 cup white vinegar
1 cup dry white wine
½ cup oil
1 teaspoon ground cloves
1 teaspoon thyme
1 teaspoon coriander
salt and pepper to taste

Green Peppercorn Sauce
2 tablespoons oil
1 tablespoon cornflour
125 mL sour cream
¼ cup green peppercorns

Slit surface of meat and insert small pieces of garlic. Combine vinegar, wine, oil, cloves, thyme, coriander, salt and pepper in a large bowl, add meat and marinate 2–3 hours. Drain, retaining 250 mL of marinade.

Preheat browning dish on high 5 minutes. Cook venison on medium high 8 minutes, turning after 4 minutes.

Transfer meat to a shallow roasting dish, pour over marinade and cover. Cook on medium 30 minutes, turn and cook a further 20–30 minutes or until fork tender. Stand covered for 10 minutes before carving.

During standing time prepare sauce by combining oil, cornflour, sour cream and peppercorns. Cook on high 3 minutes. Stir vigorously and serve with venison.   JW

Roasted Rosemary Leg of Lamb

Veal Fillets with Avocado and Hollandaise Sauce

Time: 17 minutes — Serves 6

1 tablespoon oil
6 veal fillets
1 large ripe avocado, peeled and sliced

Hollandaise Sauce

100 g butter
3 egg yolks
2 tablespoons lemon juice or white wine or tarragon vinegar
salt and pepper to taste

To prepare sauce, place butter in bowl and melt on high 1 minute. Beat together egg yolks, lemon juice, salt and pepper and stir into the melted butter. Cook on defrost 4 minutes, stirring every 30–45 seconds. Beat sauce while it cools. Sauce will thicken on cooling.

Preheat browning dish on high 4 minutes. Add oil and cook veal fillets, 3 at a time, on high 4 minutes, turning once. Repeat for remaining fillets.

Serve veal topped with avocado slice and hollandaise sauce. JW

Hollandaise Sauce: **Step 1** Combine lemon juice, egg yolks, and seasonings

Step 2 Add melted butter and whisk

Bechamel (White) Sauce

Time: 5½ minutes — Makes 1 cup

1 tablespoon butter
1 tablespoon cornflour
1 cup milk
salt and pepper to taste

Place butter into glass jug. Cook on high 30 seconds. Blend cornflour, milk, salt and pepper and cook on high 3–5 minutes. Sauce will become firm, similar to a semi-set jelly. Beat vigorously with wooden spoon or balloon whisk.

For a thicker sauce, cook a further 1–2 minutes on high.

To thin sauce, continue beating, gradually adding extra liquid.

Variations

Brandy and Mushroom Sauce

1 cup bechamel
1 tablespoon brandy
¼ cup sliced button mushrooms
1 tablespoon chopped parsley

Place brandy, mushrooms and parsley in glass jug. Cover and cook on high 2 minutes. Combine mushroom mix with white sauce.

Serve with pork, beef or veal.

Step 3 Cook on defrost stirring every 30–45 seconds

Mustard and Onion Sauce

1 cup bechamel
1 tablespoon wholegrain mustard
1 small onion, finely chopped

Place mustard and onion into glass jug, cover and cook on high 1 minute. Combine mustard and onion mix with bechamel.

Serve with pork, beef, veal or lamb. JW

Veal Fillets with Avocado and Hollandaise Sauce

Vegetables and Salads

Vegetables and salads are no longer seen as mere accompaniments to meat, fish or poultry dishes. It is not unusual for a main course to consist of only vegetables — or of one or two specially selected, carefully prepared and beautifully presented vegetables. The salad has also undergone change: a variety of fruits or vegetables raw or blanched with a harmonious dressing, served with the main course, or following it, will freshen the palate for the delights to follow.

Celeriac Salad

Time: 7 minutes — Serves 4

500 g celeriac, peeled and sliced
250 mL boiling salted water
2 teaspoons vinegar
2 tablespoons sugar
1 onion, finely chopped
freshly ground black pepper
3 tablespoons olive oil
1 tablespoon lemon juice
2 tablespoons chopped walnuts

Combine celeriac, boiling salted water, vinegar and sugar. Cover. Cook on high 7 minutes. Drain celeriac. Place in serving bowl. Add onion and pepper.

Combine olive oil, lemon juice and walnuts. Toss through salad. Serve hot or cold.   JW

Celery and Almond Saute

Time: 6 minutes — Serves 6–8

8 stalks celery, cut in diagonal slices
⅓ cup chopped shallots
2 tablespoons butter
pinch garlic salt
pinch white pepper
½ teaspoon sugar
toasted almonds

In a 1 litre casserole combine celery, shallots, butter, garlic salt and pepper. Cover and cook on high 6 minutes or until crisp but still tender. After 3 minutes stir in sugar and toasted almonds.   DM

Snowpea and Onion Salad

Time: 3 minutes — Serves 4

250 g snowpeas
1 onion, sliced
1 green pepper, finely chopped

Dressing

¼ cup vinegar
4 tablespoons oil
salt and pepper to taste
½ tablespoon mustard seeds
1 egg, beaten

Combine snowpeas, onion and green pepper in a shallow dish. Cover and cook on high 3 minutes. Allow to cool. Combine dressing ingredients and toss through vegetables. Serve cold.   JW

Celery and Almond Saute

Tomatoes with Spinach Topping

Time: 10 minutes — Serves 6

300 g frozen, chopped spinach
3 large ripe tomatoes
1/8 teaspoon salt
1/8 teaspoon pepper
1/2 teaspoon sugar
1/2 teaspoon basil
1/4 cup chopped onion
1/2 cup grated cheese

Cut corner off frozen spinach bag. Cook on high 5–6 minutes. Place spinach in a bowl and drain. Cut the tomatoes in half using a decorative zig-zag cut, and sprinkle with salt, pepper, sugar and basil. Combine half the cheese and all the onion with spinach. Spoon mixture onto tomato halves and cook on high 4 minutes. Top tomatoes with remaining cheese after cooking for 3 minutes.   DM

Tomatoes with Spinach Topping

Lemon Butter Asparagus

Time: 10 minutes — Serves 4

2 bunches asparagus spears
60 g butter
juice and rind of 1 lemon
freshly ground black pepper
1 tablespoon freshly chopped parsley

Trim asparagus and place in shallow dish. Dot with butter, lemon juice, rind and pepper. Cover and cook on high 10 minutes. Drain, keeping juices.

Arrange asparagus spears on plates. Pour over butter juices and garnish with parsley.   JW

Glazed Orange Sweet Potato

Time: 13 minutes — Serves 6–8

750 g orange sweet potato
3 tablespoons butter
2 tablespoons honey
1/2 teaspoon ground ginger
1 tablespoon finely chopped parsley

Peel sweet potatoes and dice into even-sized pieces, about 2.5 cm. Place in casserole, add 2 tablespoons cold water. Cover and cook on high 8–12 minutes until fork tender. Drain.

Mix butter, honey and ginger in small bowl. Cook on high 1 minute. Pour over potato and toss to coat.

Sprinkle with finely chopped parsley and serve.   DM

Jacket Potatoes

Time: 20 minutes — Serves 6

6 medium-sized potatoes
2 bacon rashers, diced
2 tablespoons finely cut chives
6 tablespoons sour cream

Wash and dry potatoes. Prick each one several times with a skewer. Wrap individually in plastic wrap and arrange evenly in a dish. Cook on high 14–18 minutes, turning over halfway through cooking.

Remove plastic and wrap each one in a square of cooking foil to keep hot and aid presentation.

Place bacon in a basin, cover with white kitchen paper and cook on high 2 minutes. Drain well.

Cut potatoes halfway through with a sharp knife. Before serving press potatoes firmly with fingers to force cut edges to open and puff up. Top with sour cream, bacon rashers and chives.   DM

Pasta

Pasta is possibly one of the most flexible ingredients in any kitchen. It can be simply and easily served in place of potatoes, for example, or dressed-up as a mouth-watering entree or main course.

Fettucine with Calamari Sauce

Time: 22 minutes — Serves 4

Fettucine

4 cups boiling water
1 teaspoon salt
1 tablespoon oil
250 g fettucine

Calamari Sauce

125 g calamari, cleaned and sliced
1 tablespoon freshly chopped parsley
6 shallots, chopped
juice 1 lemon
freshly ground black pepper
½ cup white wine
2 tablespoons sour cream

Garnish

Parmesan cheese

Place boiling water, salt and oil into 2 litre casserole dish. Add fettucine, cover and cook on high 15 minutes. Stir and set aside.

Combine sauce ingredients, except for sour cream, in a shallow dish. Cover and cook on high 5–7 minutes. Blend in sour cream.

Drain fettucine, add sauce and serve garnished with Parmesan cheese.   JW

Basil-scented Tagliatelle

Time: 15 minutes — Serves 4–6

250 g spinach tagliatelle
4 cups boiling water
1 teaspoon salt
2 tablespoons dried basil or 4 tablespoons
  finely chopped fresh basil
4 tablespoons butter
1 clove garlic, crushed
6 shallots, chopped
4 tablespoons Parmesan cheese

Place tagliatelle, boiling water and salt into 4 litre casserole dish. Cover and cook on high 15 minutes. Drain and toss through basil, butter, garlic, shallots and Parmesan cheese. Serve hot.   JW

Fettucine with Calamari Sauce

Fettucine with Calamari Sauce: **Step 1** Add Fettucine to boiling water

Step 2 Combine sauce ingredients

Step 3 Drain fettucine, add sauce and garnish with Parmesan cheese

Desserts

A delicious dessert to follow the main course — allowing a suitable pause for conversation and digestion — will bring a light to most eyes: even those of guests who loudly proclaim that they are not 'pudding people'. Choose a recipe you can prepare well in advance or that requires few last minute preparations. Although with a microwave oven, last minute preparation is simply that. In just 2–3 minutes you can reheat desserts and serve them piping hot.

Hazelnut Pie

Time: 18 minutes — Serves 6–8

1 cup roughly chopped
   roasted hazelnuts
1 × 22 cm raw pie crust
3 eggs
½ cup brown sugar
1 cup corn syrup
2 tablespoons butter
1 tablespoon flour
1 teaspoon vanilla essence
¼ teaspoon salt

Pastry

1 cup flour
½ teaspoon salt
⅓ cup cooking margarine
2 tablespoons butter
3 tablespoons cold water

To make pastry, combine flour and salt in a medium-sized bowl. Cut in margarine and butter to resemble coarse crumbs. Blend in water and knead lightly. Let rest in refrigerator 15 minutes. Roll out, line a 22 cm pie plate and chill a further 10 minutes.

Beat 1 egg yolk lightly and brush evenly over prepared pastry case to seal. Cook on high 45 seconds until yolk has set.

Combine in mixing bowl remaining eggs — separated white and leftover beaten yolk. Add remaining ingredients except hazelnuts. Blend well. Stir in hazelnuts and cook on high 4 minutes, stirring after 2 minutes.

Pour into pastry case. Reduce power to medium and cook 10–13 minutes until filling has almost set. Let stand 6 minutes before serving. The standing time completes the cooking.

Serve hot or cold with whipped cream.   DM

Fruits de Saison

Time: 4 minutes — Serves 8–10

½ cup frozen berries
¼ cup shredded coconut
2 tablespoons finely chopped pecans
1 carton sour cream
2 tablespoons fresh cream or milk
assorted fresh fruit wedges
almond macaroons
pink and white marshmallow halves
lemon juice, strained

Hazelnut Pie: **Step 1** Line pie plate with pastry and chill

Step 2 Combine filling ingredients

Step 3 Pour cooked filling into pastry crust

Place frozen berries into bowl. Cook on high 4 minutes. Allow to cool, Mix in shredded coconut, pecans, sour cream and fresh cream.

Put berry dip in centre of glass platter and arrange selected fruit, macaroons and marshmallows around bowl. Brush apple, pear and banana pieces slightly with strained lemon juice. Refrigerate until chilled.   DM

Hazelnut Pie

Strawberry Kahlua Mousse

Time: 13 minutes — Serves 4–6

Mousse

½ cup sugar
3 teaspoons gelatine
2 tablespoons water
1 cup milk
4 egg yolks
1 tablespoon Kahlua
250 g strawberries, hulled and chopped
300 mL thickened cream

Strawberry Kahlua Sauce

¼ cup Kahlua
1 tablespoon sugar
12 strawberries, hulled and chopped finely

Combine sugar, gelatine and water in a small bowl. Cook on high 30–60 seconds. Allow to cool slightly.

Combine milk, egg yolks, Kahlua and strawberries in mixing bowl. Cook on medium 5–7 minutes, stirring occasionally until thickened. Set aside.

Whip cream until stiff. Fold gelatine, strawberry mixture and cream together. Pour into 1 litre mould and chill. When firm, unmould onto serving plate.

Combine sauce ingredients in a bowl and cook on high 5 minutes. Serve with Strawberry Kahlua Mousse.   JW

Step 1 Combine sugar, gelatine and water and cook on high

Step 2 Mix milk, yolks, Kahlua and strawberries

Step 3 Fold together gelatine, strawberry mixture and whipped cream

Strawberry Kahlua Mousse

Strawberries and Kiwifruit in Champagne

Time: 2 minutes — Serves 6

1 sugar cube
2 cups champagne
36 strawberries, hulled and halved
3 kiwi fruit, peeled and sliced
dash nutmeg

Place sugar cube, champagne and nutmeg in mixing bowl. Cook on high 2 minutes. Stir. Divide fruit equally between 6 parfait glasses. Pour over champagne. Serve chilled.

JW

Pecan Chocolate Cake

Pecan Chocolate Cake

Time: 19½ minutes — Serves 8

½ cup butter
⅔ cup brown sugar
⅔ cup coconut
⅔ cup chopped pecan nuts
1½ cups flour
1⅓ cups caster sugar
¼ cup cocoa
1½ teaspoons baking powder
1 level teaspoon salt
1 cup milk
⅔ cup butter
3 eggs
1 teaspoon vanilla essence

Line base of 2 × 22 cm souffle dishes with two rounds of greaseproof paper. Place butter in bowl and cook on high 1½ minutes. Stir in brown sugar, coconut and pecans. Spread mixture evenly in each dish and set aside.

Place remaining ingredients in mixing bowl. Blend at low speed. Beat 2 minutes on medium then divide mixture and spread evenly in each dish. Cook one cake at a time on medium for 6 minutes then increase to high and cook 2–3 minutes until cake is light and spongy to touch. Let stand 5 minutes.

Turn onto serving plate. Turn second cake out onto the topping side of first cake. Spread any topping which may cling to paper onto cake top.

DM

Strawberries and Kiwifruit in Champagne

Coffee Time

Coffee time treats finish your meal to perfection. With a microwave oven, you can create delicious chocolates in minutes to serve with freshly brewed coffee, Irish coffee or cappuccino.

Mint Slice

Time: 1½ minutes — Makes 25

180 g cooking chocolate
3 tablespoons butter
1 cup icing sugar
⅛ teaspoon peppermint essence
3-5 drops green food colouring
3-4 teaspoons milk

Cut chocolate into small cubes and combine with 2 tablespoons butter in a small bowl. Cook on high 1–1½ minutes or until chocolate is soft to touch. Stir until smooth. Spread in 20 × 20 cm square dish and chill until set.

In a medium-sized bowl combine icing sugar, 1 tablespoon butter, peppermint essence and green food colouring. Beat with electric hand mixer until smooth. Spread over chilled chocolate and refrigerate until firm.

Cut into squares. Store, covered, in refrigerator.

Note: For a thicker base, double the amount of chocolate butter. DM

Ginger Nut Chocolate

Time: 3 minutes — Makes 24

200 g dark chocolate
½ cup ginger in syrup, drained and chopped
¼ cup hazelnuts, crushed

Break chocolate into pieces and place in mixing bowl. Cook on high 2–3 minutes. Stir and fold through chopped ginger and crushed hazelnuts. Spread mixture on a greased cookie slide. When set, break into bite-sized pieces. JW

Maraschino Chocolate Clusters

Time: 3 minutes — Makes 24

200 g dark cooking chocolate
30 g butter
1 teaspoon maraschino cherry juice
90 g maraschino cherries, chopped
60 g almond slivers

Break chocolate into pieces. Place chocolate, butter and maraschino juice in mixing bowl and cook on high 2–3 minutes. Stir. Fold through chopped cherries and almond slivers. Spoon into small paper cases and allow to set. JW

Irish Coffee (top); Ginger Nut Chocolate (centre); Maraschino Chocolate Clusters and Mint Slice (bottom)

Cappuccino

Time: 4 minutes — Serves 2

2–3 teaspoons brown sugar or coffee crystals
2 teaspoons instant coffee
1⅓ cups hot water
¼ cup orange liqueur
whipped cream
cocoa

In a jug, combine sugar, instant coffee and hot water. Cover and cook on high 3–4 minutes until boiling. Stir to dissolve sugar then mix in liqueur. Pour into coffee cups and top with whipped cream. Sprinkle lightly with cocoa. DM

Cappuccino

Irish Coffee

Time: 13 minutes — Serves 6–8

¼ cup brown sugar or coffee crystals
9 teaspoons instant coffee
5½ cups water
1½ cups Irish whiskey
whipped cream
cinnamon sugar

In a 2 litre jug, combine sugar, instant coffee and water and cook on high 13 minutes or until very hot. Stir in whisky and pour into individual cups. Top with cream and sprinkle lightly with cinnamon sugar. DM

243

The Buffet

Buffets are the ultimate in flexible entertaining. They can enhance your barbecue, or alleviate the hunger pangs of a cocktail party, and they're the perfect solution for Christmas entertaining. You can hold a buffet indoors or out, or you can throw open the French windows and have it both ways.

The Art of the Buffet and Barbecue

Remember when the great Australian buffet consisted of a leg of ham, roast chicken, the perennial trio of potato, three bean mix and rice salads, and a cream-bedecked pav? At one time you could practically stake your life on its inevitability.

One of the main reasons why the ham and chicken partnership was so popular is that these are foods that feed a lot of people for minimal cost and you can leave them largely unattended. Fine virtues, but the duo isn't the only variation on that theme. Curries, stews, pates, terrines, cold roast meats, quiches and indeed anything encased in pastry fit the same bill. Similarly, the potato variety isn't the only salad impervious to time. Pasta, artichoke, carrot, mushroom, hearts of palm, orange and onion salads all stand up well too.

Serving appetisers as a lead-up to a buffet always says, 'Look, I care; I bothered'. Warning: over-indulgence in 'tidbits' can blunt the effect of the most meticulously prepared dishes. If you offer too many irresistibles, bird-like eaters will fill up on them and overeaters will wolf them down and go on to overeat at table.

The microwave oven is one of the best appliances to use for preparing those short-order run-ups to a buffet meal. Appetisers can be prepared the night or morning before. Good microwave appetisers include meatballs, stuffed mussels, bacon-wrapped oysters or water chestnuts, hot vegetable and cheese dips, herbed scallops and easy pate or seafood canapes.

Pull out all the stops — selectively
One of the main drawcards of buffet entertaining is that you can have the choice of two main dishes, two salads, or a vegetable and a salad, and two desserts. Too many dishes will erode your valuable time and patience. Most of us like a bit of everything, so make sure all the selected recipes blend harmoniously, thus avoiding taste conflict.

Buffet food should always be easy to manage. No matter how delicious the food tastes or how ravenous they are, people are apt to throw in the towel if they have to struggle and juggle. Go for fork food, and keep away from any recipe that demands too much last minute attention. Dishes that can be wholly or partly cooked ahead are the ones to seek out.

French Bean and Zucchini Salad, Green and White Salad, Rice Pilaf and Apricot Brandy Jelly (top, left to right); Pork Sate, Chicken in Spicy Sauce, Ratatouille with Coconut Sauce and Rollmops (bottom, left to right)

244

Party Cheese Ball

In these days of astronomical food prices think in terms of market 'specials' like chicken, turkey, minced meat, continental sausages, eggs, cheese, less costly meat cuts that can be boned and stuffed, and then look for exciting ways to prepare them. Ethnic cuisines throughout the world offer thousands of dishes that eke out the protein part of the menu with cheaper ingredients such as beans, pasta, chickpeas, rice, potatoes and root vegetables. An excellent chilli con carne, paella, lasagne, moussaka or stuffed crepe can be the best of buffet dishes. Big parties with small price tags needn't be an impossible dream.

Barbecue supreme
Cooking for a mob out of doors is more of an Australian tradition than inviting them inside. The barbecue is the Aussie large gathering supreme. One of the greatest pleasures of eating in the fresh air is that almost any kind of food goes. In the relaxed atmosphere of the garden, bush or backyard, you can allow yourself great freedom of choice in the type and range of food you serve. Sophistication is the new keynote of the Antipodean barbie. Virtually every type of meat and seafood is now a candidate for barbecuing — pork, beef, lamb, chicken, fish, prawns and lobster. But what really makes modern barbecues so deliciously different is the widespread use of marinades. Without these exciting flavouring agents, barbecued meats and fish dishes are just outdoor grills.

The imaginative use of spices, herbs, fresh vegetables, wines, yoghurt, citrus juices and vinegar can elevate a plain steak or chop into something special. There are two types of marinade — cooked and uncooked. Cooked marinades are often used for larger cuts of meat, such as leg and shoulder of lamb, loin of pork, rolled beef roast and whole chickens. Uncooked marinades are the number one choice for smaller cuts of meat, such as chops, steaks, poultry pieces and seafood. There are also two types of barbecue sauce — the basting sauces and the accompaniment sauces. Both can add immeasurably to the occasion.

Quicker barbecuing
Speed up the cooking time of barbecued food by using the microwave oven. Or, use the microwave oven to reheat leftover charcoaled foods. By grilling extras over the coals, you can have a barbecue meal stored away for another occasion without heating the grill.

For example, pre-cook barbecued spare ribs in the microwave for 20 minutes, then transfer to the barbecue for a finishing off period of 15 minutes. Marinated chicken can be micro-cooked for 18 minutes, then grilled over the coals for 10 minutes to achieve the proper sheen. Zappy pork chops also benefit from two layer cooking. Simply microwave for 12–15 minutes, shift the action to the grill tray and cook for a further 10 minutes.

Cheese: A fine dessert
No food complements a good meal better than a well-chosen cheese. One of the benefits of concluding a meal with cheese is that it spares the cook having to prepare a more exotic dessert. Orchestrating a cheese platter is like conducting a symphony — harmony is all.

There's no need to offer a vast assortment of cheese, either. Two to four compatible cheeses are adequate, and for a light buffet luncheon or supper one good cheese — or party cheese ball — is all you need.

For ease and comfort
Whether the party takes place inside or out, an important consideration is to always provide adequate sit-down space for everyone, and put salt and pepper shakers out so they can season their food to their own taste. The same feeling of largesse should also apply to plates and glasses.

At large gatherings really good wines go unnoticed and unappreciated. Reasonably cheap and cheerful is the right course to steer. Buy up big on the flagons and casks.

Menu Number 3

Luncheon Buffet for 6–8

Rollmops
Pork Sate
Chicken in Spicy Sauce
Ratatouille with Coconut Sauce
French Bean and Zucchini Salad
Green and White Salad
Rice Pilaf
Cheese Damper
Apricot Brandy Jelly

This menu provides a delicious luncheon buffet with its clean, cool salad tastes and textures contrasting with the spicy hot dishes.

Preparation Timetable

Week ahead: Prepare Rollmops. Place in shallow dish and cover with lid or a layer of plastic wrap then foil. Refrigerate.

Day ahead: Prepare Apricot Brandy Jelly. Set into bowl or individual dishes. Refrigerate.

Prepare Pork Sate. Marinate pork pieces in a shallow dish covered with plastic wrap. Refrigerate.

Prepare Chicken in Spicy Sauce. Place chicken into a shallow dish, coat with oil and sauce, sprinkle with paprika, celery salt and pepper. Cover with plastic wrap and refrigerate.

Prepare Rice Pilaf. Cook rice but do not add ham, peas, capsicum, seasonings and toasted almonds. Place rice covered with plastic wrap in refrigerator. Dice ham and capsicum, placing in separate containers covered with plastic wrap. Refrigerate.

Place wine, beer and cold drinks into refrigerator to chill. Check tablecloth, napkins, glassware, dinnerware and cutlery. Ensure that all are clean and polished, ready to use.

3 hours before: Set table with tablecloth, napkins, glassware, dinnerware and cutlery. Arrange table decoration. Prepare drinks tray and appetisers.

2 hours before: Prepare Ratatouille with Coconut Sauce. Cook Ratatouille and set aside covered with plastic wrap. Prepare Coconut Sauce, set aside covered. Ensure that plastic wrap rests on surface of sauce to prevent skin from forming.

Prepare Cheese Damper but do not cook. Set aside covered with plastic wrap.

Prepare salads. For Green and White Salad, cook cauliflower florets and drain. Combine remaining ingredients in serving bowl. Refrigerate until serving time. Prepare garlic, salt, oil and vinegar for dressing. Keep in airtight container. Refrigerate.

1 hour before: Cook Cheese Damper. When cooked, place on cake rack to cool. Cover with teatowel till serving time.

Cook Chicken in Spicy Sauce for 20 minutes. Remove dish from microwave and set aside. Cook Pork Sate for 5 minutes, cover with plastic wrap and set aside.

30 minutes before: Remove Rollmops from refrigerator. Drain and serve on one large platter, garnished with onions and capers from mixture. Add lemon quarters and parsley. Set aside in refrigerator. Uncork red wine and allow to breathe.

15 minutes before: Whip cream for Apricot Brandy Jelly. Add to cream 1 teaspoon gelatine dissolved in ½ tablespoon water. Cook on high 30 seconds. Fold through whipped cream. Pipe cream rosettes onto jelly to decorate. Return to refrigerator until serving time.

Toss ham, capsicum, peas, seasonings and toasted almonds through rice, place on serving dish and set aside.

Buffet time: Serve Rollmops. Cook Chicken in Spicy Sauce for remaining 10 minutes. Heat Ratatouille on high for 3 minutes. Heat Pork Sate uncovered on high for 5 minutes. Pour vinegar and garlic dressing over Green and White Salad. Pour Coconut Sauce over Ratatouille.

Serve Pork Sate, Chicken in Spicy Sauce, Ratatouille with Coconut Sauce, Salads, Rice Pilaf, Cheese Damper on buffet table.

Serve Apricot Brandy Jelly.

Rollmops

Time: 5 minutes — Serves 10–12

1 litre cold water
2 salt herrings, cleaned and filleted
1 onion, thinly sliced
1 cup water
1 tablespoon peppercorns
1 bay leaf
1 tablespoon capers
1 tablespoon dried dill
parsley sprigs

Place herring fillets into cold water. Allow to soak 3 hours. Drain. Place herring and onion rings in layers in a shallow dish.

Combine water, peppercorns, bay leaf, capers and dill. Pour over herrings. Cover and cook on medium 5 minutes.

Allow to chill overnight in refrigerator. Drain off liquid. Remove bay leaf. Serve herring, onions and capers garnished with parsley sprigs.　　　　　JW

Pork Sate

Time: 10 minutes — Serves 6

750 g pork meat, cut into 2 cm cubes
2 teaspoons turmeric
2 teaspoons ground cumin
rind ½ lemon
1 teaspoon salt
1 tablespoon sugar
4 tablespoons coconut cream
1 tablespoon water

Thread pork meat onto wooden skewers. Blend turmeric, cumin, lemon rind, salt, sugar, coconut cream and water and coat sate. Marinate 1 hour. Drain and place into shallow dish and cook on high 5 minutes. Turn and cook further 5 minutes or finish cooking on barbecue.　　JW

Chicken in Spicy Sauce

Time: 30 minutes — Serves 6–8

2 × 1.5 kg whole roasting chickens
1 tablespoon oil
1 teaspoon chilli sauce
1 tablespoon paprika
1 teaspoon celery salt
freshly ground black pepper

Cut chicken into quarters. Combine oil and chilli sauce and coat chicken quarters. Place chicken portions in shallow dish.

Combine paprika, celery salt and pepper. Sprinkle over chicken.

Cover and cook on medium high 20 minutes.

Uncover and cook further 10 minutes. Stand 5 minutes. Alternatively, barbecue 10 minutes to complete cooking.

JW

Cold Ratatouille

Time: 15 minutes — Serves 6–8

500 g white onions, peeled and quartered
500 g green and red capsicum, cut into 2.5 cm pieces
500 g eggplant, chopped
4 tomatoes, skinned and quartered
500 g zucchini, sliced
1 teaspoon dried thyme
1 bay leaf
2 tablespoons basil
freshly ground black pepper
2 cloves garlic, crushed

Combine all ingredients in a shallow dish. Cover and cook on high 10–15 minutes. Serve with Coconut Sauce (see recipe).

JW

Coconut Sauce

Time: 1 minute — Makes 1¼ cups

½ small coconut
1 teaspoon oil
1 clove garlic, crushed
salt to taste
½ teaspoon sugar
½ teaspoon cayenne pepper
½ cup white wine
juice ½ lime

Combine all ingredients. Cook on high 1 minute. Serve with Cold Ratatouille or other vegetable dishes.

JW

248

French Bean and Zucchini Salad

Time: 6 minutes — Serves 8–10

375 g green beans
375 g small zucchini
1 bay leaf
1 clove garlic, peeled
½ teaspoon salt
1 onion sliced
1 red capsicum, shredded
iced water

Dressing

1 clove garlic, chopped
½ teaspoon salt
½ teaspoon white pepper
¼ cup olive oil
¼ cup tarragon vinegar
2 teaspoons sesame oil

String beans and cut into 2 cm lengths. Trim zucchini, cut into 1 cm rings. Place vegetables into casserole dish and add bay leaf, garlic, salt and 3 tablespoons cold water. Cover and cook on high 6 minutes. Drain, chill in iced water and drain again.

Combine all dressing ingredients in a jar and shake well.

To serve, arrange vegetables in salad bowl and toss with dressing.

DM

Green and White Salad

Time: 7 minutes — Serves 8–10

½ small head cauliflower
1 head fresh green lettuce
½ bunch curly endive
250 g artichoke hearts, drained
12 black olives
¼ cup salad oil
2 tablespoons tarragon or white vinegar
½ teaspoon salt
1 clove chopped garlic

Cut cauliflower into small florets each with a portion of stalk. Wash in cold water. Place into casserole dish and add 1–2 tablespoons cold water. Cover and cook on high 6–7 minutes until crispy tender. Rinse cauliflower in iced water to prevent overcooking.

Wash lettuce and endive and separate leaves from stalk, Refrigerate until crisp. Tear greens into bite-sized pieces and dry by shaking in a clean teatowel. Place into glass salad bowl, cut artichokes into quarters and add to bowl with olives and cauliflower. Refrigerate until serving time.

Sprinkle garlic with salt and puree using side of knife. Add to oil and vinegar. Blend well, Just before serving, add to salad and toss until vegetables are well coated.

DM

Rice Pilaf

Time: 12 minutes — Serves 8

1 tablespoon butter
1 small onion, finely chopped
clove garlic, finely chopped
1 cup washed long grain rice
1¾ cups boiling chicken stock or canned beef consomme
¼ cup ham, diced
1 cup cooked peas
½ red capsicum, diced
½ green capsicum, diced
2 tablespoons toasted flaked almonds
salt to taste
ground pepper

Place butter, onion and garlic into a deep casserole dish. Cover and cook on high 3 minutes. Add rice and cook 1 minute. Add boiling stock. Cover and cook on high 8 minutes. Let stand 4 minutes.

Lightly fork in ham, peas, capsicum and seasonings and sprinkle with toasted almonds. DM

Rice Pilaf: **Step 1** Combine rice, butter, onion and garlic

Step 2 Add boiling stock

Step 3 Lightly fork through ham, peas, capsicum and seasoning

Rice Pilaf

249

Cheese Damper

Time: 13 minutes — Serves 10–12

3 cups self-raising flour
1 teaspoon salt
3 tablespoons butter
½ cup milk
¾ cup water
2 tablespoons grated Parmesan cheese (optional)
paprika

Sift flour and salt into a bowl, rub in butter until mixture resembles breadcrumbs. Make well in centre and add milk and water. Mix lightly in a cutting motion with a table knife, adding one tablespoon of grated Parmesan cheese. Turn onto floured board. Knead lightly and shape into a ball.

Shape into circle. Brush top of damper with extra milk. Sprinkle with remaining Parmesan cheese and paprika.

Heat browning dish on high 5 minutes. Sprinkle with a little plain flour and place damper carefully on top. Cook uncovered on high 7–8 minutes.   DM

Cheese Damper: **Step 1** Sift flour and salt and rub in butter

Step 2 Add milk and water

Step 3 Lightly knead and shape into ball

250

Apricot Brandy Jelly: **Step 1** Combine apricots, pears, cherries and water

Step 2 Mix brandy, gelatine and water

Step 3 Gently stir gelatine mixture into fruit

Apricot Brandy Jelly

Time: 16 minutes — Serves 6–8

125 g dried apricots
125 g dried pears, chopped
60 g glace cherries
600 mL water
¼ cup brandy
2 tablespoons gelatine
extra 4 tablespoons water
whipped cream

Combine apricots, pears, cherries and water in a 2 litre casserole. Cover and cook on high 10 minutes, then a further 5 minutes on medium.

Combine brandy, gelatine and water. Cook on high 1 minute. Stir gelatine mix into fruit. Pour into a wet flan dish. Allow to set in refrigerator. Before serving, invert onto platter and garnish with whipped cream.   JW

Cheese and Bacon Ruffs (top) and Liver Canapes (bottom)

Buffet Appetisers

These irresistible hors d'oeuvres will whet appetites and enhance appreciation of the cook's culinary skills.

Prawn and Bacon Rolls

Time: 9 minutes — Serves 12

12 green prawns or scallops, prepared
4 rashers bacon, rindless
12 cubes canned pineapple, drained
12 glace cherries
12 cocktail sticks

Cut each rasher into thirds. Wrap one strip of bacon around each prawn. Place a cherry, a cube of pineapple and one wrapped prawn on each cocktail stick.

Heat browning dish on high for 6 minutes. Arrange prawn rolls around outer edge. Cook on high 1½ minutes on each side. DM

Bacon and Cheese Ruffs

Time: 6 minutes — Makes 32

8 slices white bread, toasted
2 tablespoons melted butter
1 cup grated tasty cheese
2 egg whites
⅔ cup finely chopped capsicum
1 teaspoon chopped parsley
½ teaspoon salt
dash pepper
3 bacon rashers, finely chopped and cooked

Using a cookie cutter, cut four rounds out of each slice of bread. Brush one side with melted butter. Beat egg whites until stiff. Fold in cheese, capsicum, parsley, salt and pepper. Spoon mixture onto unbuttered side of bread and sprinkle with bacon.

Heat browning dish on high 4 minutes. Arrange 16 rounds, butter side down, in dish. Cook on high about 1 minute until cheese melts. Repeat with remaining rounds. DM

Liver Canapes

Time: 7 minutes — Makes 2 cups

2 tablespoons butter
1 onion, finely chopped
3 rashers rindless bacon, chopped
60 g mushrooms, chopped
½ teaspoon dried thyme
250 g chicken livers, washed and drained
salt and pepper to taste
1 tablespoon sherry
1 tablespoon brandy
½ cup cream
¼ cup crushed walnuts

Place all ingredients except cream and walnuts into shallow dish. Cover and cook on medium high 7 minutes.

Blend mixture till smooth. Fold through cream and walnuts. Place in bowl and chill. Spread over crackers or toast squares and serve. JW

Stuffed Mussels

Time: 25–35 minutes — Serves 4–6

30 mussels in shells
1 tablespoon oil

Rice Stuffing

100 g long grain rice
2 onions, finely chopped
2 tablespoons olive oil
60 g pine nuts
60 g currants
30 g sugar
1 tablespoon chopped parsley
salt and pepper to taste
300 mL fish stock

Place half the mussels into shallow dish, add oil and cook on high 5–10 minutes. Remove mussels from oven as shells open. Continue cooking until all shells open. Set aside.

Place ingredients for rice stuffing into 2 litre casserole dish. Cover and cook on high 10 minutes, then a further 5 minutes on medium. To serve whole stuffed mussels, follow Step 3. To serve as below, remove mussel and half of shell. Place small portion stuffing on base of shell and top with mussel. Serve cold. JW

Stuffed Mussels

Party Cheese Ball

Time: 2–3 minutes — Serves 12–14

¼ cup finely cut green capsicum
¼ cup finely chopped shallots
1 teaspoon butter
250 g cream cheese
2 cups grated Cheddar cheese
125 g blue vein cheese, crumbled
1 tablespoon canned pimiento or red capsicum, chopped
2 teaspoons prepared horseradish
2 teaspoons Worcestershire sauce
1 clove garlic, chopped very finely
1 cup chopped pecans, cashews or almond flakes

In a bowl combine green capsicum, shallots and butter. Cover and cook on high 45 seconds. Place cream cheese in a large bowl. Cook on medium 1–1½ minutes or until softened. Stir in vegetables and remaining ingredients except nuts.

Shape into ball. Wrap in plastic wrap and chill 2–3 hours. Unwrap, roll in chopped nuts and serve with assorted crackers and celery sticks.   DM

Stuffed Mussels: **Step 1** Arrange half mussels in shallow dish, add oil and cook

Step 2 Combine rice stuffing ingredients

Party Cheese Ball

Step 3 Place small portion rice stuffing into shell

Soup Starters

A chilled soup makes a wonderful starter for buffet entertaining: it can be prepared well in advance, kept in the refrigerator and simply garnished and served. No last minute preparations. And while your guests enjoy the soup, you can be putting the finishing touches to the main buffet meal or turning the meat on the barbecue.

Chilled Avocado Bisque

Time: 23 minutes — Serves 4–6

1 large ripe avocado or 2 medium-sized avocados, mashed
1 small onion, finely chopped
1 tablespoon butter
3 tablespoons flour
600 mL rich chicken stock
150 mL fresh cream or natural yoghurt
fresh dill
lemon slices
salt and pepper to taste

Place onion and butter into casserole dish and cook on high 5 minutes.

Blend in flour and cook a further minute. Warm chicken stock in a jug by heating on high for 5 minutes. Stir stock into onion mixture. Add avocado. Cook on medium 12 minutes or until boiling, stirring every 3 minutes. Chill soup before folding in cream or yoghurt. Correct seasonings. Garnish with fresh dill and lemon slices.   DM

Gazpacho

Time: 1 minute — Serves 4–6

250 g ripe tomatoes
60 g bread, crusts removed
2 tablespoons olive oil
600 mL chicken stock
1 clove garlic, peeled
1 tablespoon vinegar
salt and pepper to taste
1 teaspoon sugar

Garnish

60 g ripe tomatoes, diced
60 g green capsicum, diced
60 g cucumber, peeled, deseeded and diced
60 g croutons

Remove core from tomatoes and place in oven. Cook on high 1 minute. Peel tomatoes and chop roughly. Place tomatoes and bread into food processor or blender. Add oil and one cup of stock and puree.

Cut garlic clove in half and rub the inside of serving bowl. Pour in remaining stock and vinegar. Blend in tomato puree and refrigerate until chilled. Chill diced tomato, capsicum and cucumber. Serve garnishes along with soup in separate bowls.   DM

Gazpacho

Chilled Cherry Soup

Chilled Cherry Soup

Time: 6 minutes — Serves 4–6

500 g can cherries, pitted
2 tablespoons brown sugar
1 tablespoon cornflour
⅛ teaspoon cinnamon
½ cup orange juice or red wine
sour cream for garnish

Dice six cherries for garnish. Place remaining cherries and juice into 1 litre casserole. Mix in sugar, cornflour, cinnamon and orange juice (or red wine). Cook on high 5–6 minutes until boiling. Stir twice during cooking. Cool mixture and puree in food processor or blender.

Refrigerate until chilled. Top each serving with sour cream, sprinkle with reserved cherry pieces.   DM

255

Main Buffet Meals

Buffet food should be easy to manage. Kebabs and fork dishes are ideal. Our selection includes a wide range of easy-to-eat foods ideal on their own for just a few guests or combined with other dishes for a crowd. When catering for quantity plan a varied menu — watch for clashes — of dishes that can be prepared ahead of time so the cook isn't trapped in the kitchen far from the fun of the party. This section also includes marinades and accompaniment sauces for barbecue buffets.

Marinated Beef

Time: 30–35 minutes — Serves 8–10

1.5–2 kg whole fillet beef
1 tablespoon wholegrain mustard
1 tablespoon oil
juice and rind 1 lemon
1 tablespoon honey
½ teaspoon soy sauce

Combine mustard, oil, lemon juice and rind, honey and soy sauce. Coat fillet with mixture. Cook fillet on roasting rack on medium high 30–35 minutes. Turn once about halfway through cooking. Stand covered with foil 15 minutes. Slice beef thinly to serve.   JW

Barbecued Whole Leg of Lamb

Time: 40 minutes — Serves 6–8

2 kg leg lamb, boned
2 tablespoons honey
1 tablespoon soy sauce
freshly ground black pepper
dash cayenne pepper
1 tablespoon sesame oil
juice 1 lemon
2 tablespoons dried rosemary

Combine honey, soy sauce, pepper, cayenne pepper, sesame oil and lemon juice. Cook on high 30 seconds. Spread lamb flat and coat both sides with mixture. Sprinkle with rosemary. Cook lamb on roasting rack on medium high 40 minutes. Alternatively barbecue last 10 minutes to complete cooking.   JW

Marinated Beef and Home-made Mustard

Home-made Mustard

Time: 2 minutes — Makes 1½ cups

1 cup mustard seeds
1 tablespoon whole black peppercorns
1 cup olive oil
¼ cup vermouth
¾ cup white wine vinegar
½ tablespoon salt
½ teaspoon dried tarragon leaves
½ teaspoon dried dill

Place mustard seeds and peppercorns into blender. Blend 1 minute. Combine with remaining ingredients in a 1 litre casserole dish. Cover and cook on high 2 minutes.

Pour mustard mixture into 2 jars. Seal. Allow to stand at least 24 hours before using.   JW

Home-made Mustard: **Step 1** Pound together mustard seeds and peppercorns

Step 2 Combine remaining ingredients

Step 3 Spoon into jars and set aside

Marinades and Sauces

Orange-Sherry Marinade
Makes 2 cups

1 cup orange juice
⅔ cup sweet sherry
¼ cup vinegar
¼ cup orange marmalade
2 tablespoons parsley, chopped
1 teaspoon basil
¾ teaspoon salt

Combine all ingredients. Coat meat or poultry and leave to marinate 1–2 hours.

Red Wine Marinade
Makes 1⅔ cups

1 cup dry red wine
⅔ cup salad oil
2 cloves garlic, crushed
½ lemon, sliced
2 teaspoons parsley, chopped
1 teaspoon dried thyme
1 teaspoon dried basil
½ teaspoon salt
freshly ground black pepper

Combine all ingredients. Coat beef or lamb and leave to marinate 1–2 hours.

Marinades (left to right): Orange Sherry Marinade, Red Wine Marinade and Steak Marinade

Steak Marinade
Makes 1¾ cups

1 cup tarragon vinegar
⅔ cup salad oil
½ onion, thinly sliced
1 teaspoon salt
3 cloves garlic, sliced
8 peppercorns
1 teaspoon dried basil
1 teaspoon dried thyme
1 teaspoon dried oregano

Combine all ingredients. Coat and marinate beef or lamb for 1–2 hours.   JW

Tangy Barbecue Sauce
Time: 12 minutes — Makes 1½ cups

½ cup celery, chopped
3 tablespoons onion, finely chopped
2 tablespoons butter
1 cup tomato sauce
1 teaspoon chilli sauce
¼ cup lemon juice
2 tablespoons vinegar
2 tablespoons brown sugar
1 tablespoon Worcestershire sauce
1 teaspoon dry mustard
¼ teaspoon salt
freshly ground black pepper

Place celery, onion and butter in 1 litre casserole dish. Cook on high 2 minutes. Add remaining ingredients. Cover and cook on high 5 minutes. Turn down and cook a further 5 minutes on medium. Allow to cool before serving. JW

Whole Silver Bream with Chilli Ginger Sauce

Time: 20 minutes — Serves 8–10

1 × 1 kg silver bream or snapper
2 tablespoons lemon juice
½ teaspoon salt

Sauce

3 tablespoons oil
4 red chillies, deseeded, finely chopped
3 slices green ginger, finely chopped
2 cloves garlic, finely chopped
3 tablespoons onion, finely chopped
1½ tablespoons dry sherry
4 tablespoons tomato sauce
3 tablespoons sugar
3 tablespoons white vinegar
2 shallots, shredded, for garnish

Place oil into basin, add chillies, ginger, garlic and onion. Cook on high 4 minutes stirring every minute. Add sherry, tomato sauce, sugar and vinegar. Cook on medium 5–6 minutes stirring every 2 minutes. Sauce can be made in advance and stored in refrigerator. Reheat just before serving.

Trim fins and tail of fish. Remove eyes using a melon baller or prick eyes to prevent them from bursting. Cut the thickest section of the fish three times on each side to enable the fish to cook evenly. Place fish onto serving plate. Rub inside of fish with salt. Squeeze lemon juice over fish. Cover with plastic wrap. Cook on high 8–10 minutes. Test with fork for doneness. The flesh should flake easily.

Drain any juice from platter. Mask fish with chilli ginger sauce and top with shredded shallots. Serve hot.   DM

Seafood Kebabs

Whole Fish with Cashew Nuts (top) and Whole Silver Bream with Chilli Ginger Sauce (bottom)

Seafood Kebabs

Time: 7½ minutes — Serves 6–8

250 g green prawns
250 g prepared scallops
250 g thick fish fillet, jewfish
2 firm tomatoes, quartered then halved
6 stuffed olives
2 tablespoons lemon or lime juice
1 tablespoon butter
2 tablespoons cut parsley
12 pineapple wedges
12 green capsicum wedges, diced
6 bamboo sate sticks

Devein and wash prawns. Cut fish fillet into 2 cm cubes. Place one piece capsicum onto each stick followed by a piece of pineapple. Alternate prawns, scallops, fish fillet and tomato. Finish with one piece pineapple, capsicum and one stuffed olive.

Place butter in basin and cook on high 30 seconds. Add strained lemon or lime juice. Brush over kebabs. Arrange kebabs in an oblong pyrex roasting dish or serving platter. Cook on high 4 minutes. Turn kebabs over and brush with butter. Continue cooking 2–3 minutes. Sprinkle with cut parsley before serving.   JW/DM

259

Chicken and Avocado Salad

Time: 10 minutes — Serves 6–8

8 chicken fillets
1 tablespoon oil
1 teaspoon paprika
1 tablespoon chopped parsley
1 teaspoon oregano
410 g can seedless grapes
2 medium-sized avocados
6 shallots, chopped
2 radishes, sliced
¼ cup sour cream
dash tabasco sauce

Chicken and Avocado Salad

Place chicken fillets in shallow dish. Coat with oil and sprinkle with paprika, parsley and oregano. Cover with plastic wrap and cook on medium high 10 minutes. Stand 5 minutes then cut chicken into strips.

Drain grapes and add to chicken pieces. Peel and roughly chop avocado. Add avocado, shallots and radishes to chicken mix. Toss salad together.

Blend together sour cream and tabasco sauce. Serve sauce on chicken and avocado salad or separately.   JW

Rice

Rice-based dishes are popular for buffet meals. They contribute to the visual appeal of the table, are ideal to eat hot or cold with a wide variety of main dishes and, thanks to the chef's imagination, can add interesting and piquant flavours to the meal. And with microwave cooking you can be guaranteed perfect, fluffy rice every time.

Saffron Brown Rice

Time: 31 minutes — Serves 8

1 cup washed brown rice
1 small onion, chopped
1 tablespoon butter
1 chicken cube, crumbled
½ teaspoon salt
⅛ teaspoon saffron powder
ground pepper
1¼ cups water
½ cup dry white wine

Place rice, onion, butter, chicken cube, salt, saffron and pepper into deep casserole dish. Combine water and wine in a bowl and cook on high 5 minutes until boiling. Pour over rice, cover and cook on high 26 minutes. Let stand covered 10 minutes to complete cooking.   DM

Spicy Rice with Peas

Time: 15 minutes — Serves 8

2 tablespoons butter
1 teaspoon cumin seeds

Spicy Rice with Peas

½ teaspoon dry crushed chilli or ⅛ teaspoon chilli powder
½ teaspoon ground pepper
1 cup washed rice
½ teaspoon turmeric
1 teaspoon salt
1 cup peas
1¾ cups boiling water or stock

Place butter into large casserole dish. Cook on high 1 minute. Add cumin seeds, chilli and pepper and cook 1 minute more. Add washed rice, turmeric and salt and cook on high 1 minute. Add peas and boiling water or stock. Cover.

Place casserole on large plate to collect any spillovers. Cook on high 12 minutes. Stand 4 minutes then fork rice up lightly. Serve hot.   DM

Vegetable Rice Ring

Time: 16 minutes — Serves 8

1 cup washed long grain rice
1½ cups water
1 teaspoon butter
⅛ teaspoon salt
1 firm tomato, diced, seeds removed
2 shallots, finely cut
1 tablespoon green capsicum, finely chopped
1 teaspoon oil
2 tablespoons cut parsley

Place water and butter in deep casserole. Cook on high 4 minutes. Add rice and salt. Cover and cook on high 8 minutes. Stand 4 minutes.

Place oil, tomato, shallots, capsicum in small basin. Cook on high 1 minute then add parsley. Fork mixture through cooked rice.

Spoon into a greased ring mould, pressing down gently. Cook on high 2–3 minutes to reheat. Invert onto round serving plate and serve hot.   DM

Salads

Salads look lovely and are delightful to eat. Crisp and crunchy or lightly blanched they are an invaluable part of any buffet.

To give a lift to a green salad add any or all of the following as the mood and the season take you: avocado, artichoke hearts, carrot, cauliflower or broccoli florets, cucumber, ham, mushrooms, radishes, onions, or zucchini. Avoid bruised vegetables and fruit, and keep greens crisp.

Arrange your salad ingredients attractively in a bowl or on a platter that's big enough to avoid spilling. Add as much or as little dressing as taste requires, toss and serve.

Salad Nicoise

Time: 9 minutes — Serves 6–8

250 g French beans
2 tablespoons water
250 g tomatoes
15 g stuffed olives
3 medium-sized potatoes, peeled and diced
15 g anchovy fillets
1 teaspoon capers
4 tablespoons vinaigrette dressing

Cut beans into 2.5 cm pieces. Blanch for 2 minutes on high in a small casserole with two tablespoons water. Place the potatoes in a bowl, cover with plastic wrap and cook on high 7 minutes. Set beans and potatoes aside to cool.

Toss potatoes, beans, tomatoes and olives together in serving bowl. Combine anchovy fillets, capers and vinaigrette dressing. Pour over the vegetables and toss. Serve chilled.   DM

Vinaigrette Dressing

3 tablespoons salad oil
1 teaspoon French mustard
1 tablespoon white or tarragon vinegar
salt and ground pepper to taste

Combine all ingredients in jar. Replace lid and shake well. Store in airtight jar.

Variations
English mustard (in place of French mustard)
chopped chives or parsley
chopped hard-boiled egg
strained lemon juice (in place of vinegar)   DM

Salad Nicoise

Pasta and Broccoli Salad

Time: 20 minutes — Serves 8–10

250 g pasta
4 cups boiling water
1 teaspoon salt
250 g broccoli spears, cut in half
1 tomato, chopped
¼ cup olive oil
freshly ground black pepper
½ teaspoon dried basil
2 tablespoons Parmesan cheese, grated

Place pasta, boiling water and salt in 4 litre casserole dish. Cover and cook on high 15 minutes. Set aside. Place broccoli in shallow dish. Cover and cook on high 5 minutes. Combine broccoli spears with tomato, olive oil, pepper and basil.

Drain pasta. Toss broccoli and pasta together. Serve sprinkled with Parmesan cheese.   JW

Pasta and Broccoli Salad with Italian Herb Loaf

Gado Gado Salad

Time: 11½ minutes — Serves 10

500 g bean or soy bean sprouts
250 g finely-shredded cabbage
250 g green beans, cut in 2 cm lengths
2 kg carrots, cut matchstick size

Sauce

1 onion, sliced
2 cloves garlic, chopped
2 teaspoons oil
¼ teaspoon salt
2 teaspoons brown sugar
1 teaspoon lemon juice
1 teaspoon soy sauce
1 teaspoon chilli sauce
125 g crunchy peanut butter
½ cup coconut milk (see recipe)

Garnish

sliced cucumber
sliced radish
sliced hard-boiled egg
parsley sprigs

Place bean sprouts, cabbage, beans and carrots into individual plastic bags with 1 tablespoon water for each bag. Fold in open edge. Place bags in oven and cook on high 3–4 minutes until vegetables are crispy tender. Rinse vegetables in cold water and drain.

Place onion, garlic and oil in bowl. Cook on high 5 minutes. Add remaining sauce ingredients and blend well.

Place peanut sauce in centre of flat salad platter. Arrange blanched vegetables. Garnish with cucumber, radish, egg and parsley. Chill and serve.

DM

Coconut Milk

¾ cup cold water
3–4 tablespoons desiccated coconut

Place water and coconut in basin. Cook on high 2½ minutes. Allow to cool, strain and squeeze through white cloth.

Gado Gado Salad: **Step 1** Place sprouts, cabbage, beans and carrots in plastic bags

Step 2 Combine onion, garlic and oil for sauce

Step 3 Add remaining sauce ingredients, mix and serve with salad

Peanut and Cabbage Salad

Time: 10 minutes — Serves 8–10

½ head cabbage, shredded
2 tablespoons flour
¾ cup sugar
¼ teaspoon salt
⅛ teaspoon pepper
2 eggs, beaten
1½ cups cold water
½ cup white vinegar
3 tablespoons prepared mustard
½ cup chopped peanuts

Wash shredded cabbage and shake dry in clean tea towel. Place in bowl and cover. Sift flour, sugar, salt and pepper into casserole dish. Combine eggs, water, vinegar and mustard then blend into dry ingredients. Cook on medium 10 minutes stirring every 2 minutes until mixture thickens and forms a sauce. Allow to cool then pour over cabbage, add peanuts, toss well. Chill and serve.　　　DM

Potato Salad with Bacon

Time: 17 minutes — Serves 6

6 medium-sized potatoes, peeled and sliced
1 stalk of celery, chopped
½ teaspoon dried basil
½ cup meat stock
25 mL olive oil
3 tablespoons white vinegar
freshly ground black pepper
60 g smoked bacon, diced

Place sliced potatoes in a shallow dish. Cover and cook on high 10–12 minutes. Set aside. Combine celery, basil, stock, olive oil, vinegar and pepper in a 4 cup measure. Cook on high 5 minutes then add bacon. Pour over potatoes to serve.　　　JW

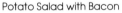
Potato Salad with Bacon

Potato Salad with Bacon: **Step 1** Layer sliced potatoes in shallow dish

Step 2 Combine celery, basil, stock, olive oil, vinegar and pepper

Step 3 Pour sauce over potatoes and serve before serving

Breads for Buffets

Most yeast breads can be proven and baked in a microwave oven. To give the loaf a crust, the clever cook sprinkles the greased loaf dish with oatmeal, crumbed crisp savoury biscuits or cracked wheat.

Dried or fresh yeast when mixed with warm water and sugar will prove only on warm setting — defrost will kill the yeast. Fresh and tasty home-made breads, speedily baked in the microwave oven are greatly appreciated by one and all in the age of sliced bread.

Wholemeal Bread

Time: About 28 minutes

1 packet dry yeast
60 mL tepid water
125 mL tepid milk
1 egg
2 tablespoons sugar
1 tablespoon salt
¼ cup butter or margarine, melted
8–10 drops yellow food colouring (optional)
3½–4 cups wholemeal flour

Soften yeast in tepid water and milk. Stir to help dissolve instantly. In large bowl combine yeast mixture with remaining ingredients, except for flour, and beat well. Add flour gradually to form a very stiff dough, beating well. Knead dough on a lightly-floured board and place in a greased bowl large enough to hold it when doubled. Cover with plastic wrap.

Prove on warm 3 minutes and then allow to stand 15 minutes. Turn dough over in bowl carefully if surface appears to be drying. Repeat cycle 2 or 3 times, proving in microwave and standing, until dough is light and doubled in size. Punch down and shape as required.

Place in loaf dish, cover and allow to double in size. Uncover and cook on medium 15 minutes. Increase to high and cook a further 1–4 minutes. Bread is cooked when it 'sounds' hollow when tapped.

Variations
Caraway and Sesame Seed Bread
¼ cup caraway seeds
¼ cup sesame seeds
egg yolk, beaten

Add caraway seeds and sesame seeds to wholemeal flour. Form proven dough into loaf shape and place in 6 cup ring mould. Brush with beaten egg yolk and sprinkle with extra caraway and sesame seeds. Cover and allow to double in size. Uncover and cook following method for Wholemeal Bread.

Wholemeal Bread (left); Caraway and Sesame Seed Rolls (top right) and Plaited Herb Loaf (bottom right)

Herb Loaf
½ tablespoon oregano
½ tablespoon ground black pepper
½ tablespoon thyme
½ tablespoon dill
egg yolk, beaten

Add herbs and pepper to wholemeal flour. Form proven dough into French loaf shape, cut into 3 lengths and plait. Place on microwave baking sheet and brush with beaten egg yolk. Sprinkle with poppy seeds or extra herbs. Cover and allow to double in size. Uncover and cook following method for Wholemeal Bread. JW

Wholemeal Bread: **Step 1** Soften yeast in tepid water and milk

Step 2 Combine sifted flour with remaining ingredients

Step 3 Knead on a lightly floured board

Cornmeal Bread

Time: 13 minutes — Makes 1 loaf

1 cup flour	salt and pepper to taste
1 cup cornmeal	410 g can creamed corn
1 tablespoon baking powder	3 eggs, beaten
2 tablespoons sugar	2 tablespoons oil
dash mustard powder	¼ cup grated Cheddar cheese
	dash paprika

Sift flour, cornmeal, baking powder, sugar, mustard, salt and pepper. Fold in creamed corn, beaten eggs and oil.

Grease 4 cup mould. Coat with grated cheese and paprika. Pour in bread mix. Cook on medium 12 minutes, then a further 1 minute on high. Stand 5 minutes before inverting. JW

Cornmeal Bread

Cornmeal Bread: **Step 1** Sift flour, cornmeal, baking powder, sugar, mustard and seasonings

Step 2 Fold in creamed corn, beaten eggs and oil

Step 3 Coat dish with grated cheese and paprika

Garlic Bread Rolls

Time: 2½ minutes — Serves 6

6 wholemeal or white bread rolls
150 g butter
¼ cup thinly sliced shallots
1–2 cloves garlic, minced

Cut each bread roll three times from the top two-thirds through the roll. Combine butter, shallots and garlic in basin. Cook on medium low 30–60 seconds until butter softens. Spread butter mixture between each cut in bread rolls. Place roll in large brown paper bag or wrap in grease-proof paper. Cook on high 1½ minutes. DM

Italian Herb Loaf

Time: 2½ minutes — Serves 12

1 loaf Italian bread
125 g butter
2 teaspoons cut parsley
¼ teaspoon dried oregano, crumbled
¼ teaspoon dried dill
1 clove garlic, finely chopped
½ cup Parmesan cheese, grated

Cut bread diagonally into 2 cm slices two-thirds through the loaf. Place butter and garlic into bowl, soften on medium low 30–60 seconds. Blend in herbs and cheese. Spread butter mixture on each slice bread. Wrap bread in a sheet of greaseproof paper and cook on high 1½ minutes.

If the bread should be too long for oven, cut in half and wrap each piece in greaseproof. Place side by side in oven and cook as above. DM

Desserts

When dessert is the crowning glory of your meal, the microwave will enable you to prepare an almost endless variety. Better yet, many of them can be made in advance, which makes entertaining so much easier.

With a microwave oven you can thaw prebaked flan cases, cook fruit pies, defrost frozen desserts and whip up superlative sauces — all in an instant.

Cinnamon Pear Upside Down Tart: **Step 1** Sprinkle sugar and cinnamon over pear halves

Step 2 Add red wine

Step 3 Roll out dough to make pie lid

Cinnamon Pear Upside Down Tart

Time: 35 minutes — Serves 4–6

4 firm pears, halved, peeled and cored
100 g sugar
½ teaspoon cinnamon
600 mL red wine

Dough

500 g flour, sifted
2 teaspoons salt
250 g butter
3 4 tablespoons iced water

Rub butter into flour and salt. Cut water through to form a soft dough. Knead lightly on floured board. Wrap in plastic wrap and refrigerate.

Arrange pear halves, cut-side up, in a 30 cm baking dish. Sprinkle over sugar and cinnamon. Pour over red wine to cover. Cover and cook on high 5 minutes, then reduce to medium and cook 10 minutes. Drain liquid into jug. Cook on high 10 minutes.

Pour sauce over pears. Roll out dough, cover dish, seal and trim edges. Cook on medium high 10 minutes. Cool 5 minutes then unmould on serving plate. Serve with whipped cream. JW

Peaches Italian Style

Time: 4 minutes — Serves 12

12 large canned peach halves
12 macaroons, crumbled
2 tablespoons Grand Marnier
4 tablespoons toasted almond slivers
300 mL whipped cream

Place peach halves in microwave roasting dish. Combine macaroons and Grand Marnier, divide mixture and fill centre of each peach. Cook on medium 4 minutes or until hot. Before serving top with whipped cream or ice cream and sprinkle with almond slivers.   DM

Strawberry Brandy Cream

Time: 3 minutes — Serves 6–8

810 g can strawberries
1/3 cup cherry brandy
6 teaspoons gelatine
2 cups cream
1/4 cup sugar
4 fresh strawberries for garnish, hulled and chopped

Drain canned strawberries and reserve syrup. Combine 1/4 cup syrup, brandy and gelatine in a bowl and stir. Cook on high 1 minute. Set aside to cool.

Whip cream and sugar till stiff. Fold in strawberries with cream. Gradually fold in gelatine mix and extra 1/4 cup syrup. Pour mixture into wet 4 cup mould. Chill.

Place remaining syrup and strawberries in glass jug. Cook on high 1–2 minutes.

To serve, unmould Strawberry Cream. Pour syrup over and garnish with chopped fresh strawberries.   JW

Fruit Salad Kebabs

Time: 6 minutes — Serves 6–8

1 red-skinned apple, cubed
250 g fresh pineapple wedges
1 can mandarin segments, drained
250 g assorted melon balls or cubes
1 firm banana, sliced in 2 cm pieces
8 strawberries

Glaze

1 tablespoon cornflour or arrowroot
1/8 teaspoon cinnamon
1/4 cup strained lemon juice
1/4 cup strained orange juice
3 tablespoons honey

Combine glaze ingredients in bowl. Place in oven and cook on high 2–3 minutes or until thick, stirring twice. One teaspoon freshly chopped mint may be added.

Select a range of seasonal and canned fruits to make a colourful kebab.

Thread fruit on wooden sate sticks and brush with glaze. Arrange in shallow dish. Heat on high 2–3 minutes or until hot. Serve.   DM

Fruit Salad Kebabs

Buffet Beverages

Fruit punches make entertaining easy. These tasty beverages look attractive, can be prepared in large quantities and are so simple to serve. Punch was originally a drink based on rum and flavoured with lemon and cinnamon. Today it can be alcoholic or not and enlivened with fruit juices, fresh fruits and carbonated drinks for extra sparkle.

Punch

Champagne Punch

Time: 2 minutes — Serves 6-8

1 teaspoon sugar
1 teaspoon water
3 slices orange
3 slices lemon
rind 1 lemon
1 teaspoon Angostura Bitters
60 mL brandy
60 mL maraschino
60 mL curacao
125 mL sherry
750 ml chilled champagne
750 mL soda water

Combine sugar, water, orange and lemon slices in shallow dish. Cook on high 2 minutes. Place in punch bowl. Add remaining ingredients and stir gently. JW

White Wine and Vermouth Punch

Time: 5 minutes — Serves 12-15

1 cup sugar
1 cup orange juice
1 teaspoon cinnamon
2 cups hulled strawberries
1 lemon, sliced
4 mint leaves, bruised
2 cups vermouth
2 × 750 mL bottles sweet white wine
750 mL bottle soda water
ice cubes

Place sugar and orange juice in jug. Cook on high 5 minutes. Pour into punch bowl. Add strawberries, lemon slices, mint leaves and vermouth. Stand covered 1 hour.

Before serving add white wine, soda water and ice cubes. JW

Cherry Punch

Time: 10 minutes — Serves 8-10

2 cups sugar
2 cups water
2 oranges, thinly sliced
250 mL maraschino cherries, drained
250 mL cherry brandy
2 × 750 mL bottles soda water
crushed ice

Place sugar and water in 2 litre casserole dish. Cook on high 6 minutes. Stir twice. Add orange slices. Cook on high 4 minutes. Add maraschino cherries and cherry brandy. Cover and chill.

To serve, pour cherry brandy mixture into punch bowl, add soda water and crushed ice. JW

Pineapple Punch

Serves 10

25 mL pineapple juice
25 mL grenadine
90 mL maraschino
45 mL dry gin
juice 3 lemons
2 teaspoons Angostura Bitters
1¼ litres moselle
750 mL soda water
1 pineapple, cut into cubes

Combine all ingredients in a punch bowl. Add ice just before serving. JW

Champagne Punch

Parties for Young People

The young from 12–21 are all still growing — their capacity to consume will amaze you. Turned loose, they are quite capable of gorging on sweet and junk food, making themselves ill in the process. Afterwards, they may want to know why you let them do it! So make the main meal delicious, nutritious and filling, and titillate their palates with the 'befores' and 'afters'.

Food for Thought

Adolescence used to be a phase, then it became a rite of passage, now it is a profession. Like all professions it exacts a toll from its associates, nowhere more so than in the realm of entertainment.

What sort of party do you give someone aged between 12 and 20? At 12 you still have a dependent youngster: at 20 that 'youngster' is standing on the threshold of adult life. They all seem to enjoy a party whether to celebrate a birthday, congratulate the winning team or simply a get-together with friends — old and new. Parents always remember the seemingly simpler pleasures of their youthful parties. But times have changed and tastes have changed along with them. These days, a theme seems to help the party along.

Chocolate Flake Cheesecake

Entertaining 12–14-year-olds

Let's start with the 12–14-year-olds, the teenyboppers. Nine times out of ten they are in the thrall of some pop idol. Get the boys to dress like their heroes (lines can be drawn at newly pierced ears though). The girls can have all the fun they want as glitz and glitter Cyndi Lauper or the current number one hit. The nearest one to approximate a jumble sale takes the prize. The music, is of course, a foregone conclusion.

Now that you have a theme, your next task is to feed them. Not extravagantly (in the sense of your time and money), just well. Incipient teenagers outside of French novels aren't noted for their sophisticated palates. A good idea is to serve up home-made fast foods like burgers, pizzas and hot dogs, preferably in an outdoors or barbecue setting. Simply lay on the buns, the meat patties and all the additions — tomatoes, beetroot, lettuce, onions and pickles. Point them towards the grill plate and let them serve themselves.

Pizza is always popular. To make it easy on yourself on the day — make the pizzas in advance on a puff pastry base and simply reheat in the microwave as required. Or, still on the microwave note, offer hot dogs. Spread a home-made tomato sauce over frankfurts, heat them through and slip them into the waiting buns.

Count on the partygoers downing one burger, one hot dog and a wedge of pizza each. Let them wash it all down with the usual array of 'in' soft drinks. For dessert, indulge in rich, rich chocolate nut ice cream cake or chocolate flake cheesecake.

Puff Pastry Pizzas

The mid-teens

Fifteen to seventeen-year-olds are hard core video kids — given a chance. Be the first in your street to have a VCR party. Again, go for a dress-up theme, anyone from 8 to 80 loves the challenge. How about a horror night? Hire horror movie videos. Let them think up the best of their worst, and offer an 'Oscar' for the most imaginative get-up.

The food should be in keeping with the mood. For example, make up really hot and spicy microwave frankfurts to send tingles down the spine. A recipe of 1 kg cocktail frankfurts, 1 cup chilli sauce, 3 tablespoons dry sherry, 1 finely chopped clove of garlic and the grated rind of half a lemon takes only 5 minutes to cook on high. Just layer the frankfurts in a shallow baking dish, pour over the chilli mix, cover and cook. You can serve it straight away, but it's best if made in advance and left to marinate for an hour or two then reheated for 2 minutes. Accompany with tacos, shredded lettuce and grated cheese.

Rare roast beef is another option. Microwave a 1½–2 kg beef roast. Carve off thin slices, and make roast beef sandwiches with accompaniments such as beetroot, tabouli, coleslaw and dill pickles. Follow up with a

Spicy Frankfurts

Mexican Tacos

Halloween-type pumpkin pie. All the drinks should be red such as Bloody Marys (without the vodka) or a non-alcoholic punch coloured with grenadine.

Not children anymore: The 18–20-year-olds

You can hardly call 18–20-year-olds children anymore. In most cases they dwarf you, look like men and women and feel they are adult — though you may not always agree. Thinking up a special theme for this age group is fraught with danger. A milestone, such as passing an exam, is an obvious candidate, but avoid anything that sounds too cutesy. Most probably they will come up with their own theme.

The good thing about the late teen years is that most now just want their close friends around them. The stimulation of good company is usually enough. The excitement of the evening should lie with the food.

The cardinal rule for entertaining in quantity with ease is not to plan a menu that traps anyone in the kitchen. No last minute souffles, no fried foods, not too many choices. Instead, prepare everything that you possibly can ahead of time.

Drink is a thorny question in this age group. Few parents are comfortable at the sight of their 'little ones' swigging beer, wine or spirits. On the other hand, many young people do drink in the company of their friends, and they are legally old enough to do so. So, along with orange juice and Coke or Pepsi, offer white wine, mineral water and low alcohol beer, you have to face the truth sometime.

Wine punches are popular for large gatherings because they are easy to prepare and economical. It is difficult to estimate how much punch you need, but reckon on 2–3 glasses per person. For example, a mixture of 2 litres of white wine, 1 cup apple juice, 2 tablespoons sugar, 2 tablespoons lemon juice, ¼ cup each lime juice and gin, 1 sliced lemon and 1 sliced orange will serve 12. Presuming you invite 25 people, you'll need to make up 4–6 times the recipe. One caveat should be entered here: punchbowls can all too easily be spiked, particularly by those who are still wallowing in 'cool'. If you think this is a possibility, don't serve punch.

As for the music — relax. They will look after that. You won't have to do a thing.

Hiring

So you have decided to have a party! You have the occasion, the date and the friends and family — but where do you go from here? The most important point is to have a plan of action. No party will be a success unless it is meticulously planned. Give yourself lots of time. No one needs the hassle of a last minute panic.

When it comes to the food, decorations and the music, you can always choose to do all the work yourself — and have the party in your lounge room. But for an occasional fling, or a special occasion like a 21st birthday, the increasingly popular alternative is to hire.

Why hire?
These days the options are incredible. You can hire anything from cups to camels! The advantages of hiring are obvious. Firstly, because of the range of food, music, decorations available for hire, you can give the kind of party you'd never be able to arrange all by yourself.

Most importantly, hiring can save you enormous amounts of time and trouble. There are hundreds of experienced caterers in Australia who will look after your every whim. Some just supply the food. Others bring the crockery and cutlery too. At the top of the scale, there are caterers who will organise everything for your party — from the food and decorations, to the entertainment and the cleaning up. Once again, it depends on the budget.

You can hire staff to act as waiters and cleaners, leaving you free to enjoy the party. You can hire instant entertainment and wonderful decorations, creating a terrific atmosphere and ensuring that everyone has a good time.

Few homes have enough glassware, cutlery or crockery for lots of guests. Hiring quickly solves that problem. Hiring also solves the problem of location. If your house won't do, why not erect a marquee in the back garden?

If you want to do all the cooking yourself, hiring can make the task easier. You can hire microwave ovens or pie warmers to help out. The same applies to the barbecue. If you can't fit enough meat on your own, you can always hire a spit or rotisserie.

What you can hire
A quick check through your telephone book will reveal the full extent of the wonderful world of hiring. To start with, you can hire glasses, often from your local hotel. There is usually an extensive range including beer glasses, wine glasses, champagne flutes and liqueur glasses. If you search around you may also find a company which hires the best quality crystal glassware. A variety of cutlery is available too, from ordinary stainless steel to ornate silver. The same range of styles applies to crockery. You can hire simple, plain dinner plates or a complete English china dinner service with gold trim.

Marquees now come in a variety of sizes, shapes and colours. Almost gone forever are the pieces of green tarpaulin that used to pass for a marquee. Hire a simple, old-fashioned marquee or choose a magnificent, white, silk-lined one.

To furnish the marquee, tables are available in many sizes and shapes — round, square, oblong, trestle-style, high or low. You will even be able to hire crisp white cloths and flounces to dress up the tables. Naturally there are chairs for the tables, too.

You can either hire an expert caterer to do the cooking for you — usually in your own home with their equipment — or you can hire the equipment and do the cooking yourself. Popular are rotisseries, or spit roasts which you can hire with or without meat and with or without a chef. You can also choose electric or gas barbecues, pie ovens, hot water urns and microwave ovens.

Hired staff, including experienced bar staff, will enhance the atmosphere as well as making the party more enjoyable for everyone. Waiters and waitresses in black and white look very smart, or they will dress in national costumes or novelty outfits such as jockey silks.

Entertaining the party
Entertainment is a vital ingredient in any good party. Discos are very popular, especially for young people. You can either hire a full disco complete with disc jockey, light show, dance floor and professional sound system, or just the sound system and/or dance floor. Live bands are also popular — and during the breaks you can play music videos on a giant, hired video screen. For small children there are clowns, magicians, puppeteers, even bushrangers for hire.

The party mood or atmosphere can also be helped along by hiring — especially with a theme party. A children's choir or string quartet will set the scene for a delightful Viennese afternoon tea, or a jazz band for a 'twenties party. If you decide to go Arabian, why not hire a camel? It is bound to impress your guests! Children will be delighted with a mini farm including ducks, sheep and rabbits. If you have something special to announce at a party, why not call on the services of a costumed town crier.

Decorations set the scene. Hire plants such as palms and orchids, or helium balloons, flags and kites. Some caterers offer a design service where they organise the entire party, including the decorations, and can offer intriguing novelties such as elaborate ice carvings for the tables. To record the fun for posterity, why not video it all? And, for a quick getaway, you can arrange for a helicopter to come and collect you!

A word about breakages: In virtually every instance, the hirer is responsible for damages and breakages. And, while all companies will have some form of public liability insurance (if, for example, someone trips over a marquee rope and hurts themselves) you may also like to insure yourself.

All companies will deliver and most expect cash on delivery. If you employ a catering company, they will expect a substantial deposit some time before the date of the party.
JM

Menu Number 4

Supper Party for 8–10 Hungry Young

Crudites with Curry Dip
Mexican Nachos
Crunchy Tuna Pie
Veal Scaloppine
Baby Buttered Potatoes
Green Salad
Chocolate Flake Cheesecake

This party starts with two spicy entrees, combining the smooth and crunchy textures of dips with the heat of curry and chilli. There are two main dishes — don't count on your young eating only from one of them. The simple salad and potato dishes can be easily prepared in large quantities, and are sure to please everyone. There's no need to keep them *only* for the young. The dessert is a rich creamy cheesecake, chocolate-flavoured, the high note of the meal, as your young guests are sure to tell you.

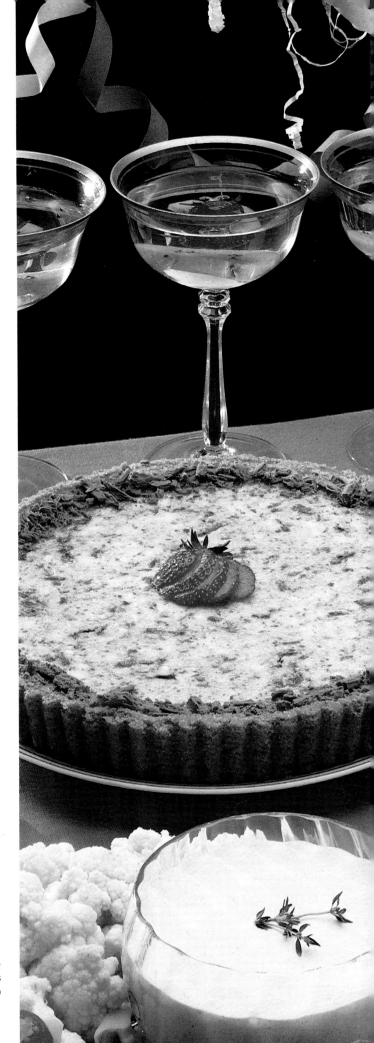

Baby Buttered Potatoes and Green Salad (top); Chocolate Flake Cheesecake, Veal Scaloppine and Mexican Nachos (centre); Crudites with Curry Dip and Crunchy Tuna Pie (bottom)

Preparation Timetable

Week Ahead: Buy party fare: hats, balloons, paper napkins, tablecloths etc.

Day Ahead: Prepare Mexican Bean Dip. Set aside covered in refrigerator.

Prepare Guacamole. Set aside covered in refrigerator.

Cut vegetables for crudites. Place into bowl. Cover with water and plastic wrap. Refrigerate.

Prepare and cook Crunchy Tuna Pie. Do not add potato straws. Cover pie and refrigerate.

Prepare Veal Scaloppine. Do not complete last 10 minutes of cooking. Cover and refrigerate.

Prepare Chocolate Flake Cheesecake. Decorate with extra flakes and refrigerate.

Place cold drinks into refrigerator to chill. Check tablecloth, napkins, glassware, dinnerware and cutlery. Make sure that all are clean and polished, ready to use. Prepare any after-dinner chocolates and store in an airtight container.

3 hours before: Set table with tablecloth, napkins, glassware, dinnerware and cutlery and arrange decoration. Prepare tray for pre-dinner drinks and party starters.

2 hours before: Prepare Curry Dip. Place into serving bowl, cover and refrigerate.

1 hour before: Remove Crunchy Tuna Pie and Veal Scaloppine from refrigerator. Set aside on bench uncovered.

Peel potatoes for Baby Buttered Potatoes. Place in dish and cover. Cook and set aside. Grate cheese for Nachos and set aside.

30 minutes before: Prepare Green Salad, arrange in serving bowl but do not add dressing. Cover and refrigerate.

Cook Baby Buttered Potatoes. Leave covered. Set aside.

15 minutes before: Cut cheesecake into portions.

Cook Veal Scaloppine on medium high 10 minutes. Top Crunchy Tuna Pie with potato straws. Cook on medium 10 minutes.

Suppertime: Drain vegetables and place around Curry Dip ready to serve.

Place Mexican Bean Dip in serving bowl. Top with corn chips and cheese and cook on high 3 minutes per bowl. Add 2 tablespoons Guacamole and 1 tablespoon sour cream in each bowl. Serve hot with corn chips.

Place Crunchy Tuna Pie, Veal Scaloppine, Baby Buttered Potatoes and Green Salad on table and let the young people serve themselves.

Serve Chocolate Flake Cheesecake.

Crudites with Curry Dip

Time: 1½ minutes — Serves 6–8

250 g cream cheese
2 tablespoons milk
1 teaspoon curry paste
¼ teaspoon onion salt
1 cup sour cream

Crudites

green beans, blanched
broccoli and cauliflower florets, blanched
carrot matchsticks
button mushrooms
celery slices
green and red capsicum, finely sliced

Cut cream cheese into cubes and place in a bowl. Cook on high 30–40 seconds.

Blend in milk, curry paste and onion salt and cook on high 1 minute. Stir to blend.

Mix in sour cream and serve with crudites.   DM

Mexican Nachos

Time: 10½ minutes — Serves 10–12

300 g corn chips
2 cups grated Cheddar cheese
300 mL sour cream

Mexican Bean Dip

410 g can red kidney beans, drained
2 teaspoons chilli sauce
freshly ground black pepper
1 green chilli, chopped
1 small onion, finely chopped

Guacamole

1 tomato
1 large ripe avocado, halved and seeded
1 tablespoon finely chopped onion
1 teaspoon olive oil
1 teaspoon lemon juice
½ teaspoon salt
freshly ground black pepper
1 clove garlic, crushed

Place all ingredients for Mexican Bean Dip in blender bowl. Chop roughly. Set aside.

For Guacamole, slit skin around outside of tomato and place in oven. Cook on high 30 seconds. Peel tomato and chop finely.

Scoop out flesh of avocado and mash. Combine tomato pulp, avocado, onion, olive oil, lemon juice, salt, pepper and garlic. Blend till smooth.

In each of 4 shallow serving bowls, place 2 tablespoons Mexican Bean Dip. Top with half the corn chips and all the grated Cheddar cheese. Cook 2 bowls at a time on high 4–5 minutes. Spoon over 2 tablespoons Guacamole and top with 1 tablespoon sour cream. Serve hot, with rest of corn chips.   JW

Crunchy Tuna Pie

Time: 20 minutes — Serves 8–10

125 g noodles
4 cups boiling water
½ teaspoon salt
125 g grated Cheddar cheese
⅔ cup sour cream
4 hard-boiled eggs, shelled and chopped
1 teaspoon tomato paste
5 cups drained and flaked tuna
salt and pepper to taste
75 g packet potato straws

Place noodles, water and salt into 2 litre casserole dish. Cover and cook on high 10 minutes. Stand in hot water for 10 minutes. Drain noodles. Combine with Cheddar cheese, sour cream, hard-boiled eggs, tomato paste, tuna, salt and pepper.

Place mixture in shallow baking dish. Top with potato straws. Cook uncovered on medium 10 minutes. Serve hot.
JW

Veal Scaloppine: **Step 1** Coat veal with breadcrumbs, Parmesan cheese, parsley and seasonings

Step 2 Arrange veal in shallow dish and add tomato mixture and mozzarella cheese

Crunchy Tuna Pie: **Step 1** Combine cooked noodles with cheese, sour cream, eggs, tomato paste, tuna and seasonings

Step 2 Top with potato chips

Veal Scaloppine

Time: 22 minutes — Serves 8–10

8 veal steaks
¼ cup seasoned breadcrumbs
⅓ cup Parmesan cheese
1 tablespoon chopped parsley
salt and pepper to taste
1 teaspoon basil
1 egg beaten
810 g can whole peeled tomatoes
125 g mozzarella cheese, grated

Pound veal steaks and slice in half. Combine seasoned breadcrumbs, tablespoon Parmesan cheese, parsley, salt, pepper and basil. Dip veal in egg and coat with crumb mixture. Place veal on microwave roasting rack. Cook on medium high uncovered 10–12 minutes turning once.

Chop whole tomatoes. Layer veal steaks, tomato mixture and mozzarella cheese in shallow dish. Sprinkle surface with rest of Parmesan cheese. Cook on medium high 10 minutes. Serve hot with a green salad garnished with orange segments.
JW

Baby Buttered Potatoes

Time: 12 minutes — Serves 8–10

500 g baby potatoes
60 g butter
2 tablespoons chopped parsley
celery salt

Place potatoes, butter and parsley in shallow dish. Cover with plastic wrap. Cook on high 12 minutes. Stand covered 5 minutes. Serve hot, sprinkled with celery salt.   JW

Chocolate Flake Cheesecake

Time: 23 minutes — Serves 8–10

1½ cups semi-sweet biscuit crumbs
2 tablespoons sugar
½ teaspoon cinnamon
½ teaspoon nutmeg
6 tablespoons butter, melted
4 cups cream-style cottage cheese
1 cup sour cream
6 eggs, beaten
1½ cups sugar
½ cup flour
pinch salt
3 chocolate flake bars, crumbled
1 teaspoon rum essence

Combine semi-sweet biscuit crumbs, sugar, cinnamon, nutmeg and butter. Press mixture into base and sides of 25 cm cake dish. Cook on high 3 minutes. Chill till set.

Combine cottage cheese, sour cream, eggs and sugar. Beat thoroughly. Fold in sifted flour and salt. Fold in 2 flake bars and rum essence. Pour mixture into biscuit crust. Cook on medium 15–20 minutes. Stand 10 minutes. Decorate with extra flake bar. Serve cold.   JW

Party Starters

Nibbles are very popular with the young. Not only are they tasty, but you can use them to break the ice by giving a platter to someone a bit shy. Offering the nibbly bits around encourages them to move from one group to another, while finding their feet.

Pork Balls with Dipping Sauce

Time: 10 minutes — Makes 48

375 g pork, minced
1 cup seasoned breadcrumbs
¼ cup Parmesan cheese
1 tablespoon finely chopped parsley
⅛ teaspoon cayenne pepper
2 eggs

Crumble pork into a bowl and cook on high 4 minutes, stirring after 2 minutes. Drain well. Blend in remaining ingredients.

Using a teaspoon, shape mixture into small balls. Chill for 15 minutes. Put a toothpick into each ball.

Line a 30 cm plate with paper towel and place 24 balls evenly around the edge. Cook on high for 3 minutes or until firm and heated through. Repeat with remaining balls.

Dipping Sauce

1 tablespoon French mustard
½ cup bechamel sauce (see recipe)

Blend mustard into the sauce. Serve in a small bowl.
DM

Prune and Bacon Rolls

Time: 9 minutes — Makes 12

12 pitted prunes
12 blanched almonds
4 bacon rashers
12 cocktail sticks

Place one almond in each pitted prune. Cut bacon rashers into thirds and wrap one strip around each prune. Fasten with a cocktail stick.

Heat browning dish on high 6 minutes. Cook bacon rolls on high 1½ minutes, turn and cook a further 1½ minutes. Serve hot.   DM

Pork Balls with Dipping Sauce (top); Chinese Ravioli (centre) and Salami Whirls (bottom)

Salami Whirls

Time: 30 minutes — Makes 36

2 sheets ready-rolled frozen puff pastry, thawed
1 egg yolk, beaten
1 tablespoon chopped parsley
1 tablespoon sesame seeds
8 slices salami
extra sesame seeds

Lightly brush one side of pastry with egg yolk and sprinkle with parsley and sesame seeds. Arrange the salami slices on pastry then carefully roll up into a log shape. Brush with egg and sprinkle with sesame seeds.

Slice log into 5 cm wide pieces and place flat on greaseproof paper on 2 or 3 microwave-safe platters. Cook each platter on high 8–10 minutes. When cooked, allow to cool on a cake rack and serve cold. JW

Salami Whirls: **Step 1** Sprinkle parsley and sesame seeds over pastry

Step 2 Spread salami over pastry

Step 3 Roll up pastry and slice into 5cm wide pieces

Chinese Ravioli

Time: 20 or 35 minutes — Makes 30

250 g pork mince
125 g raw prawn meat, minced
4 dried mushrooms, soaked in warm water for 20 minutes and finely chopped
1 shallot, finely chopped
1 tablespoon soy sauce
½ teaspoon salt
½ teaspoon sesame oil
1 beaten egg yolk
30 dim sim pastry skins
1 egg white
6–8 cups boiling water
¼ cup oil

Combine pork and prawn meat, mushrooms and shallots together in a small bowl. Mix in the soy sauce, salt and sesame oil and stir in the beaten egg yolk so that the mixture resembles a thick paste.

Place 1 teaspoon of filling into centre of each pastry skin. Brush edges with egg white. Fold over pastry to form a triangle or fold opposite corners together. Press edges to seal.

Steamed method: Pour boiling water into a large casserole. Add half the triangles, cover and cook on medium 10 minutes. Drain and repeat with remaining triangles.

Fried method: Preheat browning dish on high 5 minutes. Add oil and cook in batches of 6 on high for 4–6 minutes turning once while each batch is cooking.

Serve with Pork Balls Dipping Sauce (*see recipe*) or ready-made chilli sauce. DM

Puff Pastry Pizzas

Time: 36 minutes — Serves 8

2 sheets ready-rolled frozen puff pastry, thawed
½ cup tomato paste
1 onion, finely chopped
1 teaspoon oregano
salt to taste
freshly ground black pepper
60 g mushrooms, sliced
¼ cup black olives
16 slices salami
1 tablespoon chopped parsley
250 g mozzarella cheese, grated
paprika

Cut pastry sheets into quarters. Combine tomato paste, onion, oregano, salt and pepper. Spread a small amount of topping over each square and top with mushrooms, olives and salami. Sprinkle with mozzarella, parsley and paprika.

Preheat browning dish on high 6 minutes. Cook squares, 4 at a time, on high 15 minutes a batch. Stand 1 minute before serving. JW

Cheese and Liverwurst Roll

Cheese and Liverwurst Roll

Time: 1½ minutes — Serves 6–8

250 g cream cheese
250 g liverwurst
2 finely chopped shallots
½ teaspoon Worcestershire sauce
1 cup finely chopped parsley

Cut cream cheese into eighths. Place into bowl. Cook on medium 1½ minutes to soften. Add liverwurst, shallots and Worcestershire sauce and blend together.

Turn out onto a piece of plastic wrap 20 × 35 cm. Form into a log shape 3 cm thick by rolling in plastic wrap. Chill until set and remove plastic wrap.

Spread parsley onto pastry board, place cheese roll onto board and roll to coat evenly with parsley.

Serve garnished with Melba toast, assorted crackers and celery sticks.   DM

Cheese and Liverwurst Roll: **Step 1** Combine softened cheese, shallots, liverwurst and sauce

Melba Toast

Time: 13 minutes — Makes 48

6 slices day-old sliced white bread

Remove crusts from day-old sliced bread. Cut each slice into 4 rounds using scone cutter and then carefully cut each through the middle producing very thin rounds.

Heat browning dish on high 5 minutes. Cook 12 rounds at a time on high 1 minute on each side or until crisp.
                                                        DM

Step 2 Coat rolled cheese with chopped parsley

The Party Platter

The main course for a party needs to look good but more importantly there must be plenty of it. Depending on the number of guests, you will need two or three main dishes. Choose those that can be prepared in advance as much as possible, and take care to provide variety with taste and colour and texture. Ethnic dishes add a touch of the exotic and are popular with the 12–20 age group these days. Our international selection of party platters combines the taste of tangy herbs and spices with the unbeatable flavour of home cooking.

Mexican Tacos

Time: 20½ minutes — Serves 8–10

500 g minced beef
1 onion, finely chopped
2 tablespoons oil
¼ cup tomato paste
1 teaspoon mixed herbs
½ teaspoon chilli powder
1 green chilli, finely chopped
salt and pepper to taste
dash tabasco sauce
dash cayenne pepper
8–10 taco shells
1 lettuce, shredded
2 tomatoes, chopped
½ cup grated Cheddar cheese
300 mL sour cream

Place beef, onion, oil, tomato paste, mixed herbs, chilli powder, green chilli, salt, pepper, tabasco sauce and cayenne pepper into shallow dish. Cover and cook on high 10 minutes, stirring twice.

Uncover and cook on medium 10 minutes. Set aside.

Place 8–10 taco shells upside down on baking sheet. Cook on high 30 seconds. Serve taco shells filled with lettuce, tomato, meat mixture, sprinkled with cheese and a spoonful of sour cream.   JW

Cannelloni Crepes

Time: 35 minutes — Serves 6–8

Crepes
1¼ cups flour
pinch salt
1 egg, beaten
300 mL milk
1 tablespoon butter

Mexican Tacos

Filling

500 g veal mince
1 onion, finely chopped
1 tablespoon finely chopped parsley
salt and pepper to taste
1 clove garlic, crushed
1 tablespoon oil
810 g can whole peeled tomatoes
1 teaspoon basil
125 g mozzarella cheese, grated
½ cup Parmesan cheese

Sift flour and salt, gradually beat in egg and milk to form batter. Cover and stand 30 minutes. Grease crepe pan with small portion of butter. Drop spoonfuls of mixture onto hot pan. Tilt pan to allow batter to cover base. Cook till mixture sets. Turn. Cook for an extra few seconds. Remove and cool. Layer greaseproof paper between crepes.

Combine mince, onion, parsley, salt, pepper, garlic and oil in large casserole dish. Cover and cook in microwave on high 8–10 minutes. Stir twice during cooking.

Add tomatoes and basil. Combine evenly. Cook uncovered on high 5 minutes then reduce to medium and cook a further 5 minutes. Allow to cool slightly.

Place 2 tablespoons of meat mixture on centre of each crepe. Roll up. Place, roll side down, in shallow dish. Continue covering base of dish with crepe cannelloni. Top with half the grated mozzarella cheese and half the Parmesan cheese. Add second layer of crepe cannelloni and top with remaining mozzarella and Parmesan cheeses.

Cook on high 5 minutes then reduce to medium and cook a further 10 minutes. Allow to stand 5 minutes. Serve hot.   JW

Cannelloni Crepes: **Step 1** Make crepes in the conventional way

Step 2 Combine ingredients for filling

Cannelloni Crepes

Step 3 Fill and roll up crepes

Pork and Mushroom Stroganoff

Time: 30 minutes — Serves 6-8

500 g pork fillet, sliced thinly
1 medium onion, peeled and
  sliced
½ teaspoon basil
3 tablespoons oil
125 g button mushrooms

2 tablespoons cornflour
salt and pepper to taste
1 cup chicken stock
300 mL sour cream
1 tablespoon chopped
  parsley

Place pork, onion, basil and 1 tablespoon oil in shallow dish. Cover and cook on medium high 10 minutes stirring once. Add mushrooms and cook a further 5 minutes on medium. Set aside.

Combine rest of oil, cornflour, salt, pepper and stock in glass jug. Cook on high 3-5 minutes. Stir vigorously when cooked. Fold through pork mixture. Cover and cook on medium 5 minutes. Add sour cream and parsley. Stir through evenly. Cook uncovered on high 5 minutes. Serve hot with rice or noodles.   JW

Step 1 Combine pork, onion, basil and oil

Step 2 Add mushrooms

Step 3 Add oil, cornflour, stock and seasonings

Pork and Mushroom Stroganoff served with pasta

286

Drum Favourites

Time: 25 minutes — Serves 6–8

8 chicken or 6 turkey drumsticks

Poppy Seed Coating
¾ cup cornmeal (polenta)
2 tablespoons poppy seeds
2 teaspoons paprika
Dip: 2 beaten eggs
4 tablespoons melted butter

Basil Coating
1½ cups seasoned stuffing mix
¾ teaspoon basil
⅛ teaspoon garlic powder
Dip: 1 beaten egg
2 tablespoons milk or 1 additional beaten egg
4 tablespoons melted butter

Remove skin from drumsticks. Combine coating ingredients in a shallow dish. Cool melted butter and beat into eggs. Combine dip ingredients and brush over drumsticks. Dredge in coating, pressing into each drumstick.

Place drumsticks on microwave roasting rack with the thick end near the outer edge. Cook on high 10 minutes. Turn and cook further 8–15 minutes or until juice runs clear.
DM

Tangy Barbecue Baste
juice and rind 1 orange
1 tablespoon honey
½ teaspoon chilli sauce
1 tablespoon barbecue sauce
freshly ground black pepper
1 tablespoon oil
1 teaspoon dried thyme

Combine orange juice and rind, honey, chilli sauce, barbecue sauce, pepper, oil and thyme in glass jug. Cook on high 1 minute.

Coat drumsticks with baste. Place in shallow dish with thick end near the edge of dish. Cook on medium high 15 minutes, turn and cook further 10 minutes or until juice runs clear.
JW

Spicy Rice Salad and Turkey Drumsticks with Tangy Barbecue Coating

Sate Chicken Teriyaki

Time: 28 minutes — Serves 6–8

500 g chicken fillets
6 shallots

Marinade

½ cup soy sauce
¼ cup honey
1 clove garlic, crushed
½ teaspoon ground ginger
2–3 tablespoons oil

Cut fillets into 2 cm cubes. Combine marinade ingredients with 2 tablespoons oil in bowl. Add chicken and toss to coat. Marinate 30 minutes.

Trim shallots and cut into 2 cm lengths. Place 5 chicken cubes onto each sate stick with a piece of shallot in between. Brush chicken with oil. Heat browning dish on high 8 minutes. Place 6 sates on dish and cook on high 10 minutes turning sticks every 3 minutes. Brush with remaining marinade and oil. Cook remaining sates and serve arranged on rice platter. DM

Savoury Lasagne

Savoury Lasagne

Time: 31 minutes — Serves 8–10

8 sheets short lasagne
2 cups boiling water
½ teaspoon salt
810 g can whole peeled tomatoes, chopped
½ teaspoon basil
250 g peperoni sausage, sliced
1 onion, finely chopped
1 clove garlic, crushed
freshly ground black pepper
250 g ricotta cheese
2 eggs, beaten
½ cup cream
250 g mozzarella cheese, grated
¼ cup Parmesan cheese

Place 4 sheets short lasagne in a shallow dish, add boiling water and salt. Cover with plastic wrap and cook on high 4 minutes. Carefully lift out pasta and allow to drain. Cook remaining lasagne on high 4 minutes and drain.

Mix together tomatoes, basil, peperoni sausage, onion, garlic and black pepper and set aside. Combine ricotta cheese, eggs and cream in glass jug. Cook on high 3 minutes, stirring twice.

Starting with lasagne sheets, arrange lasagne, tomato and sausage mixture and ricotta sauce in layers in a greased shallow dish. Sprinkle ricotta layer with grated mozzarella and Parmesan cheeses. Top with ricotta mix and Parmesan cheese.

Cook on medium high 10 minutes, then reduce power and cook on medium 10 minutes. Stand 5 minutes uncovered. Serve hot. JW

Sweet and Sour Meat Kebabs

Time: 30 minutes — Makes 30 kebabs

1.5 kg leg lamb, deboned
12 bacon rashers, rind removed

Marinade

½ cup raisins
1 cup tomato sauce
1 cup dry white wine
¼ cup brown sugar
2 teaspoons Worcestershire sauce
½ teaspoon ground ginger
salt and pepper to taste

Cut lamb meat into 2.5 cm cubes and thread alternately onto wooden sate sticks with bacon rolls. Place kebabs in shallow dish.

Combine raisins, tomato sauce, white wine, sugar, Worcestershire sauce, ginger, salt and pepper. Baste kebabs with marinade. Cover with plastic wrap and marinate 1–2 hours. Drain.

Arrange 15 kebabs in a circular pattern on microwave safe platter. Cook on medium high 15 minutes. Repeat cooking remaining kebabs. Reheat all kebabs (arrange the cooler ones on top) on high 2 minutes. Serve immediately. JW

Salad Time

Salads are the perfect party food. They are easy on the eye, contributing to the festive air. They are simple to make and easy to eat single-handed: fork food. With fresh fruit and vegetables available all year round, the salad is a popular party choice. Here we have included cooked salads, using the microwave, to extend your salad vocabulary.

Sour Cream Potato Salad

Time: 22 minutes — Serves 10–12

4 large potatoes
4 tablespoons vinaigrette (see recipe)
½ cup peeled and seeded cucumber or dill cucumber, cut into 2 cm dice
½ cup celery, in 2 cm dice
4 shallots, in 2 cm dice
4 hard-boiled eggs, in 2 cm dice
1 cup microwave mayonnaise (see recipe)
½ cup sour cream
1 tablespoon horseradish
salt and ground pepper to taste
2 rashers rindless bacon
finely cut chives

Place bacon rashers between 2 sheets of white paper towel. Cook on high 3 minutes. Cut into cubes.

Prick each potato several times with skewer. Wrap potatoes in plastic wrap. Space out evenly in oven. Cook 15 minutes or until tender, turning over halfway through cooking. Remove plastic wrap.

Peel potatoes, cut into 2 cm cubes, place in bowl and pour over vinaigrette. When cool add cucumber, celery, shallots and eggs.

Blend mayonnaise, sour cream and horseradish together. Pour over salad and toss lightly. Garnish with bacon and chives.   DM

Microwave Mayonnaise

Time: 7 minutes — Makes 1½ cups

3 egg yolks, beaten
300 mL cream
¼ cup dry white wine
2 teaspoons prepared French mustard
1 tablespoon lemon juice
freshly ground black pepper
1 tablespoon finely chopped parsley

Place all ingredients in glass jug. Cook on medium 5–7 minutes, stirring every minute, to thicken. Serve over vegetables or salad.   JW

Broccoli Salad

Time: 6 minutes — Serves 6–8

650 g fresh broccoli
3 hard-boiled eggs, chopped
90g dried red pimiento or capsicum, finely diced
10 black olives, stoned and chopped

Prepare broccoli by cutting into florets. Place into plastic bag with 1 tablespoon water and fold in open edge. Cook on high 5–6 minutes. Plunge broccoli in chilled water and drain well.

Arrange broccoli on flat salad platter. Moisten with Italian dressing (*see recipe*). Garnish with chopped eggs, pimiento or capsicum and olives.   DM

Italian Dressing

¼ cup olive oil
2 tablespoons strained lemon juice
1 teaspoon grated lemon zest
salt to taste
½ teaspoon oregano
1 clove garlic, finely chopped
1 tablespoon grated Parmesan cheese
½ teaspoon freshly ground pepper

Combine all ingredients, mix well and chill. Store in an airtight container. Mix again before using.   DM

Broccoli Salad

Spicy Rice Salad

Time: 19 minutes — Serves 4–6

250 g long grain rice
2 cups water
2.5 cm piece green ginger
salt and pepper to taste
dash nutmeg
½ teaspoon powdered coriander seed
1 tablespoon lemon juice
1 shallot, finely chopped
5 tablespoons olive oil
60 g raisins
60 g currants
4 dried apricots, chopped
30 g toasted almonds (see recipe)

Combine all ingredients, except almonds. Place in 2 litre casserole dish. Cover and cook on high 10 minutes, then a further 5 minutes on medium. Allow to stand 5 minutes before serving. Serve hot or cold.

Toasting Almonds

Place 3 tablespoons butter and almonds into small bowl. Microwave on high 3–4 minutes until golden, stirring every minute.

Use almond flavoured butter for basting vegetable and chicken kebabs.   DM

Spicy Rice Salad: **Step 1** Combine rice and vegetables

Step 2 Add 2 cups water, then cover and cook on high

Avocado Jelly Salad

Time: 6 minutes — Serves 10

1 tablespoon gelatine
2 tablespoons cold water
1 × 125 g packet lime jelly
2 cups hot water
1 cup mashed ripe avocado
½ cup ready-made mayonnaise
½ cup sour cream
fresh dill or mint sprigs for garnish

Place water and gelatine in small bowl. Stir to dissolve. The gelatine will absorb the water. Place in oven and cook on medium 30–60 seconds until dissolved.

Place 2 cups water in large bowl. Cook on high 5 minutes. Blend in jelly crystals and gelatine, stir to dissolve. Chill until partially set. Fold in avocado, mayonnaise and cream. Pour into a ring or jelly mould greased with extra mayonnaise. Chill until firm.

Unmould onto a bed of crisp salad greens. Garnish with fresh fruit or seafood, sprigs of fresh dill or mint. Serve chilled.   DM

Pineapple and Vegetable Kebabs

Time: 15 minutes — Serves 6–8

500 g can pineapple pieces
1 large red capsicum, cut into 2 cm pieces
1 large green capsicum, cut into 2 cm pieces
1 large onion, cut into 2 cm pieces
6–8 bamboo sate sticks

Glaze
½ cup honey
1 tablespoon French mustard

Combine honey and mustard in small basin. Heat on medium 3–4 minutes then set aside. Place pieces of pineapple, onion, red capsicum, pineapple, green capsicum alternately on sate sticks. Repeat if sticks are long.

Heat browning dish on high 5 minutes. Place one tablespoon of oil in dish. Using a piece of white paper towel, spread oil over dish. Brush kebabs with honey glaze and cook 6 minutes on high turning and basting after 3 minutes. Pour remaining glaze over kebabs before serving.   DM

The Staff of Life

An essential nutrient, bread is often the life and soul of a party too — or at least of the eating side of it. Bread is easy 'finger' food, and an excellent basis for the most exotic topping you can think of, or the simplest. After you try these recipes, you may not want to 'dress' the bread at all.

Wholemeal Bread Sticks

Time: Microwave 60 minutes — Makes 4
        Conventional 25 minutes

½ Vitamin C tablet
2 tablespoons brown sugar
2 tablespoons compressed yeast
2½ cups lukewarm water
½ cup wholemeal flour
60 g butter

Place all ingredients in a bowl. Blend together and cook on warm 15–20 minutes or until mixture doubles in bulk.

½ cup vegetable oil
4 cups wholemeal flour
½ cup cracked wheat
½ cup gluten flour
3 teaspoons warm salted water
½ cup rolled oats

Blend oil and dry ingredients in a large bowl. Stir in yeast mixture and mix with table knife to form a dough. Knead 5 minutes on lightly-floured board. Return dough to basin and press out onto the sides of the basin until 2.5 cm thick. Cover with plastic wrap. Cook on warm 20 minutes or until doubled in bulk.

Punch down dough to release the carbon dioxide gas. Knead for 5 minutes. Cut dough into quarters and shape into four bread sticks. Place on large tray and cover lightly with plastic wrap. Cook on warm 20 minutes or until doubled in bulk.

Transfer to a greased tray. Brush each stick with warm water and sprinkle with rolled oats. Bake in conventional oven at 200°C for 20–25 minutes until bread is well risen and crisp and sounds hollow when tapped. Cool before serving.   DM

Wholemeal Bread Sticks

Pumpkin Scone Ring

Time: 8 minutes — Makes 1 ring

2 tablespoons butter
2 tablespoons sugar
1 cup cooked pumpkin, mashed
1 small onion, finely chopped
2 tablespoons finely chopped parsley
1 egg, beaten
½ cup milk
2½ cups self-raising flour, sifted
½ teaspoon salt
assorted vegetable and cheese sticks:
   carrot, celery, red and green capsicum, cucumber

Grease and line a ring mould. Cream butter and sugar. Add pumpkin, onion and parsley. Blend in beaten egg and milk. Add flour and salt. Mix with a table knife to form a dough. Place in ring mould. Cook on high 7–8 minutes. Let stand 3–4 minutes before turning out to cool.

Fill centre of scone ring with assorted vegetable and cheese sticks.

Note: For 1 cup of pumpkin you will require 375 grams raw pumpkin. Peel and seed pumpkin, prick with skewer. Wrap in plastic wrap. Cook on high 4–5 minutes until tender then mash and leave to cool.

DM

Cheese and Bacon Ring

Time: 9 minutes — Makes 1 loaf

15 g dried yeast
150 mL warm milk
125 mL warm water
1 tablespoon oil
1 egg, beaten
3½ cups wholemeal flour
1 teaspoon salt
1 tablespoon brown sugar
¼ cup bacon, diced
¼ cup Cheddar cheese, diced
½ teaspoon mustard powder
4 slices Swiss cheese
paprika
1 tablespoon finely chopped parsley

Combine yeast, milk and water. Blend till smooth. Add oil and beaten egg. Combine 3 cups wholemeal flour, salt and sugar. Add bacon, cheese and mustard powder. Mix together.

Pour in milk and yeast mixture. Sprinkle over remaining ½ cup flour. Cover with plastic wrap. Allow to stand in a warm place till mixture 'bubbles'. Uncover and combine ingredients to form soft dough ball.

Place mixture into greased ring mould. Cover with plastic wrap. Stand 30 minutes in a warm place until doubled in size.

Cook on medium 7 minutes, then top with Swiss cheese and sprinkle with paprika and parsley. Cook a further 1–2 minutes on high. Allow to cool slightly in mould 10 minutes. Turn out onto cake rack. Serve warm.

JW

292

Cheese and Ham Loaf

Time: 2 minutes — Serves 8–10

1 stick French bread
8–10 slices Swiss cheese
8–10 slices ham

Slice French bread into 8–10 portions. Between each slice place 1 slice cheese and 1 slice ham. Place loaf into serving basket. Cook on high 1–2 minutes. Cheese will melt. Serve slices with melted cheese and ham.

JW

Cheese and Bacon Ring: **Step 1** Combine cheese, bacon and dry ingredients

Step 2 Add dissolved yeast, oil, and egg, milk and water

Cheese and Ham Loaf (top); Cheese and Bacon Ring (bottom)

The Sweet Tooth

Some of these rich desserts are designed to tempt and delight the younger teens, some are better offered to the older teens. They are visually the centre of attention and the 'point' of the party with a purpose, such as birthdays or victory feasts.

Pavlova

Time: 3 minutes — Serves 8–10

Base

1 egg white
1 cup icing sugar

Marshmallow Pavlova

4 egg whites
½ cup caster sugar
¼ teaspoon cream of tartar
300 mL whipped cream
½ cup chopped strawberries
¼ cup almond flakes
1 orange, halved and thinly sliced
dark chocolate, melted

Combine egg white and icing sugar to form a soft dough. Roll out to fit 25–30 cm microwave-safe platter and set aside.

Whisk egg whites for marshmallow pavlova till stiff. Beat in caster sugar and cream of tartar. Ensure that mixture is very stiff. Pipe pavlova mixture around edge of base to form nest shape. Spoon remaining mixture into centre of base. Smooth with knife.

Cook on high 3 minutes. Stand in oven for 5 minutes. Remove and decorate with whipped cream, strawberries, almond flakes, orange slices and piped chocolate. Crushed walnuts and passionfruit also make an attractive garnish.
JW

Chocolate Truffles

Time: 4 minutes — Makes 18–22 balls

150 g butter
300 g milk cooking chocolate
1 tablespoon rum
¼ cup sour cream
extra 60 g chocolate, grated

Break up chocolate. Place butter, chocolate and rum into 2 litre mixing bowl. Cook on high 3–4 minutes. Stir to melt chocolate. Fold in sour cream. Pour mixture into shallow dish. Allow to chill for 1 hour in refrigerator.

Quickly spoon 1 teaspoon of mixture onto grated chocolate, working to form a ball. Coat with extra grated chocolate. Chill till set.
JW

Pineapple Fruit Salad Meringue

Time: 3 minutes — Serves 12

1 firm ripe pineapple
1 can fruit salad or two fruits, drained
4 tablespoons Cointreau or Grand Marnier

Meringue

3 egg whites
½ cup caster sugar
¼ cup toasted almond slivers
12 glace cherries

Cut pineapple in half lengthwise through top. Remove flesh from each pineapple half. Cut out core, dice pineapple into 2 cm pieces and combine with fruit salad and Cointreau. Marinate 15 minutes. Return mixture to pineapple cases.

Beat egg whites until stiff peaks form. Gradually beat in sugar, spread meringue over fruit and top with cherries and almonds. Cook on high 2–3 minutes until set. DM

Chocolate Truffles

Chocolate Nut Ice Cream Cake

Time: 25 minutes — Serves 10–12

Cake

250 g almond flakes
1 packet chocolate cake mix
60 g butter, melted
2 eggs
½ cup milk
1 tablespoon rum

Ice Cream

6 egg yolks, beaten
2 cups sugar
100 g milk chocolate
1¾ cups icing sugar
1 tablespoon drinking chocolate
4 × 300 mL cream, whipped

Garnish (optional)

4 strawberries
1 kiwi fruit, peeled and sliced
2 tablespoons cherry brandy

Combine almond flakes, chocolate cake mix, butter, 2 eggs and milk. Blend together till smooth. Pour batter into a 22 cm cake dish. Cook on medium 15 minutes. Stand 10 minutes, uncovered.

Crumble cake, add rum to crumbs. Set aside.

Combine egg yolks and sugar in 2 litre casserole dish. Cook on medium 5–7 minutes. Stir twice. Set aside. Break up chocolate into glass jug. Cook on high 2–3 minutes. Stir.

Sift together icing sugar and drinking chocolate. Fold together egg yolk mixture, melted chocolate, icing sugar, drinking chocolate and cream. Blend evenly.

Press 1 cup cake crumble into 20 cm spring-form cake tin then pour over 2 cups ice cream mix. Repeat layering ¾ cup crumble and 2 cups ice cream finishing with ice cream. Freeze for 6–8 hours.

One hour before serving, carefully release spring-form tin. Mark surface of cake into slices. Decorate with strawberries and kiwi fruit. Freeze for 1 hour.

Pour over cherry brandy and serve immediately.   JW

Step 1 Combine almonds, chocolate cake mix, butter, eggs and milk

Step 2 Fold together egg yolks, melted chocolate, icing sugar, drinking chocolate and cream

Step 3 Layer cake and ice cream mixtures in springform tin

Cinnamon Shortbread

Time: 17½ minutes — Makes about 48

2 cups flour
½ cup icing sugar
½ teaspoon cream of tartar
½ teaspoon bicarbonate of soda
1 teaspoon ground cinnamon
½ cup melted butter
1 egg
milk to mix if required
¼ cup caster sugar
¼ cup crushed hazelnuts

Combine flour, icing sugar, cream of tartar, bicarbonate of soda and cinnamon in mixing bowl. Blend in butter and egg to form soft biscuit dough. If dough is too dry, add small quantity of milk and knead into dough.

Divide dough into 5 portions. Shape each portion into 22 cm roll on greaseproof paper. Place greaseproof paper and dough on microwave baking sheet. Press down dough. Sprinkle with crushed hazelnuts and sugar.

Cook each roll on medium for 3–3½ minutes. Remove from oven. When cool, slice each portion into 2.5 cm wide strips. Cool completely and store in airtight container between layers of greaseproof paper.   DM

Cinnamon Shortbread: **Step 1** Mix together melted butter and dry ingredients

Step 2 Shape dough into 22 cm long rolls

Step 3 Sprinkle rolls with crushed hazelnuts and sugar before cooking

Rocky Road

Time: 3 minutes

375 g cooking chocolate
1 tablespoon butter
2 eggs
1¼ cups sifted icing sugar
1½ teaspoons vanilla essence
1½ cups roasted peanuts
1 cup coconut
2 cups marshmallows

Cook chocolate and butter on high 2–3 minutes or until soft. Beat eggs, sugar and vanilla until sugar dissolves. Blend in peanuts, coconut and chocolate mixture. Fold in marshmallows. Pour into oblong dish to set. Cut into serving pieces.   DM

Chocolate Thick Shake

Time: 1 minute — Serves 2

3 scoops chocolate ice cream
3 tablespoons milk
2 tablespoons chocolate syrup
4 whole marshmallows
2 tablespoons whipped cream

Place all ingredients into a large glass or jug. Cook on medium 1 minute, stirring twice during cooking. Top with whipped cream.   DM

Hot Mocha Chocolate

Time: 6–8 minutes — Serves 6

½ cup cocoa
¼ cup instant coffee
4–6 teaspoons coffee crystals
4 cups hot water
whipped cream
chocolate curls

Combine coffee, cocoa and coffee crystals. Heat water in jug on high for 6–8 minutes until almost boiling. Stir in coffee mixture.

Pour into serving cups, top with whipped cream and chocolate curls and serve.   DM

Hot Mocha Chocolate with Cinnamon Shortbread

Index

(1) Indicates recipe for one.

Printed in Singapore